Fifth Edition

NorthStar 4

Listening & Speaking

Authors: Tess Ferree
           Kim Sanabria

Series Editors: Frances Boyd
                  Carol Numrich

Dedication

To Jay and Carlos, Kelly and Victor.
—Tess Ferree and Kim Sanabria

NorthStar: Listening & Speaking Level 4, Fifth Edition

Copyright © 2020, 2015, 2009, 2004 by Pearson Education, Inc.
All rights reserved.

No part of this publication may be reproduced, stored in a retrieval system, or transmitted in any form or by any means, electronic, mechanical, photocopying, recording, or otherwise, without the prior permission of the publisher.

Pearson Education, 221 River St, Hoboken, NJ 07030

Staff credits: The people who made up the *NorthStar: Listening & Speaking Level 4, Fifth Edition* team, representing content creation, design, manufacturing, marketing, multimedia, project management, publishing, rights management, and testing, are Pietro Alongi, Stephanie Callahan, Gina DiLillo, Tracey Cataldo, Dave Dickey, Warren Fishbach, Sarah Hand, Lucy Hart, Gosia Jaros-White, Stefan Machura, Linda Moser, Dana Pinter, Karen Quinn, Katarzyna Starzynska - Kosciuszko, Paula Van Ells, Claire Van Poperin, Joseph Vella, Peter West, Autumn Westphal, Natalia Zaremba, and Marcin Zimny.

Project consultant: Debbie Sistino
Text composition: ElectraGraphics, Inc.
Development editing: Leigh Stolle
Cover design: Studio Montage

Library of Congress Cataloging-in-Publication Data

A Catalog record for the print edition is available from the Library of Congress.

Printed in the United States of America

ISBN-13: 978-0-13-522702-2 (Student Book with Digital Resources)
ISBN-10: 0-13-522702-X (Student Book with Digital Resources)

6 2021

ISBN-13: 978-0-13-522694-0 (Student Book with MyEnglishLab Online Workbook and Resources)
ISBN-10: 0-13-522694-5 (Student Book with MyEnglishLab Online Workbook and Resources)

6 2021

CONTENTS

WELCOME TO NORTHSTAR

A Letter from the Series Editors

We welcome you to the 5th edition of *NorthStar Listening & Speaking Level 4*.

Engaging content, integrated skills, and critical thinking continue to be the touchstones of the series. For more than 20 years *NorthStar* has engaged and motivated students through contemporary, authentic topics. Our online component builds on the last edition by offering new and updated activities.

Since its first edition, *NorthStar* has been rigorous in its approach to critical thinking by systematically engaging students in tasks and activities that prepare them to move into high-level academic courses. The cognitive domains of Bloom's taxonomy provide the foundation for the critical thinking activities. Students develop the skills of analysis and evaluation and the ability to synthesize and summarize information from multiple sources. The capstone of each unit, the final writing or speaking task, supports students in the application of all academic, critical thinking, and language skills that are the focus of unit.

The new edition introduces additional academic skills for 21st century success: note-taking and presentation skills. There is also a focus on learning outcomes based on the Global Scale of English (GSE), an emphasis on the application of skills, and a new visual design. These refinements are our response to research in the field of language learning in addition to feedback from educators who have taught from our previous editions.

NorthStar has pioneered and perfected the blending of academic content and academic skills in an English Language series. Read on for a comprehensive overview of this new edition. As you and your students explore *NorthStar*, we wish you a great journey.

Carol Numrich and Frances Boyd, the editors

New for the FIFTH EDITION

New and Updated Themes

The new edition features one new theme per level (i.e., one new unit per book), with updated content and skills throughout the series. Current and thought-provoking topics presented in a variety of genres promote intellectual stimulation. The real-world-inspired content engages students, links them to language use outside the classroom, and encourages personal expression and critical thinking.

Learning Outcomes and Assessments

All unit skills, vocabulary, and grammar points are connected to GSE objectives to ensure effective progression of learning throughout the series. Learning outcomes are present at the opening and closing of each unit to clearly mark what is covered in the unit and encourage both pre- and post-unit self-reflection. A variety of assessment tools, including online diagnostic, formative, and summative assessments and a flexible gradebook aligned with clearly identified unit learning outcomes, allow teachers to individualize instruction and track student progress.

Note-Taking as a Skill in Every Unit

Grounded in the foundations of the Cornell Method of note-taking, the new note-taking practice is structured to allow students to reflect on and organize their notes, focusing on the most important points. Students are instructed, throughout the unit, on the most effective way to apply their notes to a classroom task, as well as encouraged to analyze and reflect on their growing note-taking skills.

Explicit Skill Instruction and Fully-Integrated Practice

Concise presentations and targeted practice in print and online prepare students for academic success. Language skills are highlighted in each unit, providing students with multiple, systematic exposures to language forms and structures in a variety of contexts. Academic and language skills in each unit are applied clearly and deliberately in the culminating writing or presentation task.

Scaffolded Critical Thinking

Activities within the unit are structured to follow the stages of Bloom's taxonomy from *remember* to *create*. The use of APPLY throughout the unit highlights culminating activities that allow students to use the skills being practiced in a free and authentic manner. Sections that are focused on developing critical thinking are marked with 🔍 to highlight their critical focus.

Explicit Focus on the Academic Word List

AWL words are highlighted at the end of the unit and in a master list at the end of the book.

The Pearson Practice English App

The **Pearson Practice English App** allows students on the go to complete vocabulary and grammar activities, listen to audio, and watch video.

ExamView

ExamView Test Generator allows teachers to customize assessments by reordering or editing existing questions, selecting test items from a bank, or writing new questions.

MyEnglishLab

New and revised online supplementary practice maps to the updates in the student book for this edition.

THE NORTHSTAR UNIT

1 FOCUS ON THE TOPIC

Each unit begins with an eye-catching unit opener spread that draws students into the topic. The learning outcomes are written in simple, student-friendly language to allow for self-assessment. Focus on the Topic questions connect to the unit theme and get students to think critically by making inferences and predicting the content of the unit.

Exploring Genius

LEARNING OUTCOMES

> Infer important ideas
> Take notes with bullets and dashes
> Recognize emphasis

> Use the passive voice
> Contract and reduce *be* and *have*
> Give your opinion

Go to **MyEnglishLab** to check what you know.

2 UNIT 1

1 FOCUS ON THE TOPIC

1. The photo shows a *prodigy*—a young person with exceptional abilities. Do you know of anyone who could be considered a prodigy? What does this person do that is different or special?

2. If a child shows unusual talent in a particular area, how should the parents react? Should they push the child to develop that talent, or allow the child to develop it naturally?

3. Why do some children show advanced abilities at an early age? Are they born with a special talent, or do they learn it somehow?

Exploring Genius **3**

MyEnglishLab

The "Check What You Know" pre-unit diagnostic checklist provides a short self-assessment based on each unit's GSE-aligned learning outcomes to support the students in building an awareness of their own skill levels and to enable teachers to target instruction to their students' specific needs.

2 FOCUS ON LISTENING

A vocabulary exercise introduces words that appear in the listenings, encourages students to guess the meanings of the words from context, and connects to the theme presented in the final speaking task.

Go to MyEnglishLab lines indicate when additional practice is available online.

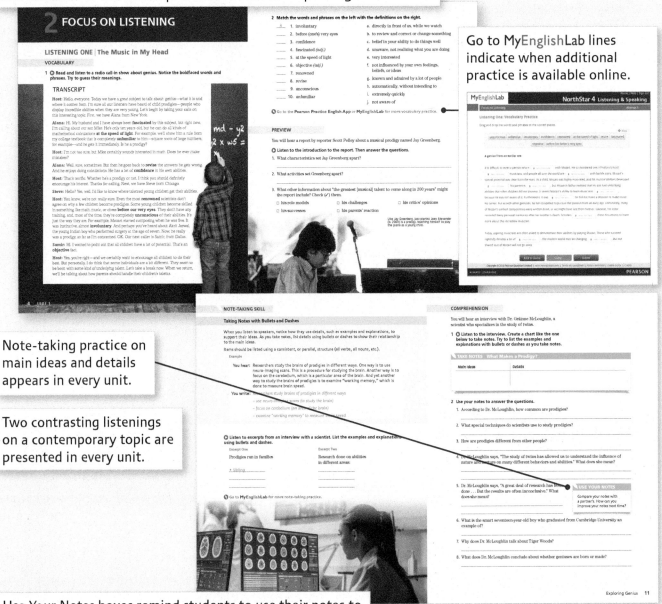

Note-taking practice on main ideas and details appears in every unit.

Two contrasting listenings on a contemporary topic are presented in every unit.

Use Your Notes boxes remind students to use their notes to complete exercises that support language, academic skills, production and critical thinking.

Every unit focuses on noting main ideas and details and features an additional note-taking skill applicable to the listenings. Activities are designed to support students in successfully completing the final speaking tasks.

EXPLICIT SKILL INSTRUCTION AND PRACTICE

Step-by-step instructions and practice guide students to move beyond the literal meaning of the listenings. 🔍 highlights activities that help build critical thinking skills.

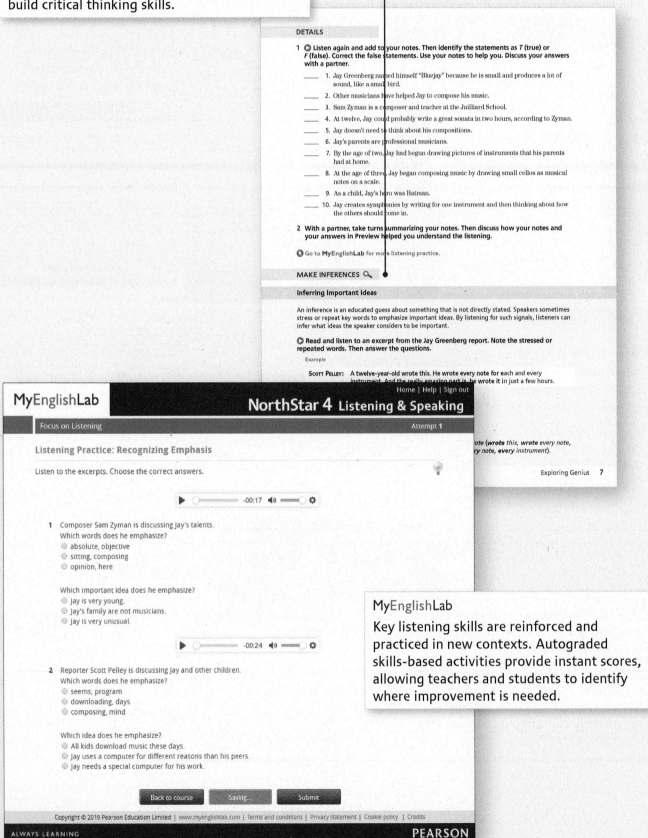

DETAILS

1 ▶ Listen again and add to your notes. Then identify the statements as *T* (true) or *F* (false). Correct the false statements. Use your notes to help you. Discuss your answers with a partner.

_____ 1. Jay Greenberg named himself "Bluejay" because he is small and produces a lot of sound, like a small bird.

_____ 2. Other musicians have helped Jay to compose his music.

_____ 3. Sam Zyman is a composer and teacher at the Juilliard School.

_____ 4. At twelve, Jay could probably write a great sonata in two hours, according to Zyman.

_____ 5. Jay doesn't need to think about his compositions.

_____ 6. Jay's parents are professional musicians.

_____ 7. By the age of two, Jay had begun drawing pictures of instruments that his parents had at home.

_____ 8. At the age of three, Jay began composing music by drawing small cellos as musical notes on a scale.

_____ 9. As a child, Jay's hero was Batman.

_____ 10. Jay creates symphonies by writing for one instrument and then thinking about how the others should come in.

2 With a partner, take turns summarizing your notes. Then discuss how your notes and your answers in Preview helped you understand the listening.

🌐 Go to **MyEnglishLab** for more listening practice.

MAKE INFERENCES 🔍

Inferring Important Ideas

An inference is an educated guess about something that is not directly stated. Speakers sometimes stress or repeat key words to emphasize important ideas. By listening for such signals, listeners can infer what ideas the speaker considers to be important.

▶ Read and listen to an excerpt from the Jay Greenberg report. Note the stressed or repeated words. Then answer the questions.

Example

SCOTT PELLEY: A twelve-year-old wrote this. He wrote every note for each and every instrument. And the really amazing part is, he wrote it in just a few hours.

ote (**wrote** this, **wrote** every note,
ry note, **every** instrument).

Exploring Genius **7**

MyEnglishLab

NorthStar **4** Listening & Speaking

Home | Help | Sign out

Focus on Listening   Attempt **1**

Listening Practice: Recognizing Emphasis

Listen to the excerpts. Choose the correct answers.

▶ ○————— -00:17 ◀)) ———○ ⚙

1 Composer Sam Zyman is discussing Jay's talents.
   Which words does he emphasize?
   ○ absolute, objective
   ○ sitting, composing
   ○ opinion, here

   Which important idea does he emphasize?
   ○ Jay is very young.
   ○ Jay's family are not musicians.
   ○ Jay is very unusual.

▶ ○————— -00:24 ◀)) ———○ ⚙

2 Reporter Scott Pelley is discussing Jay and other children.
   Which words does he emphasize?
   ○ seems, program
   ○ downloading, days
   ○ composing, mind

   Which idea does he emphasize?
   ○ All kids download music these days.
   ○ Jay uses a computer for different reasons than his peers.
   ○ Jay needs a special computer for his work.

[Back to course]   [Saving...]   [Submit]

ALWAYS LEARNING   **PEARSON**

MyEnglishLab
Key listening skills are reinforced and practiced in new contexts. Autograded skills-based activities provide instant scores, allowing teachers and students to identify where improvement is needed.

3 FOCUS ON SPEAKING

Productive vocabulary targeted in the unit is reviewed, expanded upon, and used creatively.

Grammar presentations focus on skills that are used in the listenings and applied in the final speaking task. A concise grammar skills box serves as a reference point for students throughout the unit and beyond.

MyEnglishLab
Auto-graded vocabulary and grammar practice activities reinforce meaning, form, and function. Meaningful and instant feedback guides students to self-correct and provides students and teachers with essential information to monitor progress.

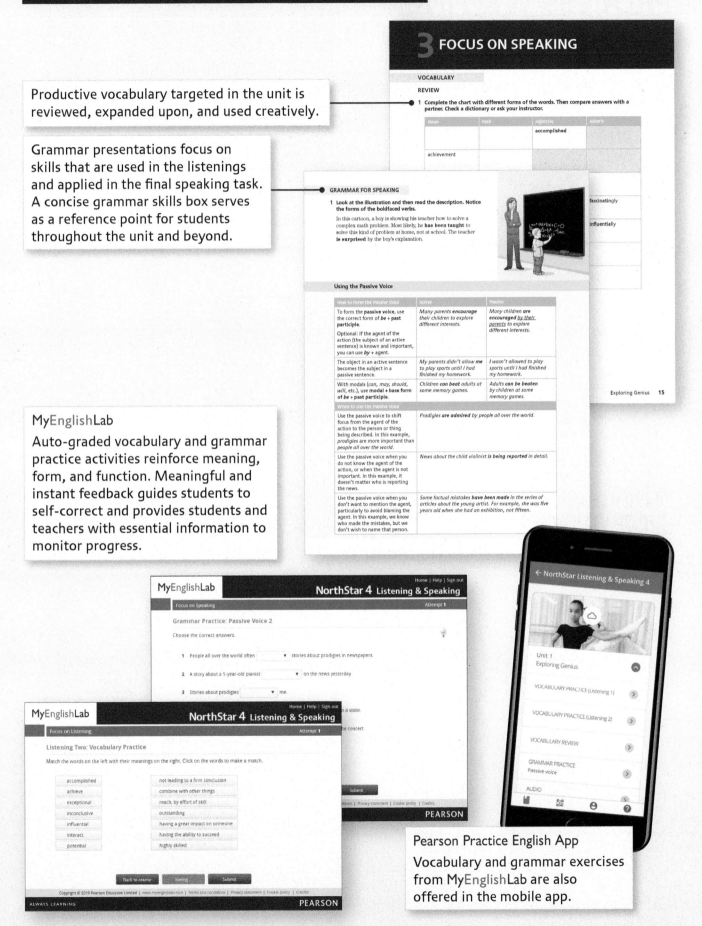

3 FOCUS ON SPEAKING

VOCABULARY

REVIEW

1 Complete the chart with different forms of the words. Then compare answers with a partner. Check a dictionary or ask your instructor.

Noun	Verb	Adjective	Adverb
		accomplished	
achievement			
			fascinatingly
			influentially

GRAMMAR FOR SPEAKING

1 Look at the illustration and then read the description. Notice the forms of the boldfaced verbs.

In this cartoon, a boy is showing his teacher how to solve a complex math problem. Most likely, he **has been taught** to solve this kind of problem at home, not at school. The teacher **is surprised** by the boy's explanation.

Using the Passive Voice

How to Form the Passive Voice	Active	Passive
To form the **passive voice**, use the correct form of **be + past participle**. Optional: If the agent of the action (the subject of an active sentence) is known and important, you can use **by** + agent.	Many parents **encourage** their children to explore different interests.	Many children **are encouraged** by their parents to explore different interests.
The object in an active sentence becomes the subject in a passive sentence.	My parents didn't allow **me** to play sports until I had finished my homework.	**I** wasn't allowed to play sports until I had finished my homework.
With modals (can, may, should, will, etc.), use **modal + base form of be + past participle**.	Children **can beat** adults at some memory games.	Adults **can be beaten** by children at some memory games.
When to Use the Passive Voice		
Use the passive voice to shift focus from the agent of the action to the person or thing being described. In this example, prodigies are more important than people all over the world.	Prodigies **are admired** by people all over the world.	
Use the passive voice when you do not know the agent of the action, or when the agent is not important. In this example, it doesn't matter who is reporting the news.	News about the child violinist **is being reported** in detail.	
Use the passive voice when you don't want to mention the agent, particularly to avoid blaming the agent. In this example, we know who made the mistakes, but we don't wish to name that person.	Some factual mistakes **have been made** in the series of articles about the young artist. For example, she was five years old when she had an exhibition, not fifteen.	

Exploring Genius 15

MyEnglishLab

Home | Help | Sign out

NorthStar 4 Listening & Speaking

Focus on Speaking   Attempt 1

Grammar Practice: Passive Voice 2

Choose the correct answers.

1 People all over the world often ▼ stories about prodigies in newspapers.

2 A story about a 5-year-old pianist ▼ on the news yesterday.

3 Stories about prodigies ▼ me.

Submit

MyEnglishLab

Home | Help | Sign out

NorthStar 4 Listening & Speaking

Focus on Listening   Attempt 1

Listening Two: Vocabulary Practice

Match the words on the left with their meanings on the right. Click on the words to make a match.

accomplished	not leading to a firm conclusion
achieve	combine with other things
exceptional	reach, by effort of skill
inconclusive	outstanding
influential	having a great impact on someone
interact	having the ability to succeed
potential	highly skilled

Back to course   Saving   Submit

ALWAYS LEARNING   PEARSON

← NorthStar Listening & Speaking 4

Unit 1
Exploring Genius

VOCABULARY PRACTICE (Listening 1) ›

VOCABULARY PRACTICE (Listening 2) ›

VOCABULARY REVIEW ›

GRAMMAR PRACTICE
Passive voice ›

AUDIO

Pearson Practice English App
Vocabulary and grammar exercises from MyEnglishLab are also offered in the mobile app.

A TASK-BASED APPROACH TO PROCESS WRITING

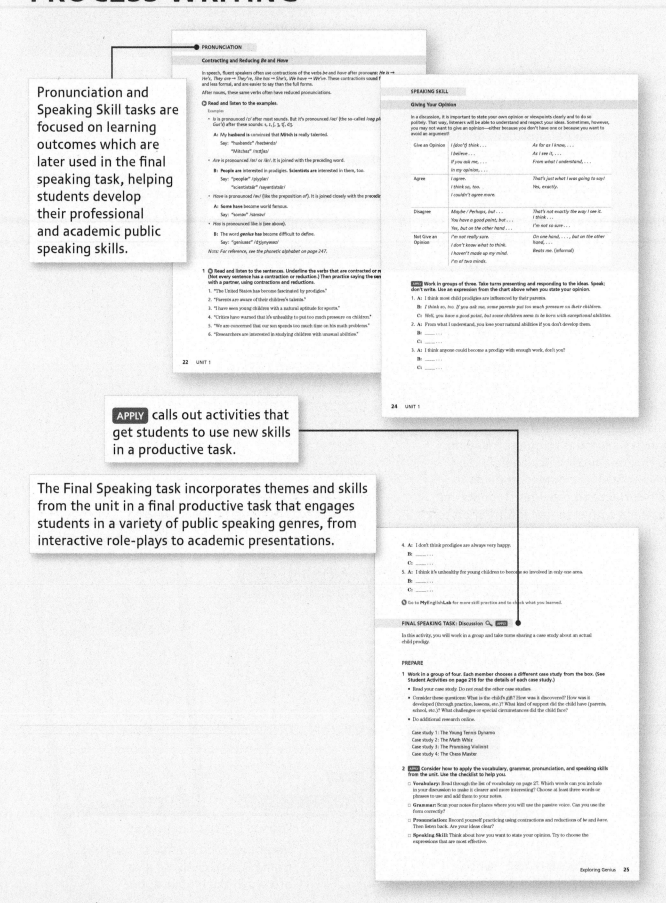

Pronunciation and Speaking Skill tasks are focused on learning outcomes which are later used in the final speaking task, helping students develop their professional and academic public speaking skills.

APPLY calls out activities that get students to use new skills in a productive task.

The Final Speaking task incorporates themes and skills from the unit in a final productive task that engages students in a variety of public speaking genres, from interactive role-plays to academic presentations.

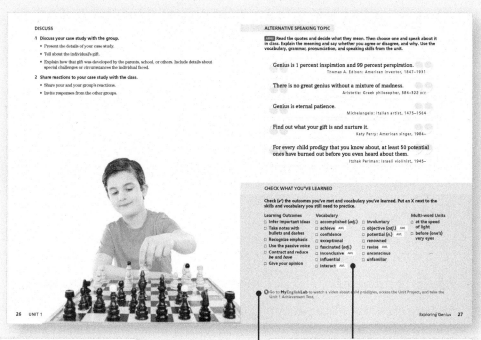

DISCUSS

1 Discuss your case study with the group.
   • Present the details of your case study.
   • Tell about the individual's gift.
   • Explain how that gift was developed by the parents, school, or others. Include details about special challenges or circumstances the individual faced.

2 Share reactions to your case study with the class.
   • Share your and your group's reactions.
   • Invite responses from the other groups.

ALTERNATIVE SPEAKING TOPIC

Read the quotes and decide what they mean. Then choose one and speak about it in class. Explain the meaning and say whether you agree or disagree, and why. Use the vocabulary, grammar, pronunciation, and speaking skills from the unit.

Genius is 1 percent inspiration and 99 percent perspiration.
Thomas A. Edison: American inventor, 1847–1931

There is no great genius without a mixture of madness.
Aristotle: Greek philosopher, 384–322 BCE

Genius is eternal patience.
Michelangelo: Italian artist, 1475–1564

Find out what your gift is and nurture it.
Katy Perry: American singer, 1984–

For every child prodigy that you know about, at least 50 potential ones have burned out before you even heard about them.
Itzhak Perlman: Israeli violinist, 1945–

CHECK WHAT YOU'VE LEARNED

Check (✓) the outcomes you've met and vocabulary you've learned. Put an X next to the skills and vocabulary you still need to practice.

Learning Outcomes	Vocabulary		Multi-word Units
☐ Infer important ideas	☐ accomplished (adj.)	☐ involuntary	☐ at the speed of light
☐ Take notes with bullets and dashes	☐ achieve AWL	☐ objective (adj.) AWL	☐ before (one's) very eyes
☐ Recognize emphasis	☐ confidence	☐ potential (n.) AWL	
☐ Use the passive voice	☐ exceptional	☐ renowned	
☐ Contract and reduce *be* and *have*	☐ fascinated (adj.)	☐ revise AWL	
☐ Give your opinion	☐ inconclusive AWL	☐ unconscious	
	☐ influential	☐ unfamiliar	
	☐ interact AWL		

Go to **MyEnglishLab** to watch a video about child prodigies, access the Unit Project, and take the Unit 1 Achievement Test.

At the end of the unit, students are directed to MyEnglishLab to watch a video connected to the theme, access the Unit Project, and take the Unit Achievement Test.

Academic Word List words are highlighted with [AWL] at the end of the unit.

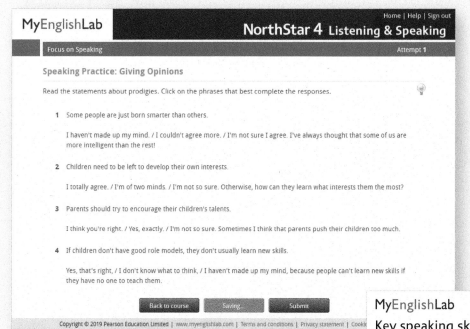

MyEnglishLab

Home | Help | Sign out

NorthStar 4 Listening & Speaking

Focus on Speaking   Attempt **1**

Speaking Practice: Giving Opinions

Read the statements about prodigies. Click on the phrases that best complete the responses.

1 Some people are just born smarter than others.

   I haven't made up my mind. / I couldn't agree more. / I'm not sure I agree. I've always thought that some of us are more intelligent than the rest!

2 Children need to be left to develop their own interests.

   I totally agree. / I'm of two minds. / I'm not so sure. Otherwise, how can they learn what interests them the most?

3 Parents should try to encourage their children's talents.

   I think you're right. / Yes, exactly. / I'm not so sure. Sometimes I think that parents push their children too much.

4 If children don't have good role models, they don't usually learn new skills.

   Yes, that's right, / I don't know what to think, / I haven't made up my mind, because people can't learn new skills if they have no one to teach them.

[Back to course]   [Saving...]   [Submit]

Copyright © 2019 Pearson Education Limited | www.myenglishlab.com | Terms and conditions | Privacy statement | Cooki

ALWAYS LEARNING

MyEnglishLab
Key speaking skills and strategies are reinforced and practiced in new contexts. Autograded skills-based activities provide instant scores, allowing teachers and students to identify where improvement is needed.

COMPONENTS

Students can access the following resources on the Pearson English Portal.

- **Classroom Audio and Videos**

  Classroom audio (the readings for the Reading & Writing strand and the listenings and exercises with audio for the Listening & Speaking strand) and the end-of-unit videos are available on the portal.

- **Etext**

  Offering maximum flexibility in order to meet the individual needs of each student, the digital version of the student book can be used across multiple platforms and devices.

- **MyEnglishLab**

  MyEnglishLab offers students access to additional practice online in the form of both auto-graded and teacher-graded activities. Auto-graded activities support and build on the academic and language skills presented and practiced in the student book. Teacher-graded activities include speaking and writing.

- **Pearson Practice English App**

  Students use the Pearson Practice English App to access additional grammar and vocabulary practice, the listenings and readings from the student books, and the end-of-unit videos on the go with their mobile phone.

INNOVATIVE TEACHING TOOLS

With instant access to a wide range of online content and diagnostic tools, teachers can customize learning environments to meet the needs of every student. Digital resources, all available on the Pearson English Portal, include **MyEnglishLab** and ExamView.

Using MyEnglishLab, *NorthStar* teachers can

Deliver rich online content to engage and motivate students, including

- student audio to support listening and speaking skills, in addition to audio versions of all readings.
- engaging, authentic video clips tied to the unit themes.
- opportunities for written and recorded reactions to be submitted by students.

Use diagnostic reports to

- view student scores by unit, skill, and activity.
- monitor student progress on any activity or test as often as needed.
- analyze class data to determine steps for remediation and support.

Access Teacher Resources, including

- unit teaching notes and answer keys.
- downloadable diagnostic, achievement and placement tests, as well as unit checkpoints.
- printable resources including lesson planners, videoscripts, and video activities.
- classroom audio.

Using ExamView, teachers can customize Achievement Tests by

- reordering test questions.
- editing questions.
- selecting questions from a bank.
- writing their own questions.

SCOPE AND SEQUENCE

	1 Exploring Genius Pages: 2–27 Listening 1: The Music in My Head Listening 2: What Makes a Prodigy?	**2 Pushing Boundaries** Pages: 28–53 Listening 1: Artist Opens Others' Eyes Listening 2: An Athlete's Inspiring Journey
Inference	Inferring important ideas	Inferring the meaning of figurative language
Note-Taking	Taking notes with bullets and dashes	Taking notes using key words
Listening	Recognizing emphasis	Distinguishing main ideas from details
Grammar	Passive voice	Gerunds and infinitives
Pronunciation	Contracting and reducing *be* and *have*	Identifying and using thought groups
Speaking	Giving your opinion	Introducing a presentation
Final Speaking Task	Discussion: anecdotes about child prodigies	Presentation to a group: report on a person who overcame obstacles
Video	Child prodigies	A girl with autism
Assessments	Pre-Unit Diagnostic: Check What You Know Checkpoint 1 Checkpoint 2 Unit Achievement Test	Pre-Unit Diagnostic: Check What You Know Checkpoint 1 Checkpoint 2 Unit Achievement Test
Unit Project	Research a famous prodigy	Review a movie about overcoming obstacles

3 Early to Bed, Early to Rise	4 Animal Intelligence
Pages: 54–79 Listening 1: How Can Teenagers Get Enough Sleep? Listening 2: Get Back in Bed!	Pages: 80–105 Listening 1: Who's Smart? Listening 2: What Motivates Animals?
Inferring a speaker's assumptions	Inferring a speaker's attitude
Taking notes with symbols and abbreviations	Avoiding non-essential words when taking notes
Recognizing claims and evidence	Identifying parts of oral paragraphs
Present unreal conditionals	Reported speech
Using contrastive stress	Using intonation on *yes / no* questions with *or*
Asking for clarification	Stating reasons and giving support
Role-play: a meeting about sleep deprivation in hospitals	Research presentation: a topic related to animal ethics
Sleep deprivation and health issues	Talking to animals

Pre-Unit Diagnostic:
  Check What You Know
Checkpoint 1
Checkpoint 2
Unit Achievement Test
	Pre-Unit Diagnostic:
	  Check What You Know
	Checkpoint 1
	Checkpoint 2
	Unit Achievement Test

Research and share causes / remedies for jet lag	React to quotations

SCOPE AND SEQUENCE

	5 The Golden Years Pages: 106–131 Listening 1: The Longevity Project Listening 2: Tobey Dichter, Generations Online	**6 Giving to Others: Why Do We Do It?** Pages: 132–159 Listening 1: Why We Give Listening 2: The Mystery Donor
Inference	Inferring a speaker's intention	Inferring the degree of certainty
Note-Taking	Taking notes with a diagram	Annotating your notes
Listening	Identifying and understanding relationships between ideas	Identifying the purpose of direct quotations
Grammar	Comparing past forms	Relative pronouns in adjective clauses
Pronunciation	Using word blends with *you*	Listing intonation
Speaking	Making suggestions	Ranking ideas
Final Speaking Task	Discussion: different viewpoints on elderly care	Presentation: a public service announcement (PSA)
Video	The long lives of the residents of Acciaroli	Philanthropy

Assessments	Pre-Unit Diagnostic:
	  Check What You Know
	Checkpoint 1
	Checkpoint 2
	Unit Achievement Test
		Pre-Unit Diagnostic:
		  Check What You Know
		Checkpoint 1
		Checkpoint 2
		Unit Achievement Test

Unit Project	Research images of seniors in advertisements	Research and write a report on a philanthropist

7 Water, Water, Everywhere?	8 Video Games: Friend or Foe?
Pages: 160–185 Listening 1: Water Shortage: Past the Tipping Point? Listening 2: Putting Water to Work	Pages: 186–215 Listening 1: The Darker Side of Video Games Listening 2: Truths and Myths in Gaming
Inferring the purpose of questions	Inferring contrasting information
Taking notes with handouts	Taking notes with an outline
Listening for multiple details	Identifying counterarguments
Causal verbs	Phrasal verbs
Pronouncing stressed and unstressed vowels	Using stress with adverbial particles
Referring to a Visual Aid	Making concessions
Presentation with visual aid: water issues	Debate: pros and cons of video games
Water conservation in college dormitories	Video games

Pre-Unit Diagnostic:
    Check What You Know
Checkpoint 1
Checkpoint 2
Unit Achievement Test
	Pre-Unit Diagnostic:
	    Check What You Know
	Checkpoint 1
	Checkpoint 2
	Unit Achievement Test

Research and write a report on water scarcity	Write a report on a popular online game

ACKNOWLEDGMENTS

To friends, family, and colleagues who have supported us throughout the fifth edition of *NorthStar*, our heartfelt thanks. Each of you has left an imprint on these pages.

The project has again been enriched by the contributions of many individuals. We thank Frances Boyd and Carol Numrich, our *NorthStar* series editors, as well as the wonderful editorial staff at Pearson Education. Our gratitude goes to editors Dana Pinter, Leigh Stolle, Linda Moser, Autumn Westphal, and Peter West. Their positive attitude and tactful expertise have been critical as we developed the manuscript. In addition, the many interviewees and commentators heard in the listenings, are a part of *NorthStar*.

Most of all, we thank our loving families and friends.

—Tess Ferree and Kim Sanabria

REVIEWERS

Chris Antonellis, Boston University – CELOP; Gail August, Hostos; Aegina Barnes, York College; Kim Bayer, Hunter College; Mine Bellikli, Atilim University; Allison Blechman, Embassy CES; Paul Blomquist, Kaplan; Helena Botros, FLS; James Branchick, FLS; Chris Bruffee, Embassy CES; Joyce Cain University of California at Fullerton; Nese Cakli, Duzce University; Molly Cheny, University of Washington; María Cordani Tourinho Dantas, Colégio Rainha De Paz; Jason Davis, ASC English; Lindsay Donigan, Fullerton College; Mila Dragushanskaya, ASA College; Bina Dugan, BCCC; Sibel Ece Izmir, Atilim University; Érica Ferrer, Universidad del Norte; María Irma Gallegos Peláez, Universidad del Valle de México; Vera Figueira, UC Irvine; Rachel Fernandez, UC Irvine; Jeff Gano, ASA College; Emily Ellis, UC Irvine; María Genovev a Chávez Bazán, Universidad del Valle de México; Juan Garcia, FLS; Heidi Gramlich, The New England School of English; Phillip Grayson, Kaplan; Rebecca Gross, The New England School of English; Rick Guadiana, FLS; Sebnem Guzel, Tobb University; Esra Hatipoglu, Ufuk University; Brian Henry, FLS; Josephine Horna, BCCC; Judy Hu, UC Irvine; Arthur Hui, Fullerton College; Zoe Isaacson, Hunter College; Kathy Johnson, Fullerton College; Marcelo Juica, Urban College of Boston; Tom Justice, North Shore Community College; Lisa Karakas, Berkeley College; Eva Kopernacki, Embassy CES; Drew Larimore, Kaplan; Heidi Lieb, BCCC; Patricia Martins, Ibeu; Cecilia Mora Espejo, Universidad del Valle de México; Oscar Navarro University of California at Fullerton; Eva Nemtson, ASA College; Kate Nyhan, The New England School of English; Julie Oni, FLS; Willard Osman, The New England School of English; Olga Pagieva, ASA College; Manish Patel, FLS; Paige Poole, Universidad del Norte; Claudia Rebello, Ibeu; Amy Renehan, University of Washington; Lourdes Rey, Universidad del Norte; Michelle Reynolds, FLS International Boston Commons; Mary Ritter, NYU; Ellen Rosen University of California at Fullerton; Dana Saito-Stehiberger, UC Irvine; Dariusz Saczuk, ASA College; Miryam Salimov, ASA College; Minerva Santos, Hostos; Sezer Sarioz, Saint Benoit PLS; Gail Schwartz, UC Irvine; Ebru Sinar, Tobb University; Beth Soll, NYU (Columbia); Christopher Stobart, Universidad del Norte; Guliz Uludag, Ufuk University; Debra Un, NYU; Hilal Unlusu, Saint Benoit PLS; María del Carmen Viruega Trejo, Universidad del Valle de México; Reda Vural, Atilim University; Douglas Waters, Universidad del Norte; Emily Wong, UC Irvine; Leyla Yucklik, Duzce University; Jorge Zepeda Porras, Universidad del Valle de México

LEARNING OUTCOMES

> Infer important ideas
> Take notes with bullets and dashes
> Recognize emphasis

> Use the passive voice
> Contract and reduce *be* and *have*
> Give your opinion

🖱 Go to **MyEnglishLab** to check what you know.

Exploring Genius

1 FOCUS ON THE TOPIC

1. The photo shows a *prodigy*—a young person with exceptional abilities. Do you know of anyone who could be considered a prodigy? What does this person do that is different or special?

2. If a child shows unusual talent in a particular area, how should the parents react? Should they push the child to develop that talent, or allow the child to develop it naturally?

3. Why do some children show advanced abilities at an early age? Are they born with a special talent, or do they learn it somehow?

LISTENING ONE | The Music in My Head

VOCABULARY

1 ▶ **Read and listen to a radio call-in show about genius. Notice the boldfaced words and phrases. Try to guess their meanings.**

TRANSCRIPT

Host: Hello, everyone. Today we have a great subject to talk about: genius—what it is and where it comes from. I'm sure all our listeners have heard of child prodigies—people who display incredible abilities when they are very young. Let's begin by taking your calls on this interesting topic. First, we have Alana from New York.

Alana: Hi. My husband and I have always been **fascinated** by this subject, but right now, I'm calling about our son Mike. He's only ten years old, but he can do all kinds of mathematical calculations **at the speed of light**. For example, we'll show him a rule from my college textbook that is completely **unfamiliar** to him—square roots of large numbers, for example—and he gets it immediately. Is he a prodigy?

Host: I'm not too sure, but Mike certainly sounds interested in math. Does he ever make mistakes?

Alana: Well, sure, sometimes. But then he goes back to **revise** the answers he gets wrong. And he enjoys doing calculations. He has a lot of **confidence** in his own abilities.

Host: That's terrific. Whether he's a prodigy or not, I think you should definitely encourage his interest. Thanks for calling. Next, we have Steve from Chicago.

Steve: Hello? Yes, well, I'd like to know where talented young children get their abilities.

Host: You know, we're not really sure. Even the most **renowned** scientists don't agree on why a few children become prodigies. Some young children become skilled in something like math, music, or chess **before our very eyes**. They don't have any training, and, most of the time, they're completely **unconscious** of their abilities. It's just the way they are. For example, Mozart started composing when he was five. It was instinctive, almost **involuntary**. And perhaps you've heard about Akrit Jaswal, the young Indian boy who performed surgery at the age of seven. Now, he really was a prodigy, as far as I'm concerned. OK. Our next caller is Samir, from Dallas.

Samir: Hi. I wanted to point out that all children have a lot of potential. That's an **objective** fact.

Host: Yes, you're right—and we certainly want to encourage all children to do their best. But personally, I do think that some individuals are a bit different. They seem to be born with some kind of underlying talent. Let's take a break now. When we return, we'll be talking about how parents should handle their children's talents.

2 Match the words and phrases on the left with the definitions on the right.

_h_ 1. involuntary

_A_ 2. before (one's) very eyes

_C_ 3. confidence

_e_ 4. fascinated *(adj.)*

___ 5. at the speed of light

_F_ 6. objective *(adj.)*

_H_ 7. renowned

_B_ 8. revise

_G_ 9. unconscious

_D_ 10. unfamiliar

a. directly in front of us, while we watch

b. to review and correct or change something

c. belief in your ability to do things well

d. unaware, not realizing what you are doing

e. very interested

f. not influenced by your own feelings, beliefs, or ideas

g. known and admired by a lot of people

h. automatically, without intending to

i. extremely quickly

j. not aware of

👆 Go to the **Pearson Practice English App** or **MyEnglishLab** for more vocabulary practice.

PREVIEW

You will hear a report by reporter Scott Pelley about a musical prodigy named Jay Greenberg.

▶ **Listen to the introduction to the report. Then answer the questions.**

1. What characteristics set Jay Greenberg apart?

   greatest talent in 200 years.

2. What activities set Greenberg apart?

   _____

3. What other information about "the greatest [musical] talent to come along in 200 years" might the report include? Check (✓) them.

   ☐ his role models   ☐ his challenges   ☐ his critics' opinions

   ☐ his successes   ☐ his parents' reaction

Like Jay Greenberg, jazz pianist Joey Alexander (b. 2003) is a prodigy, teaching himself to play the piano as a young child.

STEINWAY & SONS

1 ▶ **Listen to the whole report. Create a chart like the one below to take notes.**

TAKE NOTES   The Music in My Head

Main Ideas	Details
Reporter:	
Jay Greenberg = musical prodigy	- studies at Juilliard
	- is greatest talent in 200 yrs
	- has written 5 full-length symphonies
	- is 12 yrs old

2 Compare your notes with a partner's. How can you improve your notes?

▶ Go to **MyEnglishLab** to view example notes.

MAIN IDEAS

Answer the questions. Use your notes to help you.

1. What does Jay's teacher Sam Zyman say about Jay's talent?

   No idea how to handle Jay.

2. What does Jay say about how he creates compositions?

   In Jay's head

3. What role have Jay's parents played in the development of his talent?

   One look Jay to the music store.

4. Why doesn't Jay go back and revise his work?

   The first h's correct.

DETAILS

1 ▶ **Listen again and add to your notes. Then identify the statements as _T_ (true) or _F_ (false). Correct the false statements. Use your notes to help you. Discuss your answers with a partner.**

__T__ 1. Jay Greenberg named himself "Bluejay" because he is small and produces a lot of sound, like a small bird.

__F__ 2. Other musicians have helped Jay to compose his music.

__F__ 3. Sam Zyman is a composer and teacher at the Juilliard School.

__T__ 4. At twelve, Jay could probably write a great sonata in two hours, according to Zyman.

__T__ 5. Jay doesn't need to think about his compositions.

__F__ 6. Jay's parents are professional musicians. _thuu are teacher ipaint_

__F__ 7. By the age of two, Jay had begun drawing pictures of instruments that his parents had at home.

__T__ 8. At the age of three, Jay began composing music by drawing small cellos as musical notes on a scale.

__F__ 9. As a child, Jay's hero was Batman.

__T__ 10. Jay creates symphonies by writing for one instrument and then thinking about how the others should come in.

2 **With a partner, take turns summarizing your notes. Then discuss how your notes and your answers in Preview helped you understand the listening.**

▶ Go to **MyEnglishLab** for more listening practice.

MAKE INFERENCES 🔍

Inferring Important Ideas

An inference is an educated guess about something that is not directly stated. Speakers sometimes stress or repeat key words to emphasize important ideas. By listening for such signals, listeners can infer what ideas the speaker considers to be important.

▶ **Read and listen to an excerpt from the Jay Greenberg report. Note the stressed or repeated words. Then answer the questions.**

Example

SCOTT PELLEY: A twelve-year-old wrote this. He wrote every note for each and every instrument. And the really amazing part is, he wrote it in just a few hours.

1. Which words does the reporter stress or repeat?

2. Which idea does the reporter want to emphasize?

   a. Jay has an unusual background.

   b. Jay is incredibly talented.

ANSWERS: 1. He stresses _twelve_ and _a few hours_. He repeats _wrote_ (**wrote** this, **wrote** every note, **wrote** it in just a few hours) and stresses and repeats _every_ (**every** note, **every** instrument).
2. b

▶ **Listen to excerpts from the Jay Greenberg report and answer the questions.**

Music teacher Sam Zyman comments on Jay Greenberg's skills.

1. Which words does Zyman repeat? _prodigy_____

2. Which idea does Zyman emphasize?

   a. Jay is one of the greatest music prodigies in history.

   b. Jay's parents are responsible for his composition skills.

Excerpt Two

Jay's mother Orna Greenberg comments on her son.

1. Which word does she repeat? _____

2. Which idea does she emphasize?

   a. She thought she should encourage her son's interest in music.

   b. Jay became obsessed with cellos when he was a young child.

DISCUSS 🔍

Work with a partner or in a small group. Discuss the questions.

1. Why are Jay's teacher and mother so surprised by Jay's talents?

2. What kinds of feelings does Jay experience when he is composing?

3. What do you predict for Jay's future in music and in life?

🡒 Go to **MyEnglishLab** to give your opinion about another question.

> **USE YOUR NOTES**
>
> **APPLY** Find information in your notes to use in your discussion.

LISTENING TWO | What Makes a Prodigy?

VOCABULARY

1 **Work with a partner. Take turns reading the words in the box aloud. Try to guess their meanings. Check a dictionary if necessary.**

accomplished *(adj.)*	exceptional	influential	potential *(n.)*
achieve	inconclusive	interact	

2 Complete the transcript with the words from Exercise One. The transcript is from a lecture and about the so-called "nature / nurture debate," which considers the origin of unusual abilities. Then take turns with a partner reading the lecture aloud.

LECTURER: Hello, everyone. Today, we're going to continue our discussion about prodigies. As early as the seventeenth century, scientists began to ask where unusual abilities come from, and we are still fascinated by this question today. Why are some children especially intelligent and _____ in certain
1.
areas while others are not? Why do some have _____ talent?
2.
Are they simply born with the _____ to do well at something,
3.
or do they somehow acquire their talent from their environment and by how they _____ with the world?
4.

This question is now referred to as "the nature / nurture debate." *Nature* refers to natural, inborn ability. For example, some people are born with the ability to run faster than others, to do mathematical calculations in their head, or to _____ success in chess, even if they get very little
5.
encouragement from their families or teachers.

Nurture, on the other hand, refers to the impact of people's environment on their success. For example, some great musicians have had the help and support of _____ teachers or parents who have made their
6.
children practice for hours every day. Sometimes, an uncle or sibling may inspire a child to take up a particular activity. Researchers say that these influences are also very important.

Today, scientists have a greater ability to study nature and nurture. They use modern methods, like neuro-imaging scans, to study the human brain, particularly areas like the cerebellum. However, in the end, research about whether our genes or environment are responsible for our successes is _____.
7.

▶ Go to the **Pearson Practice English App** or **MyEnglishLab** for more vocabulary practice.

Taking Notes with Bullets and Dashes

When you listen to speakers, notice how they use details, such as examples and explanations, to support their ideas. As you take notes, list details using bullets or dashes to show their relationship to the main ideas.

Items should be listed using a consistent, or parallel, structure (all verbs, all nouns, etc.).

Example

You hear: Researchers study the brains of prodigies in different ways. One way is to use neuro-imaging scans. This is a procedure for studying the brain. Another way is to focus on the cerebellum, which is a particular area of the brain. And yet another way to study the brains of prodigies is to examine "working memory," which is done to measure brain speed.

You write: *Researchers study brains of prodigies in different ways*

– use neuro-imaging scans (to study the brain)

– focus on cerebellum (an area of the brain)

– examine "working memory" to measure brain speed

▶ **Listen to excerpts from an interview with a scientist. List the examples and explanations using bullets and dashes.**

Excerpt One

Prodigies run in families

• *Sibling* _____

_____

_____

Excerpt Two

Research done on abilities
in different areas:

_____

_____

_____

↖ Go to **MyEnglishLab** for more note-taking practice.

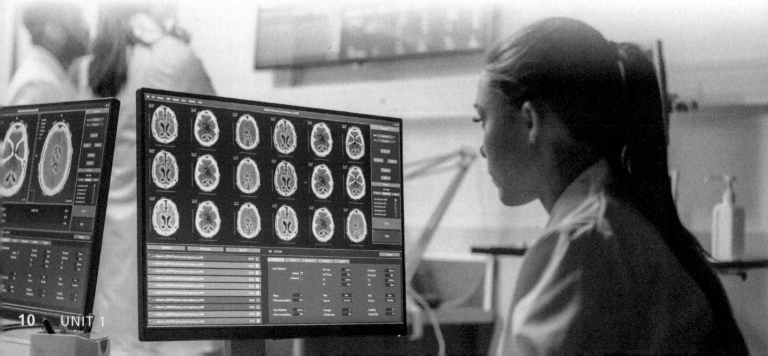

COMPREHENSION

You will hear an interview with Dr. Gráinne McLoughlin, a scientist who specializes in the study of twins.

1 ▶ **Listen to the interview. Create a chart like the one below to take notes. Try to list the examples and explanations with bullets or dashes as you take notes.**

TAKE NOTES What Makes a Prodigy?	
Main Ideas	**Details**

2 **Use your notes to answer the questions.**

1. According to Dr. McLoughlin, how common are prodigies?

_____

2. What special techniques do scientists use to study prodigies?

_____

3. How are prodigies different from other people?

_____

4. Dr. McLoughlin says, "The study of twins has allowed us to understand the influence of nature and nurture on many different behaviors and abilities." What does she mean?

_____

_____

5. Dr. McLoughlin says, "A great deal of research has been done . . . But the results are often inconclusive." What does she mean?

_____

_____

> **USE YOUR NOTES**
>
> Compare your notes with a partner's. How can you improve your notes next time?

6. What is the smart seventeen-year-old boy who graduated from Cambridge University an example of?

_____

7. Why does Dr. McLoughlin talk about Tiger Woods?

_____

8. What does Dr. McLoughlin conclude about whether geniuses are born or made?

_____

1 ▶ **Listen to an excerpt from the interview with Dr. McLoughlin. How does her voice change when she says "differently"?**

Recognizing Emphasis

When speakers want to emphasize an important idea, they often slow down and stress one word or phrase, speaking loudly and clearly. The word or phrase can indicate the speaker's view.

▶ **Read and listen to an excerpt from the interview with Dr. McLoughlin. Then answer the question.**

Example

DR. McLOUGHLIN: Actually, prodigies are quite rare.

What does she say?

a. Actually, prodigies are quite **rare**. (This emphasis indicates that the information—that prodigies are very uncommon—is important or surprising.)

b. Actually, prodigies **are** quite rare. (This emphasis indicates confirmation or agreement with the information—that prodigies are very uncommon.)

ANSWER: a - Dr. McLoughlin emphasizes *rare* to express her feeling that the information (that prodigies are very uncommon) is important and may be surprising.

2 ▶ **Listen to excerpts from the interview with Dr. McLoughlin. Circle the correct answers.**

Excerpt One

1. Which word does Dr. McLoughlin emphasize?

    (a.) . . . *a person can be **made** a genius.*

    b. . . . *a person **can** be made a genius.*

2. What does she mean?

    a. Tiger Woods's experience, not his abilities, influenced his success.

    (b.) Many people would disagree with this statement, but it's true.

Excerpt Two

1. Which word does Dr. McLoughlin emphasize?

    (a.) *It could be that we all have the **potential** for genius . . .*

    b. *It could be that we **all** have the potential for genius . . .*

2. What does she mean?

    (a.) Each one of us could become a genius, under the right circumstances.

    b. Perhaps we have natural abilities.

▶ Go to **MyEnglishLab** for more skill practice.

ORGANIZE

What do we understand about prodigies? Complete the chart with details from the listenings.

USE YOUR NOTES

APPLY Review your notes from Listening One and Two. Use the information in your notes to complete the chart.

	PRODIGIES	
	LISTENING ONE: *The Music in My Head* *Jay Greenberg's Experience*	**LISTENING TWO:** *What Makes a Prodigy?* *General Research*
1. What are some outward signs of a prodigy?		
2. What does science know about the biology of prodigies?		
3. What role does nature play in the making of a prodigy?		
4. How much of a factor is environment on the development of a prodigy?		

SYNTHESIZE

What does the research of Dr. Gráinne McLoughlin tell us about prodigies? How does the case of Jay Greenberg support or not support these ideas? Discuss the questions with a partner. Give examples from the listenings.

- **STUDENT A:** Explain the main points of Dr. McLoughlin's research.

- **STUDENT B:** Talk about how Jay Greenberg's experience fits into those findings.

  Example

  A: Prodigies are rare.

  B: That explains why we're fascinated by them. Hearing music composed by a twelve-year-old is fascinating.

🔖 Go to **MyEnglishLab** to check what you learned.

FOCUS ON SPEAKING

VOCABULARY

REVIEW

1 **Complete the chart with different forms of the words. Then compare answers with a partner. Check a dictionary or ask your instructor.**

Noun	Verb	Adjective	Adverb
accomplishment	to accomplish	**accomplished**	*[illegible]*
achievement	to achieve		
confidence	to feel confidence	confident	
fascination	to fascinate	**fascinated** fascinating	fascinatingly
influence	to influence	**influential**	influentially
interaction	to interact	interactive	interactionally
volunteer	to volunteer	voluntary **involuntary**	volunteerly

2 Work with a partner. Complete the conversation by circling the correct word form. Then read the conversation aloud.

WOMAN: Good morning, Doctor. I have newborn identical twins, and I want to make sure I treat them differently because I want them both to **(1) achievement / achieve** their full potential. Can you advise me?

DOCTOR: Raising twins is a **(2) fascination / fascinating** experience. And, of course, this experience must be very difficult for you, because even one baby is a lot of work. Two is "double the trouble," as they say! Now, every infant needs individual attention, so try to spend quality time with each one. That way you can develop a different kind of **(3) interaction / interactive** with each twin.

WOMAN: Yes, I'd like to. But I'm not feeling very **(4) confidence / confident**. I'm worried that other people will treat them both the same. After all, they look identical. When people see them, they'll always assume they have the same personality and the same skills. I suppose that's a(n) **(5) volunteer / involuntary** reaction when you see identical twins.

DOCTOR: Perhaps, but try not to be too concerned. As they grow, make sure you understand how they are different and what each one is interested in. It's important to encourage their individual interests, talents, and **(6) influences / influential** so that as they grow up, they can set their own goals and **(7) accomplish / accomplishments** different things. In the meantime, try to find someone who can **(8) volunteer / voluntary** to help you get things done. You need to take care of yourself, too!

identical twins

EXPAND

Read the opinions about how people become geniuses. Then write each boldfaced word from the text next to its definition.

HOW DO PEOPLE BECOME GENIUSES?
A parent, a teacher, and a prodigy offer their opinions.

Kimberly Lewis, parent

My daughter seems to have an **innate** talent for music. One day, when she was only about seven years old, we took her to a store where they sold instruments, and, **out of the blue**, she picked up a guitar and started to play it. She seemed to have an **instinctive** feeling about chords and notes. There are no musicians in my family, so I think that she is naturally **predisposed** to be good at music. How else can you explain her talent?

126 views   2 Shares   71 Likes

Dan Medina, teacher

Everyone is born with potential, and it's a teacher's job to **motivate** his or her students to develop it. I**'m in favor of** giving all my students the chance to experiment with different things—music, math, languages, and so on. Then, if they enjoy it, they can explore it **on their own**. Of course, you have to **take into account** people's natural abilities: After all, some students pick up certain subjects faster than others. But everyone deserves the chance to succeed.

318 views   4 Shares   128 Likes

Carly Michaels, prodigy

I've been really good at art since I was a child. **In actual fact**, many people tell me that my work—my paintings—really affect them emotionally. I believe that people **inherit** some of their characteristics from their parents: That's just **common sense**. Now I'm a successful digital designer working with all kinds of **complex** computer codes. I've been encouraged by a lot of different people in my life, but I also think that I was born with a natural aptitude for art.

459 views   3 Shares   198 Likes

1. ~~take into~~ account: to pay attention to, allow for
2. predisposed: naturally inclined to
3. out of the blue: without warning
4. on their own: by themselves
5. instinctive: by instinct
6. innate: natural, inborn

7. inherit: to acquire, genetically, from your parents
8. motivate: to encourage
9. complex: not easy to understand
10. common sense: sound judgment: what most people would say
11. in favor of: to be for, supportive of
12. in actual fact: in truth

CREATE

APPLY **Work in a small group. Follow the steps.**

1. Read the discussion forum. Which group of students should the school invest the money in? What would be the benefits of each approach?

2. Discuss your reaction.

3. Try to use the vocabulary from Review and Expand.

Seabury Middle School | Forum: Additional funding

Kendra Bauer, Seabury Principal   3 hours ago

Seabury Middle School is facing a difficult decision about which programs to support. I'm opening this forum to ask for parents' opinions. We've been given some additional funding to support a program of our choice, and we're trying to decide whether to allocate it to the honors program or to an after-school program for struggling students.

 27 hearts   REPLY

---

proudpapa123   RE: Additional funding   2 hours ago

My son's a really good student, and I think he needs to be encouraged more in his classes. You should invest this money in the honors program. That way, students like my son can be pushed to do even better.

---

m_vasquez   RE: Additional funding   24 minutes ago

All of our students need to be supported, not just the best ones in the school! We've had a lot of discussions about this in our parents' group, and we feel that the after-school program would be a much better choice. Students could be given the chance to explore different subjects, like math, art, or music. All students deserve the chance to succeed!

---

avs_fan17:   RE: Additional funding   13 minutes ago

I don't see why the money couldn't be divided. Obviously, some of the more advanced students need to be challenged, but sometimes children need support in a subject they find difficult. Not everyone is good at everything, so why not expose all the students to different subjects?

🔊 Go to the **Pearson Practice English App** or **MyEnglishLab** for more vocabulary practice.

GRAMMAR FOR SPEAKING

1 Look at the illustration and then read the description. Notice the forms of the boldfaced verbs.

In this cartoon, a boy is showing his teacher how to solve a complex math problem. Most likely, he **has been taught** to solve this kind of problem at home, not at school. The teacher **is surprised** by the boy's explanation.

Using the Passive Voice

How to Form the Passive Voice	Active	Passive
To form the **passive voice**, use the correct form of *be* + **past participle**. Optional: If the agent of the action (the subject of an active sentence) is known and important, you can use *by* + agent.	*Many parents **encourage** their children to explore different interests.*	*Many children **are encouraged** <u>by their parents</u> to explore different interests.*
The object in an active sentence becomes the subject in a passive sentence.	*My parents didn't allow **me** to play sports until I had finished my homework.*	***I** wasn't allowed to play sports until I had finished my homework.*
With modals (*can, may, should, will*, etc.), use **modal + base form of *be* + past participle**.	*Children **can beat** adults at some memory games.*	*Adults **can be beaten** by children at some memory games.*

When to Use the Passive Voice		
Use the passive voice to shift focus from the agent of the action to the person or thing being described. In this example, *prodigies* are more important than *people all over the world*.	*Prodigies **are admired** by people all over the world.*	
Use the passive voice when you do not know the agent of the action, or when the agent is not important. In this example, it doesn't matter who is reporting the news.	*News about the child violinist **is being reported** in detail.*	
Use the passive voice when you don't want to mention the agent, particularly to avoid blaming the agent. In this example, we know who made the mistakes, but we don't wish to name that person.	*Some factual mistakes **have been made** in the series of articles about the young artist. For example, she was five years old when she had an exhibition, not fifteen.*	

2 Complete the news report transcript. Use the passive voice and the verbs and forms indicated. Then take turns with a partner reading the report aloud.

NEWSCASTER: Now, some news about prodigies from around the world.

Over the past two weeks, live audiences around the world _____ as the
                                                              1. (*captivate*, present perfect)
Chinese pianist Lang Lang (1982–) performed his latest work. One of these concerts was filmed

and _____ on public television next week.
        2. (*show*, future)

On this day in 2013, Shakuntala Devi died at the age of 83. Born in southern India, Devi

_____ as the "human computer" because she could calculate large numbers in
      3. (*know*, past)
her head. People thought she _____ special instruction in mathematics, but in
                                   4. (*give*, past perfect)
fact, she had no formal education. She _____ to do complex calculations by
                                            5. (*teach*, past)
her father, who was a circus performer.

Coming up next month is the annual Capablanca Memorial Chess Tournament, held in

memory of José Raúl Capablanca y Graupera (1888–1942), the "human chess machine." Born

in Cuba, Capablanca _____ one of the greatest chess players of all time.
                          6. (*consider*, present)
Unlike other famous players, he _____ for his simple playing style, but he
                                      7. (*know*, past)
played at the speed of light. This, together with his exceptional skill, made it almost impossible

for other players to beat him.

3 Rewrite the active sentences in the passive voice. Omit the agent.

1. A teacher told my son to practice piano more often.

   My son was told to practice piano more often.

2. My father didn't allow me to play soccer.

   _____

3. Your friends have always told you that you're good at art.

   _____

4. They're not going to release their new album until next week.

   _____

5. People can see Julie's work at the local art museum.

   _____

4 Work with a partner. Take turns reading and responding. Then complete the chart by writing the correct forms.

STUDENT A: Cover the second column. Read one of the statements or questions.

STUDENT B: Cover the first column. Respond, using the passive voice and the verb form indicated.

Statement / Question	Response
1. People are born with a certain amount of natural ability.	Yes, but environment is also important. If you _____ in a musical family, *bring up*, present for example, you are more likely to be good at music.
2. Dr. McLoughlin says that nature and nurture are both important.	Yes. She seems to think that they _____ . *can't separate*, present
3. Scientists seem to have done a lot of studies on prodigies.	Yes, and one thing was very interesting to me: It sounds like a lot of studies _____ on twins. *conduct*, present perfect
4. Were you a good math student?	No, not really. But I think if I _____ more, I would have *encourage*, past perfect done much better.
5. I do think Jay Greenberg is a genius, but he's had a lot of education, too.	Right. Jay _____ to all *expose*, present perfect kinds of music instruction.
6. Jay has become really famous.	I know. Now he _____ by *contact*, present progressive musicians all over the world.
7. I think he's going to be doing a lot of international performances.	Yes, I heard that he _____ *invite*, future to Japan next fall.
8. I'm learning to play the piano, but I feel bad when I see young children play so much better than I do.	You _____ by them. Not *shouldn't intimidate / present* everyone can be a prodigy!

🔾 Go to the **Pearson Practice English App** or **MyEnglishLab** for more grammar practice. Check what you learned in **MyEnglishLab**.

Contracting and Reducing *Be* and *Have*

In speech, fluent speakers often use contractions of the verbs *be* and *have* after pronouns: *He is* → *He's, They are* → *They're, She has* → *She's, We have* → *We've*. These contractions sound friendlier and less formal, and are easier to say than the full forms.

After nouns, these same verbs often have reduced pronunciations.

▶ **Read and listen to the examples.**

Examples

- *Is* is pronounced /z/ after most sounds. But it's pronounced /əz/ (the so-called *long plural*: *Gus's*) after these sounds: s, z, ʃ, ʒ, tʃ, dʒ.

  A: My **husband is** convinced that **Mitch is** really talented.

  Say: "husbandz" /həzbəndz/

  "Mitchəz" /mɪtʃəz/

- *Are* is pronounced /ər/ or /är/. It is joined with the preceding word.

  B: **People are** interested in prodigies. **Scientists are** interested in them, too.

  Say: "peoplər" /piyplər/

  "scientistsär" /sayəntistsär/

- *Have* is pronounced /əv/ (like the preposition *of*). It is joined closely with the preceding word.

  A: **Some have** become world famous.

  Say: "someəv" /səməv/

- *Has* is pronounced like *is* (see above).

  B: The word *genius* **has** become difficult to define.

  Say: "geniusəz" /dʒiynyəsəz/

NOTE: *For reference, see the phonetic alphabet on page 247.*

1 ▶ **Read and listen to the sentences. Underline the verbs that are contracted or reduced. (Not every sentence has a contraction or reduction.) Then practice saying the sentences with a partner, using contractions and reductions.**

1. "The United States has become fascinated by prodigies."

2. "Parents are aware of their children's talents."

3. "I have seen young children with a natural aptitude for sports."

4. "Critics have warned that it's unhealthy to put too much pressure on children."

5. "We are concerned that our son spends too much time on his math problems."

6. "Researchers are interested in studying children with unusual abilities."

2 ▶ **Read and listen to an excerpt from a podcast about prodigies. As you listen, fill in the verbs you hear.**

HOST: Painting prodigy Aelita Andre, born in Melbourne, Australia, in 2007, has captured the world's attention with her colorful work. However, people _____are_____ often surprised when they
_{1.}
hear that she started when she was only nine months old. The media _____have_____ called her the "youngest professional painter
_{2.}
in the world." Aelita's parents are themselves artists, and they _____have_____ always encouraged their daughter to paint.
_{3.}
They say she can spend hours working on a canvas. The public _____has_____ responded enthusiastically to Aelita's work—
_{4.}
in fact, one of her paintings sold for $50,000. Some critics _____have_____ called Aelita's work "surrealist
_{5.}
abstract expressionism."

3 APPLY **Prepare to retell Aelita's story to your partner. Mark the transcript in Exercise Two with the contractions and reductions you plan to make. Then read the transcript aloud.**

SPEAKING SKILL

Giving Your Opinion

In a discussion, it is important to state your own opinion or viewpoints clearly and to do so politely. That way, listeners will be able to understand and respect your ideas. Sometimes, however, you may not want to give an opinion—either because you don't have one or because you want to avoid an argument!

Give an Opinion	*I (don't) think . . .*	*As far as I know, . . .*
	I believe . . .	*As I see it, . . .*
	If you ask me, . . .	*From what I understand, . . .*
	In my opinion, . . .	
Agree	*I agree.*	*That's just what I was going to say!*
	I think so, too.	*Yes, exactly.*
	I couldn't agree more.	
Disagree	*Maybe / Perhaps, but . . .*	*That's not exactly the way I see it. I think . . .*
	You have a good point, but . . .	
	Yes, but on the other hand . . .	*I'm not so sure . . .*
Not Give an Opinion	*I'm not really sure.*	*On one hand, . . . , but on the other hand, . . .*
	I don't know what to think.	
	I haven't made up my mind.	*Beats me.* (informal)
	I'm of two minds.	

APPLY **Work in groups of three. Take turns presenting and responding to the ideas. Speak; don't write. Use an expression from the chart above when you state your opinion.**

1. **A:** I think most child prodigies are influenced by their parents.

   B: *I think so, too. If you ask me, some parents put too much pressure on their children.*

   C: *Well, you have a good point, but some children seem to be born with exceptional abilities.*

2. **A:** From what I understand, you lose your natural abilities if you don't develop them.

   B: _____ . . .

   C: _____ . . .

3. **A:** I think anyone could become a prodigy with enough work, don't you?

   B: _____ . . .

   C: _____ . . .

4. **A:** I don't think prodigies are always very happy.

   B: _____ . . .

   C: _____ . . .

5. **A:** I think it's unhealthy for young children to become so involved in only one area.

   B: _____ . . .

   C: _____ . . .

🔍 Go to **MyEnglishLab** for more skill practice and to check what you learned.

FINAL SPEAKING TASK: Discussion 🔍 APPLY

In this activity, you will work in a group and take turns sharing a case study about an actual child prodigy.

PREPARE

1 **Work in a group of four. Each member chooses a different case study from the box. (See Student Activities on page 216 for the details of each case study.)**

   • Read your case study. Do not read the other case studies.

   • Consider these questions: What is the child's gift? How was it discovered? How was it developed (through practice, lessons, etc.)? What kind of support did the child have (parents, school, etc.)? What challenges or special circumstances did the child face?

   • Do additional research online.

   Case study 1: The Young Tennis Dynamo
   Case study 2: The Math Whiz
   Case study 3: The Promising Violinist
   Case study 4: The Chess Master

2 APPLY **Consider how to apply the vocabulary, grammar, pronunciation, and speaking skills from the unit. Use the checklist to help you.**

   ☐ **Vocabulary:** Read through the list of vocabulary on page 27. Which words can you include in your discussion to make it clearer and more interesting? Choose at least three words or phrases to use and add them to your notes.

   ☐ **Grammar:** Scan your notes for places where you will use the passive voice. Can you use the form correctly?

   ☐ **Pronunciation:** Record yourself practicing using contractions and reductions of *be* and *have*. Then listen back. Are your ideas clear?

   ☐ **Speaking Skill:** Think about how you want to state your opinion. Try to choose the expressions that are most effective.

DISCUSS

1 **Discuss your case study with the group.**

- Present the details of your case study.

- Tell about the individual's gift.

- Explain how that gift was developed by the parents, school, or others. Include details about special challenges or circumstances the individual faced.

2 **Share reactions to your case study with the class.**

- Share your and your group's reactions.

- Invite responses from the other groups.

ALTERNATIVE SPEAKING TOPIC

APPLY Read the quotes and decide what they mean. Then choose one and speak about it in class. Explain the meaning and say whether you agree or disagree, and why. Use the vocabulary, grammar, pronunciation, and speaking skills from the unit.

> Genius is 1 percent inspiration and 99 percent perspiration.
>
> Thomas A. Edison: American inventor, 1847–1931

> There is no great genius without a mixture of madness.
>
> Aristotle: Greek philosopher, 384–322 BCE

> Genius is eternal patience.
>
> Michelangelo: Italian artist, 1475–1564

> Find out what your gift is and nurture it.
>
> Katy Perry: American singer, 1984–

> For every child prodigy that you know about, at least 50 potential ones have burned out before you even heard about them.
>
> Itzhak Perlman: Israeli violinist, 1945–

CHECK WHAT YOU'VE LEARNED

Check (✔) the outcomes you've met and vocabulary you've learned. Put an X next to the skills and vocabulary you still need to practice.

Learning Outcomes
- ☐ Infer important ideas
- ☐ Take notes with bullets and dashes
- ☐ Recognize emphasis
- ☐ Use the passive voice
- ☐ Contract and reduce *be* and *have*
- ☐ Give your opinion

Vocabulary
- ☐ accomplished (*adj.*)
- ☐ achieve AWL
- ☐ confidence
- ☐ exceptional
- ☐ fascinated (*adj.*)
- ☐ inconclusive AWL
- ☐ influential
- ☐ interact AWL
- ☐ involuntary
- ☐ objective (*adj.*) AWL
- ☐ potential (*n.*) AWL
- ☐ renowned
- ☐ revise AWL
- ☐ unconscious
- ☐ unfamiliar

Multi-word Units
- ☐ at the speed of light
- ☐ before (one's) very eyes

🔊 Go to **MyEnglishLab** to watch a video about child prodigies, access the Unit Project, and take the Unit 1 Achievement Test.

LEARNING OUTCOMES

- > Infer the meaning of figurative language
- > Take notes using key words
- > Distinguish between main ideas and details
- > Use gerunds and infinitives
- > Identify and use thought groups
- > Introduce a presentation

Go to **MyEnglishLab** to check what you know.

Pushing the Boundaries

1 FOCUS ON THE TOPIC

1. To *push the boundaries* means to exceed limits or overcome obstacles. What kinds of challenges do you predict this unit will be about?

2. The photo shows individuals racing in wheelchairs. They have not permitted their physical challenges to get in their way. What kinds of challenges have they probably faced? What personal qualities are likely to have helped them succeed?

3. How would you define the word *disability*? Provide some examples of disabilities.

LISTENING ONE | Artist Opens Others' Eyes

VOCABULARY

1 **Work with a partner. Take turns reading the boldfaced words and phrases and their definitions aloud.**

average *(adj.)*: having qualities that are typical of most people or things; ordinary

devastated *(adj.)*: extremely sad or shocked

diagnosis: identification of what illness a person has

go far beyond: to exceed the expected or usual boundary or limit

hardship: something that makes your life difficult

keep (someone) going: to give hope and encouragement

make (something) look cool: to make something seem fashionable, attractive, interesting, etc. (informal)

misconception: an idea that is wrong or untrue, but that people still believe

persevere: to continue trying to do something difficult in a determined way

stereotypical: widely held but, sometimes, incorrect opinion

this is it: expression when something concludes or ends (informal)

2 ▶ **Read and listen to a podcast. Complete the transcript with the boldfaced words and phrases from page 30. Use the correct form.**

PODCAST HOST: Hi, podcast listeners. Well, we asked you, our listeners, to call in and describe a person you admire—a person who has overcome an obstacle. Here are a few of the calls we received.

VOICE MESSAGE 1: As far as I'm concerned, my father is a hero. A few years ago, he had a terrible car accident, and the doctors gave him a scary _____: They told him he had severely
                                                                                          1.
damaged his spinal cord and would never walk again. My family was _____ by the
                                                                                          2.
news, but, you know, my father was determined to get back on his feet. He said he wasn't going to give
up—he was going to _____. And he did! Now, he's able to get around on his own. He's
                              3.
made great progress physically, but for me his achievements _____ that. He's also
                                                                              4.
become an inspiration to me because he's shown me how to face obstacles in life.

VOICE MESSAGE 2: I want to talk about Helen Keller. She's an historical figure I
really admire. Helen became blind and deaf when she was a baby, and
everyone had so many _____ about her—including her
                              5.
family! They thought she lived in a world of her own and that there was no
hope for her future. But Helen was not a(n) _____ person.
                                                            6.
Not only did she learn to communicate, but she also became a world-famous
speaker and author. And she even earned a BA along the way. In 2003, her
portrait was put on a special Alabama state quarter, and it's beautiful. It really
_____! Sadly, some people have _____
        7.   8.
ideas about the disabled, but Helen Keller is an incredible example that
disproves many of them.

Helen Keller

VOICE MESSAGE 3: I admire Mahatma Gandhi. He overcame difficulties of his own and helped other people
overcome a lot of _____ in their lives. He supported the poorest people in his country.
                              9.
His enemies made several attempts to kill him, and, in 1948, someone was successful. Gandhi was fatally
shot as he was about to make a speech, and _____ . After his death, there was an
                                                              10.
outpouring of grief across India. He was against violence, saying that "An eye for an eye only ends up
making the whole world blind." His example is what _____ when I get depressed
                                                                          11.
about world events.

▶ Go to the **Pearson Practice English App** or **MyEnglishLab** for more vocabulary practice.

You will hear a report about artist Carol Saylor.

▶ Think about the title of the listening (Artist Opens Others' Eyes) and the title of this unit (Pushing the Boundaries). What disability do you think you might hear about? Then listen to an excerpt from the report. Circle the correct answers.

Carol Saylor

1. Carol Saylor is _____ .

   a. a painter

   b. a sculptor

   c. a musician

2. She sounds _____ .

   a. devastated

   b. hopeful

   c. angry

LISTEN

1 ▶ Listen to the whole report. Create a chart like the one below to take notes.

TAKE NOTES   Artist Opens Others' Eyes

Main Ideas	Details
Carol Saylor:	• 73 yrs old
Blind and deaf artist	• art teacher, sculptor

2 Compare your notes with a partner's. How can you improve your notes?

↘ Go to **MyEnglishLab** to view example notes.

MAIN IDEAS

Circle the correct answers. Use your notes to help you.

1. According to Saylor, what do most sighted people think about blind people?

   a. They understand their difficulties.

   b. They have incorrect ideas about them.

   c. They are sympathetic to them.

2. Many student groups visit Saylor's studio. What does Saylor mainly want to teach them?

   a. how to make sculptures

   b. how to work with clay

   c. how to use their imagination

3. How do these students respond to Saylor?

   a. They are impressed by her work.

   b. They are confused about her methods.

   c. They are afraid of blindness.

4. What feelings does Saylor say her art expresses?

   a. pain and unhappiness

   b. confusion and happiness

   c. grief and hope

DETAILS

1 ▶ **Listen again and add to your notes. Then circle the correct answers to complete the summary of Saylor's story. Use your notes to help you.**

Carol Saylor, who is **(1) 62 / 73 / 81** years old, is a sculptor and art teacher. When doctors first told her she was going blind, she was very upset because she had many misconceptions about blindness. For example, she thought she would see **(2) black / colorful shapes / vibrating spots**. However, what she actually "sees" is **(3) white / beautiful / empty**.

Kate Whitman is a teacher who brings her class to see Saylor's work. She says that Saylor's story is **(4) just as important as / less important than / more important than** Saylor's art. The students are surprised and impressed by Saylor's work. One girl realizes that art is not just about what you see but also what you **(5) understand / believe / feel**.

Saylor emphasizes that her art is not art therapy, meaning that it is not only about helping herself feel better about her situation. She says that it is **(6) a way to understand the world / a part of her / a way to educate others**.

2 **With a partner, take turns summarizing your notes. Then discuss how your notes and your answers in Preview helped you understand the listening.**

◑ Go to **MyEnglishLab** for more listening practice.

MAKE INFERENCES 🔍

Inferring the Meaning of Figurative Language

Speakers sometimes use figurative language to express their feelings. Unlike literal language, figurative language involves comparing a situation, person, or object to something else, either directly or indirectly. Often, figurative language appeals to the senses (sight, sound, smell, taste, and touch). The context—the surrounding information—can help the listener determine the meaning of the figurative language.

▶ **Read and listen to an excerpt from the report about Carol Saylor. Notice the boldfaced figurative language. Then answer the question.**

Example

CAROL SAYLOR: The things that I have learned about art **go far beyond**, I think, what the average sighted person knows. And that's really what my art is all about.

What can you infer from Saylor's statement?

a. Blindness has given her deeper insight about art than she had before.

b. Sighted people do not know how to be good artists.

c. She thinks she has learned more about art than most blind people.

ANSWER: a – She uses "go far beyond" to indicate the expansion of her ideas.

▶ **Listen to excerpts from the report about Carol Saylor and circle the correct answers.**

Excerpt One

A student is explaining her reaction after she visits Saylor's studio. What is the student's intended meaning?

a. Saylor has taught her what to look for in good art.

b. Saylor has taught her to appreciate art differently.

c. Saylor has taught her to look at art much more carefully.

Excerpt Two

Saylor is explaining what art means to her. What is Saylor's intended meaning?

a. She feels that art has given her a reason to live.

b. She believes she is a naturally gifted artist.

c. She loves to teach other people to create art.

DISCUSS 🔍

Work with a partner or in a small group. Discuss the questions.

USE YOUR NOTES

APPLY Find information in your notes to use in your discussion.

1. What misconceptions do sighted people have about blind people? Carol Saylor, Kate Whitman, and others believe it is important to overcome these misconceptions. Why? Do you agree? Explain.

2. What are the biggest challenges Carol Saylor faces as an artist? What advantages, if any, does she have over sighted artists? What do you think about Saylor's answers? If you were in her shoes, what might you feel?

↻ Go to **MyEnglishLab** to give your opinion about another question.

LISTENING TWO | An Athlete's Inspiring Journey

VOCABULARY

1 **Read the entry about the Paralympic Games. Notice the boldfaced words. Try to guess their meanings.**

It began in the mid-twentieth century as a way to include athletes who were not **able-bodied** in an important sporting event. However, now the Paralympics **has transitioned** into one of the biggest international sporting events in the world. It provides a venue for athletes with a variety of disabilities to compete at the highest levels for medals in a variety of sports, including downhill skiing, cycling, and basketball. The event also raises **awareness** of the courage of disabled athletes, some of whom **have rebounded** from accidents or have faced enormous challenges. It's an **inspiring** event that celebrates athleticism and perseverance.

2 Write each word from the box next to its definition.

able-bodied	awareness	inspiring	rebound	transition

1. _awareness_ : consciousness
2. _rebound_ : to recover
3. _transition_ : to change
4. _inspiring_ : causing someone to want to do something
5. _able-bodied_ : fit, strong, and not disabled

➤ Go to the **Pearson Practice English App** or **MyEnglishLab** for more vocabulary practice.

NOTE-TAKING SKILL

Taking Notes Using Key Words

When taking notes, write the key words you hear to help you focus on the essential ideas. When you review your notes, these key words will help you to remember the information you heard. Also, use short, clear language in your notes, which will allow you to write more quickly.

Example

You hear: Held in the same year and city as the Olympic Games, the Paralympic Games is an international event that hosts athletes with a variety of physical and intellectual disabilities. The athletes compete in more than twenty different sports, including archery, tennis, and snowboarding.

You write: *Paralympic Games*

– same yr / city as Olympics

– international

– athletes w/disabilities: physical / intellectual

– 20+ sports: Ex: archery, tennis, snowboarding

Also, make sure you review your notes soon after you've written them and add important details. This will help you recall the information.

▶ **Listen to excerpts from an interview about the inspiration of athlete Ryan Chalmers. Use key words to note the main ideas and details. Be sure to use short, clear language.**

Excerpt One:

Main idea:

Stay Focused _Teaches young people to develop confidence and leadership skills._

Details:

– Ryan _Stay focused on what to achieve_

– _to persevere_ = don't give up

Excerpt Two:

Main idea:

Ryan stays mental and physical fit.

Details:

- mental fitness as important as _____

- helps in difficult situations—examples: _____

Go to **MyEnglishLab** for more note-taking practice.

COMPREHENSION

You will hear an interview with a young athlete who was inspired by athlete Ryan Chalmers and his extraordinary achievements.

1 ▶ **Listen to the interview. Create a chart like the one below to take notes. Try to identify key words as you take notes.**

TAKE NOTES An Athlete's Inspiring Journey	
Main Ideas	**Details**

Ryan Chalmers (left) with supporter
at fundraiser in New York City

36   UNIT 2

2 Use your notes to answer the questions.

1. What did Ryan Chalmers do?

   He raced across the USA

2. What realization did Natalie Escalante have after seeing Chalmers race?

   She realized that disable doesn't make good

3. In what ways has Chalmers inspired Escalante?

USE YOUR NOTES

Compare your notes with a partner's. How can you improve your notes next time?

4. What does Stay Focused teach disabled youth?

5. What does "mental fitness" mean?

LISTENING SKILL

1 ▶ **Listen to an excerpt from the interview about Ryan Chalmers and his race across the United States. What is the main idea? What kinds of details does it include?**

Distinguishing Between Main Ideas and Details

Speakers may state their main ideas directly or indirectly. They often give details, including examples, to support or illustrate their main ideas. Listening for details can help you understand the main ideas.

▶ **Read and listen to an excerpt from the interview about Ryan Chalmers and his race across the United States. Then answer the question.**

Example

HOST: His trip lasted a total of seventy-one days, during which time he raised awareness and funds for disabled teens and adults for a project called Push Across America. This is the kind of thing we in the news business should talk about more often.

Which is the main idea?

a. The journey took seventy-one days to complete.

b. The journey is the kind of event that should be in the news more.

c. The journey raised funds and awareness for the disabled.

ANSWER: c – The other choices are details that support the main idea. The details help the listener understand the difficulty of the journey and its importance.

2 ▶ **Listen to excerpts from the interview about Ryan Chalmers. Circle the correct answers.**

Excerpt One

What is the main idea of the excerpt?

a. Chalmers has played sports since the age of eight.

b. Chalmers has encouraged disabled people to play sports.

c. Chalmers has competed in the Paralympics and marathons.

Excerpt Two

1. What is the main idea of the excerpt?

a. Disabled athletes share many of the same feelings as able-bodied athletes.

b. It is just as hard to race in a wheelchair as it is to race on a bicycle.

c. Athletes choose their sport based on their individual interests.

2. What examples does Natalie Escalante give to support the idea that disabled athletes are like able-bodied athletes?

a. They both educate people about their challenges.

b. They both are passionate about what they do and want to achieve their goals.

c. They both want to convince people to compete in the same activities they do.

↻ Go to **MyEnglishLab** for more skill practice.

ORGANIZE

What similarities do the people in the listenings share? What are their differences? Complete the Venn diagram.

USE YOUR NOTES

APPLY Review your notes from Listening One and Two. Use your notes to complete the diagram.

In the individual circles, list unique challenges, goals and hopes, and personal qualities and beliefs.

In the overlapping area, list shared challenges, goals and hopes, and personal qualities and beliefs.

SIMILARITIES AND DIFFERENCES

LISTENING ONE: ARTIST OPENS OTHERS' EYES

LISTENING TWO: AN ATHLETE'S INSPIRING JOURNEY

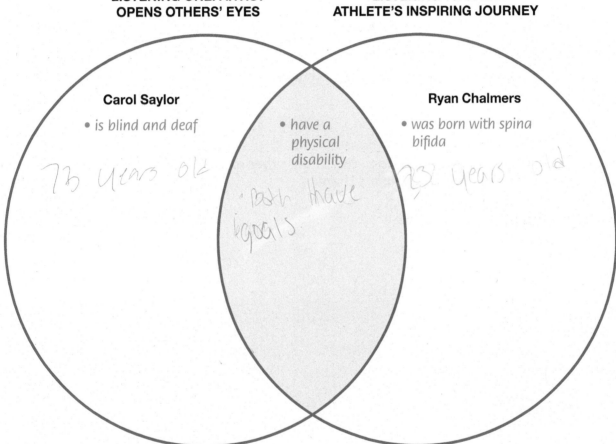

Carol Saylor

• is blind and deaf

73 years old

have a physical disability

• both have goals

Ryan Chalmers

• was born with spina bifida

23 years old

SYNTHESIZE

1 Work with a partner to prepare a role-play. Use the information in the Venn diagram and the list of questions to help you create your role-play. Add your own questions to the list.

STUDENT A: You are Carol Saylor.

STUDENT B: You are Ryan Chalmers.

Questions

- What challenges have you each faced?

- What obstacles have you each overcome?

- What do you each want to achieve?

- What personal qualities have helped each of you in life?

- What do you have in common with (Carol / Ryan)?

- What interests do you have outside of art / sports?

- _____

- _____

2 Perform your role-play for the class. Watch the other role-plays, listening for qualities that Carol Saylor and Ryan Chalmers share.

 Go to **MyEnglishLab** to check what you learned.

VOCABULARY

REVIEW

When Ryan Chalmers did the Push Across America project, fans from around the world followed him on social media. Complete the blog with the words and phrases from each box. Use the correct form.

awareness   inspirational   misconceptions   stereotypical   keep him going

KEEP ON KEEPING ON
A blog about embracing life's challenges
by Mario Blanco

Hello everyone, Mario here. I'm writing from California, where Ryan Chalmers is about to embark on a(n) _inspirational_ **1.**

journey across the United States. He'll be travelling for seventy-one days across four time zones to raise people's ___awarenesses___ **2.** of an important life lesson. Ryan is demonstrating our ability to achieve great things if we set our minds to it. But this young man is not your ___stereotypical___ **3.** athlete. He has challenged all kinds of ___misconceptions___ **4.** with his ambitious project. You see, Ryan will not be walking, running, or taking transportation. He'll be pushing his way across the country in a specially adapted racing wheelchair. And do you know what ___keep him going___ **5.**? It's the knowledge that this trip is about something bigger than himself. It's going to be a testament to the potential of people with disabilities.

(continued on next page)

devastated　　　go far beyond　　　hardships　　　rebounds　　　transitioned

I've been with Ryan over the past weeks, watching him push his chair for hours at a time, as the cool mornings turned into blisteringly hot afternoons and the days _transitioned_
6.
into nights. He's been traveling through all kinds of weather: heat, storms, wind, rain, and even snow. These are _hardships_ that _go far beyond_ what most
7.　　　　　　　　**8.**
athletes face, and there have been a few days when he looked really tired. But he stays focused and _rebounds_ after a good night's rest. Look, we would all be
9.
devastated if he failed, so I know he is going to give this challenge everything
10.
he has. A few more weeks to go, Ryan! Our hearts are with you!

able-bodied　　　average　　　diagnosis　　　persevered　　　this is it

Hello there—remember me? It's Mario, reporting on Ryan Chalmers's trip across eighteen states! _this is it_, friends: Ryan is about to cross his final bridge into New
11.
York. If you remember, he is not your _average_ athlete. He was given a(n)
12.
diagnosis of spina bifida when he was born, but he was determined to
13.
become a champion wheelchair racer. He _persevered_, and has now achieved a
14.
goal that few athletes—_able-bodied_ or disabled—have reached: He's pushed
15.
himself across the USA. And yes, now I see that the crowds are cheering Ryan Chalmers, whose determination and strength have taken him across the United States in a wheelchair, doing the equivalent of two to three marathons a day! Congratulations, Ryan! You are a role model and hero!

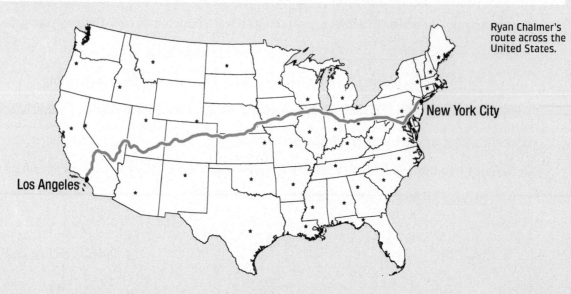

Ryan Chalmer's route across the United States.

New York City

Los Angeles

EXPAND

As you saw in Make Inferences, certain words and phrases can have both a literal meaning and a figurative meaning. Compare the two examples.

1. The view from the top of Rocky Mountains was spectacular. Chalmers *turned to* the reporters and smiled.

Here "turned to" has a literal meaning. Chalmers moved to face the reporters.

2. Ryan Chalmers's trip was frequently challenging. When he felt discouraged, he *turned to* his fans for inspiration.

Here "turned to" has a figurative meaning. Chalmers depended on his fans for inspiration.

Work with a partner. Read the sentences and notice the boldfaced phrases. Write _L_ (literal) or _F_ (figurative) for each sentence. Discuss your choices. Then explain them to the class.

1. __L__ a. Ryan Chalmers **reached a high point** in his trip as he crossed the Rocky Mountains.

   __F__ b. I **reached a high point** in tennis when I won the state tournament.

2. __L__ a. Ahmed dropped his water bottle while snowshoeing and had to **reach deep down** into the snow to find it.

   __F__ b. When the mountain climber thought she was too weak to take another step, she **reached deep down** inside herself and found the determination to make it back to camp.

3. __L__ a. My brother was born with Down Syndrome. When he **opened his eyes**, my mother knew he was different from her other children.

   __F__ b. Down Syndrome Awareness Week tries to **open people's eyes** to the contributions that disabled people make to society.

4. __F__ a. Carol Saylor wants to show her students that there is **another level** to her art. Art is not only about what you see; it's also about what you feel.

   __L__ b. Chalmers pushed up the mountain for seven hours to reach **another level**, the highest point of his journey.

5. __F__ a. New devices for hearing-impaired people allow them to **reach new heights** and achieve things they never thought were possible.

   __L__ b. Thanks to sophisticated equipment, now even relatively inexperienced mountain climbers are able to **reach new heights**.

study for test

CREATE

`APPLY` **Work with a partner. Follow the steps.**

1. Read each quote. Circle the paraphrase that best explains it.

2. Say whether you agree or disagree with the quote. Support your opinion.

3. Try to use the vocabulary from the box.

able-bodied	go far beyond	misconception	reach new heights
another level	hardship	open (one's) eyes	rebound
average	inspiring	persevere	stereotypical
awareness	keep (someone) going	reach a high point	this is it
devastated	make (something) look cool	reach deep down	transition
diagnosis			

1. **Anybody who lives long enough will eventually become disabled.**

Rachel Adams, professor and advocate for the disabled

    a. Being elderly is a type of disability.

    (b.) If you live a long time, certain body parts will fail; this happens to everyone.

2. **I have not been handicapped by my condition. I am physically challenged and differently able.**

Janet Barnes, the world's longest living quadriplegic[1]

    (a.) My condition doesn't limit me. I face the challenges in my own way.

    b. Being different is a challenge.

3. **When you have a disability, knowing that you are not defined by it is the sweetest feeling.**

Anne Wafula Strike, Paralympic wheelchair racer

    (a.) Being in a wheelchair is not the most important thing about me.

    (b.) Being in a wheelchair doesn't keep me from doing things I enjoy.

4. **Aerodynamically,[2] the bumblebee shouldn't be able to fly, but the bumblebee doesn't know that so it goes on flying anyway."**

Mary Kay Ash, businessperson and charity organizer

    a. Because of their body design, bumblebees can't fly very well.

    (b.) A positive attitude can help people to persevere despite a physical disability.

---

[1] **quadriplegic:** paralyzed in all four limbs
[2] **aerodynamically:** according to the laws of physics

 Go to the **Pearson Practice English App** or **MyEnglishLab** for more vocabulary practice.

GRAMMAR FOR SPEAKING

1 **Work with a partner. Read the conversation. What do the boldfaced words and phrases have in common? What do the underlined words have in common?**

A: Have you heard of Tanni Grey-Thompson? She's a Welsh wheelchair user who received great recognition for **winning** the London Marathon several times.

B: Is she still interested in **competing**?

A: No, she doesn't intend <u>to enter</u> the race any more. She retired several years ago. Now, she aims <u>to promote</u> sport and the Paralympics. She's also a politician, TV presenter, and educator.

B: Wow, **taking part** in all those activities is pretty amazing. She's a busy woman!

Using Gerunds and Infinitives

Gerunds	
To form a gerund, add -ing to the base form of the verb.	The story about Ryan Chalmers is about **persevering** and **overcoming** great obstacles.
Uses	
Gerunds can be the subject of a sentence.	**Pushing** himself all the way to New York was a great achievement for Chalmers.
Gerunds can follow a preposition, such as for, in, of, and about.	Carol Saylor is interested **in creating** art that people can touch.

Infinitives	
To form an infinitive, use to and the base form of the verb.	Saylor wants visitors to her studio **to learn** about using their imagination.
Uses	
Infinitives can follow be + adjective, for example: is easy, are difficult, are hard, were happy, isn't possible, aren't willing, and wasn't prepared.	It **was hard** for Chalmers **to push** his wheelchair through all kinds of weather.
Infinitives follow certain verbs, including allow, agree, decide, expect, hope, learn, manage, need, try, and want.	Chalmers **hoped to complete** his trip in less than three months, and he made it!

2 The Universal Design Movement aims to make products and buildings accessible to everyone, including disabled people. Read the poster. It contains a list of devices that can help the disabled.

Tips to Make Your Home or Community
ACCESSIBLE FOR ALL

In the 1960s, architect Selwyn Goldsmith invented the concept of the *dropped curb*, a small ramp on street corners, **allowing** people **to cross** roads more easily. His idea made a difference for thousands of people all over the world. Nowadays, there are more innovations. For example, it is common **to find** ramps at the entrances to buildings that make it easier for people in wheelchairs **to access** those buildings.

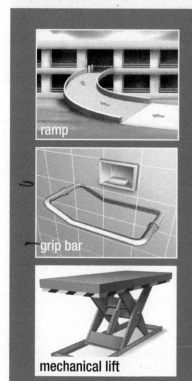

ramp

grip bar

mechanical lift

- Ramps at the entrances to buildings

- Braille signs in public elevators

- Wide doorways and hallways

- Baths / showers with grip bars

- Mechanical lifts on public buses

- Contrasting colors on ledges, counter edges, and steps

- Strobe lights on smoke and burglar alarms

- Raised buttons on appliances

- _____

- _____

With a partner, discuss how these devices could improve our everyday lives. Combine the expressions in the box with gerunds and infinitives.

. . . allow people . . .	. . . help people avoid . . .	. . . make people aware of . . .
. . . give people freedom . . .	. . . make it easier . . .	. . . stop people from . . .
. . . good for . . .	. . . make it possible . . .	

Bath Shows with grip bars

helping people avoid to make it possible

ing   helping

3 **APPLY** **Work with a partner. Follow the steps.**

1. Read the information. Think about the challenges everyday tasks present to a physically disabled person.

2. Think of a problem in your community concerning the elderly or the disabled. What could be done to make things better? Create a role-play between an advocate for the elderly / disabled and a government official. Use the prompts in the chart. Use gerunds and infinitives. Add as much information as you can.

> Since the Americans with Disabilities Act was passed in the United States in 1990, more people have become aware of the changes that must be made in public places to allow individuals with disabilities to have access to public resources and services. Government officials have a responsibility to provide such access to people with disabilities.

Advocate	Government Official
_____ is very difficult for disabled people.	As a member of the city council, I agree _____
_____ presents a real challenge for the disabled.	We representatives in the state legislature need _____
_____ can be extremely difficult.	As your congressional representative, I'm willing _____
Disabled people are forced _____	As mayor, I'm prepared _____
They often can't manage _____	As your state representative, I am ready _____ .
I'm sure they would be happy _____	As your campus chief of police, I assure you we will avoid _____

Go to the **Pearson Practice English App** or **MyEnglishLab** for more grammar practice. Check what you learned in **MyEnglishLab**.

PRONUNCIATION

Identifying and Using Thought Groups

When we speak, we group words together based on rhythm or logic, and join the groups into sentences. The groups are called thought groups. They help the listener organize the meaning of the sentence.

▶ **Read and listen.**

Examples

*   Thought groups are often grammatical phrases or structures, such as prepositional phrases or short clauses.

    A: My biggest problem is not believing in myself.

    I hate going to parties by myself.

    And I am terrified when I have to speak in class.

(continued on next page)

- Words can be combined into thought groups in different ways.

  B: When I first got the diagnosis, I was devastated.

    – Speakers sometimes choose groups of similar length to create a more pleasing rhythm.

    – In other cases, speakers group words based on logic. For example, a speaker may say two phrases in a single thought group to show that the two phrases are part of the same idea. To show that the two phrases are different ideas, the speaker will say them in two different thought groups.

    – Another basis for grouping words is to emphasize what is important.

- The words in these sentences are grouped in two ways.

  B: *I realized that everyone is born with gifts.*

  B: *I realized that everyone is born with gifts.*

    – In the first sentence, the speaker emphasizes the fact that he or she realized something important. The phrase "I realized" is emphasized.

    – In the second sentence, what the speaker realized about everyone (the fact that everyone "is born with gifts") is most important.

- Pronounce the words in a thought group together smoothly. Pause briefly after one thought group before you start the next group.

  A: My biggest problem (*pause briefly*) is lack of confidence.

  B: One of the misconceptions (*pause briefly*) is that blind people see black.

1 ▶ **Read and listen to the sentences. As you listen, mark the thought groups. Compare answers with a partner. Then take turns reading the sentences to each other. Remember to pause briefly at the end of a thought group before you start a new one.**

  1. When Saylor received her diagnosis, she thought that was it.

  2. She decided to stop painting and turn to sculpture.

  3. When people visit her studio, they realize that her art is amazing.

  4. They realize that art can involve all of your senses.

  5. Ms. Saylor's story is an inspiration for all of us.

2 APPLY **Work with a partner. Follow the steps.**

  1. Look at the two charts on the next page. Take turns creating sentences by choosing one thought group from each column.

  2. If the sentence you create is true, your partner will say, "That's right." If the sentence you create is not true, your partner will say, "I don't think that's right."

  3. Continue until you and your partner have created three true sentences for each chart. Be sure to pause briefly at the end of each thought group.

Chart A

1	2	3	4
Saylor's work	is a visual artist	she uses touch	in a different way.
A visitor to her studio	inspires other people	who is very unusual	to "see" the human body.
Carol Saylor	is impressed by the way	to think of art	because she is blind.

Chart B

1	2	3	4
Ryan Chalmers	has spoken enthusiastically	and supported the athlete	which have inspired us all.
Newspaper reporters	made the decision	to cross the United States	in his difficult moments.
Chalmers's coach	accompanied Chalmers	about the athlete's achievements,	in his racing wheelchair.

SPEAKING SKILL

Introducing a Presentation

When you give a presentation, it is important to get your audience's attention quickly. You can do this by following these steps:

- First, greet your audience in a friendly and direct manner.
- If possible, provide a particularly interesting fact or anecdote.
- Then clearly explain what you will go on to talk about and why.

1 **Answer the questions. Circle the correct answers.**

    1. Which is the best way to greet an audience?

       a. Good morning, everyone. I'm very happy to talk to you today.

       b. Hello, everyone. Stop talking and listen to me now.

       c. Look at the board, please. I wrote down a couple of dates you might want to look at.

    2. Which is the best way to say what you will talk about?

       a. Let me tell you about my father, Farid. His surname is Khadiwala.

       b. I'm going to tell you a little bit about a disabled person I admire: my father.

       c. Are you interested in skiing? A lot of people like it and so does my father.

3. Which fact is most interesting?

   a. My father, Farid Khadiwala, has a lot of medals. I think he has about five or six.

   b. My father Farid was born in 1973, on March 21. He's quite old now.

   (c.) My father, Farid Khadiwala, is disabled. However, he has won several skiing competitions.

2 Divide into two groups. Choose one of the biographical summaries. Read it and then tell your group what you find particularly interesting about the person.

Christopher Reeve (1952–2004)

- American actor who achieved great professional success in his life
- Played the superhero Superman in numerous movies
- Gifted actor, film director, and author
- Fell from a horse at the age of 43
- Became unable to move
- Needed ongoing medical care to survive
- Became a strong advocate for disabled people
- Taught paralyzed people to live independently

Stephen Hawking (1942–2018)

- World-renowned British astrophysicist
- Active as a child: enjoyed horseback riding
- Developed Lou Gehrig's disease
- Became severely disabled
- Achieved incredible things in his lifetime
- Author of the bestselling book *A Brief History of Time*
- Became happy and successful
- Took a flight into space, achieving zero gravity

3 APPLY Imagine that you are going to give a presentation about disability studies to a group of people from different fields. Disability studies is an interdisciplinary field that examines the history, representation, and experience of the disabled. Practice giving your introduction to a partner. Follow the steps.

1. Take turns greeting each other.

2. Provide an interesting fact or anecdote about Reeve or Hawking.

3. Explain what you will go on to talk about and why.

🔊 Go to **MyEnglishLab** for more skill practice and to check what you learned.

In this activity, you will give a short oral report to a small group of classmates. You will report on a person who has overcome an obstacle.

PREPARE

1 **Work in a group of 4–6. Each member chooses a different person from the box. (See Student Activities on pages 217 and 218 for the details about the person you chose.)**

- Read about your person. (Do not read about the other people.)
- Take notes.
- Optional: Do additional research online.

Jim Abbott	Millie Knight	Marla Runyan
Javid Abidi	Marlee Beth Matlin	Justin Skeesuck
Frida Kahlo		

2 **Prepare a speech about your person.**

- Think about how your person faced and overcame a challenge.
- Take notes in the outline to help you organize your ideas.

	Your Notes
Title of presentation	Frida Kahlo
Greeting	Hello Class, today I would like to talk about a artist called Frida Kahlo.
An interesting fact or anecdote	She give up th her dream of be in a medical school.
Explanation of what you will talk about and why	
Brief description of person	a strong and brave woman.
Obstacle(s) the person had to overcome	She was injured in a traffic accident when she was 18 was old.
Person's achievement(s)	She become a famour artist in because she was different of the rest.
Reason(s) this person's story is interesting to you	Frida Kahlo story is interesting to me because in my opinion she represent all women.

3 **APPLY** Consider how to apply the vocabulary, grammar, pronunciation, and speaking skills from the unit. Use the checklist to help you.

☐ **Vocabulary:** Read through the list of vocabulary on page 53. Which words can you include in your presentation to make it clearer and more interesting? Choose at least three words or phrases to use, and add them to your notes.

☐ **Grammar:** Scan your notes for gerunds and infinitives. Are you using them correctly?

☐ **Pronunciation:** Record yourself practicing using thought groups. Then listen back. Are your ideas clear?

☐ **Speaking Skill:** Think about an interesting aspect of your topic. How can you use that to draw your audience in quickly? Try different ways of getting their attention, and choose the one that is most effective.

PRACTICE

Practice with a partner from your group.

- Practice giving your presentation to your partner. Limit your talk to 2–3 minutes.
- Use the chart to give feedback to your partner.

FEEDBACK: 1 Strongly disagree 2 Disagree 3 Agree 4 Strongly agree				
The presenter began in an interesting way.	1	2	3	4
The presenter engaged the audience.	1	2	3	4
What did the presenter do well? How could he / she improve?	Comments:			

PRESENT

1 **Present to your group.**

2 **Create a chart like the one above to give feedback to the other presenters.**

ALTERNATIVE SPEAKING TOPIC

APPLY **Work in a small group. Read the information and answer the questions. Use the vocabulary, grammar, pronunciation, and speaking skills from the unit.**

The Universal Design Movement aims to make spaces and services easily accessible to all. It recommends having things like:

- wide doors to buildings
- lever handles (not twisting knobs) to open doors
- light switches that are easy to use
- enough restrooms for women and men
- closed captioning on TV
- large print labels

Questions:

– Is your campus or community accessible to everyone?

– Does it have any particular areas that make it difficult for anyone in particular?

– If you could redesign your campus or community, what three changes would you make so that it is more accessible to all users?

Do some water park and gym elevator

CHECK WHAT YOU'VE LEARNED

Check (✔) the outcomes you've met and vocabulary you've learned. Put an X next to the skills and vocabulary you still need to practice.

Learning Outcomes
- ☐ **Infer the meaning of figurative language**
- ☐ **Take notes using key words**
- ☐ **Distinguish between main ideas and details**
- ☐ **Use gerunds and infinitives**
- ☐ **Identify and use thought groups**
- ☐ **Introduce a presentation**

Vocabulary
- ☐ able-bodied
- ☐ average
- ☐ awareness AWL
- ☐ devastated (*adj.*)
- ☐ diagnosis
- ☐ hardship
- ☐ inspiring
- ☐ misconception
- ☐ persevere
- ☐ rebound (*v.*)
- ☐ stereotypical
- ☐ transition (*v.*) AWL

Multi-word Units
- ☐ go far beyond
- ☐ keep (someone) going
- ☐ make (something) look cool
- ☐ this is it

🔊 Go to **MyEnglishLab** to watch a video about a girl with autism, access the Unit Project, and t the Unit 2 Achievement Test.

LEARNING OUTCOMES

> Infer a speaker's assumptions
> Take notes with symbols and abbreviations
> Recognize claims and evidence

> Use present unreal conditionals
> Use contrastive stress
> Ask for clarification

 Go to **MyEnglishLab** to check what you know.

Early to Bed, Early to Rise

1 FOCUS ON THE TOPIC

1. An old proverb about sleep says: "Early to bed, early to rise, makes you healthy, wealthy, and wise." What does this proverb mean?

2. Some people are "early birds" (they wake up early) and others are "night owls" (they stay up late). Is one sleep routine better than the other? Why?

3. Do most people get enough sleep? Explain.

LISTENING ONE | How Can Teenagers Get Enough Sleep?

VOCABULARY

1 ▶ Many parents are concerned about their children's sleep patterns. Read and listen to the blog posts between a parent and a pediatrician. Notice the boldfaced words and phrases. Try to guess their meanings.

ADVICE FROM DR. KHAN

HOME
CONTACT
ABOUT US

Hi Dr. Khan,   9 hours ago

I'm worried about my daughter Eden, who's a middle school student with sleep issues. She **has a tendency to** stay up late, and then she's exhausted later on in the day. This sleep pattern is having a terrible effect on her schoolwork. She's falling behind in almost all her classes, and we worry that it's going to get worse **over the course of** the year. **That being said**, we think we're doing all we can. We have always told Eden that **consistency** is really important when it comes to her bedtime routine, but she doesn't seem to be able to go to bed early. I don't know—she seems to be dealing with it **pretty well**, but, obviously, we are concerned. What should we do?

Sheila Sinani

Dear Ms. Sinani,   7 hours ago

It's normal for adolescents to have problems sleeping. For example, adolescents who go to bed too early suffer from wakefulness, which can also be difficult. At this age, the body's circadian rhythm—the body's internal "clock"—is changing. But don't worry! She'll grow out of it eventually and **reset** her clock.

Of course, what you do need to worry about is **sleep deprivation**. If she wants to sleep in on weekends, let her do so. It's not a sign of slothfulness if she doesn't get up until 1 or 2 P.M., so don't think she's being lazy. It's just the body's **intrinsic** reaction to being tired. If she rests on the weekend, this will help her **recover** from the week. If you wish, you can ask her doctor about low-dose melatonin tablets, which are over-the-counter vitamin supplements that help with sleep and seem to be very effective. Most people **tolerate** those quite well. And they've been **clinically proven**[1] to work.

Good luck with Eden and don't worry too much. Try to **maintain** a positive attitude.

Dr. Khan

---

[1] You can also say *proven clinically.*

2 Write each word or phrase from the box next to its definition.

clinically proven	maintain	reset
consistency	over the course of	sleep deprivation
have a tendency to	pretty well	that being said
intrinsic	recover	tolerate

1. _Sleep dep_ : lack of sleep
2. _Recover_ : to get better after an illness, injury, shock, etc.
3. _Tolerate_ : to accept something you do not like
4. _Consistency_ : the quality of always being the same or always behaving in an expected way
5. _Pretty well_ : in a rather good, reasonable, or competent way
6. _Reset_ : to return something to a regular position or state
7. _that being said_ : in spite of what was just stated
8. _over the course of_ : during a period of time or a process
9. _Intrinsic_ : being part of the basic character or nature of someone or something
10. _Have a tendency to_ : to be likely to (do something)
11. _Clinically prov_ : shown scientifically through tests
12. _Maintain_ : to make something continue in the same way or at the same standard as before

↻ Go to the **Pearson Practice English App** or **MyEnglishLab** for more vocabulary practice.

PREVIEW

You will hear a report by Dr. Michael Howell, from the University of Minnesota, who studies sleep patterns and sleep-related issues facing adolescents.

▶ **Read the questions and predict Dr. Howell's explanation. Then listen to the introduction to Dr. Howell's report to check your predictions.**

1. Why are teenagers often sleepy? Think of several reasons.

_____

_____

2. When adolescents stay up late and wake up early, what do they begin to suffer from? What could be some of the consequences?

_____

_____

1 ▶ Listen to the whole report. Create a chart like the one below to take notes.

TAKE NOTES How Can Teenagers Get Enough Sleep?	
Main Ideas	**Details**
Howell:	
Adolescents like to stay up late	– "night owls"
→ sleep deprivation	– X choice; brains act differently
	– schedule = problems in school

2 Compare your notes with a partner's. How can you improve your notes?

↪ Go to **MyEnglishLab** to view example notes.

MAIN IDEAS

Identify the statements as *T* (true) or *F* (false). Then correct the false statements. Use your notes to help you.

___F___ 1. Middle and high school students are early birds.

___F___ 2. It is impossible to reset your body's pattern of sleep and wakefulness, or circadian rhythm.

___T___ 3. If you lose sleep during the week, your body needs to recover about half of the lost sleep time on the weekend.

___F___ 4. Most teenagers who sleep in class are lazy or uninterested in studying hard.

DETAILS

1 ▶ Listen again and add to your notes. Circle the correct answers. Use your notes to help you.

1. According to Dr. Howell, what problem is caused by adolescents' schedules?

   a. weak academic performance

   b. sleep deprivation

   c. disagreements with teachers

2. What method has been proven successful in helping people fall asleep earlier?

   a. having consistent bedtimes

   b. avoiding stressful activities

   c. limiting caffeine

3. How many minutes of morning sunlight can help reset a person's circadian rhythm?

    a. 10–20

    b. 20–30

    c. 30–40

4. When should a melatonin supplement be taken?

    a. at six o'clock in the morning

    b. six hours before bedtime

    c. at six o'clock in the evening

5. About how many hours of sleep does the adolescent that Dr. Howell discusses lose each day?

    a. one

    b. two

    c. three

6. What activities for teenagers does Dr. Howell mention?

    a. theater and gym

    b. soccer and art

    c. swimming and music

2 **With a partner, take turns summarizing your notes. Then discuss how your notes and your answers in Preview helped you understand the listening.**

Go to **MyEnglishLab** for more listening practice.

MAKE INFERENCES

Inferring a Speaker's Assumptions

Speakers sometimes make but don't directly express assumptions. To better comprehend a speaker, listeners may need to make educated guesses about, or infer, what a speaker's assumptions are.

▶ **Read and listen to an excerpt from the report by Dr. Howell. Then answer the question.**

Example

DR. HOWELL: A couple of key things to think about when you're dealing with adolescents and sleep issues is that adolescents have a tendency to be a bit of night owls. They tend to like to go to bed later and sleep in later, and this is more than just a behavioral choice on their part. Their brains actually act differently.

Dr. Howell assumes that most people think _____ stay up late and sleep in.

a. teenagers choose to

b. teenagers' brains make them

ANSWER: a – Dr. Howell implies that people believe teenagers go to bed late and sleep in because they want to, not because they need to ("this is more than just a behavioral choice"). Dr. Howell explains that teenagers' brains act differently, so they actually need to follow this sleep pattern.

▶ **Listen to excerpts from the report by Dr. Howell and circle the correct answers.**

Excerpt One

1. Dr. Howell assumes that _____ .

   a. teens are actually lazy, not tired

   b. people believe teens are not tired but lazy

2. Dr. Howell assumes that students sleeping in class _____ .

   a. supports the idea that students are lazy

   b. is an image familiar to most people

Excerpt Two

1. Dr. Howell assumes that people think starting _____ later would be enough to help teenagers.

   a. activities

   b. classes

2. Dr. Howell assumes that _____ .

   a. schools schedule multiple activities before classes

   b. teenagers don't participate in additional activities because they are too tired

DISCUSS 🔍

Work with a partner or in a small group. Discuss the questions.

1. How are teenagers' sleep patterns different from adults' sleep patterns? Why? What problems could this create?

2. How do schools make teenagers' problems worse? What could schools do instead?

3. What solutions does Dr. Howell give to address adolescent sleep issues? What other practices— like drinking caffeine, napping, and exercising—have you heard of? Which are supported by healthcare professionals?

🅝 Go to **MyEnglishLab** to give your opinion about another question.

> **USE YOUR NOTES**
>
> **APPLY** Find information in your notes to use in your discussion.

1) I think that teenagers patterns different from adults sleep

LISTENING TWO | Get Back in Bed!

1 Work with a partner. Take turns reading the words and phrases in the box aloud. Try to guess their meanings. Check a dictionary if necessary.

accumulate	critical	make (something) a priority
cranky	fatigue (n.)	touch on

2 Like teenagers, parents of small children are often sleep-deprived. Complete the conversation between two friends with the words and phrases from Exercise One. Use the correct form. Then take turns reading the conversation aloud with a partner.

KENJI: Hi, Jen, how's your new job going?

JEN: I just don't know what to do. Since my daughter was born, I'm so tired all the time. I almost fell asleep at a meeting the other day, and I started to get ___Cranky___ . My boss seemed to notice I
1.
was in a bad mood. He told me that the meeting was really important and told everyone that we should ___Make___ work ___a Priority___ . I'm
2.
sure he was making a comment about me!

KENJI: Yeah, well, you're probably just suffering from ___Fatiger___ . What time do you
3.
go to bed?

JEN: Pretty late. And my tiredness just ___accumulates___ during the week. By Thursday or
4.
Friday, I'm exhausted.

KENJI: I was watching some videos that ___touch on___ that topic. Apparently, you should
5.
sleep seven to nine hours a night. It's absolutely ___Critical___ that you get
6.
enough sleep. Otherwise you'll be yawning all day.

JEN: Nine hours? You must be joking. I don't even get six!

Go to the **Pearson Practice English App** or **MyEnglishLab** for more vocabulary practice.

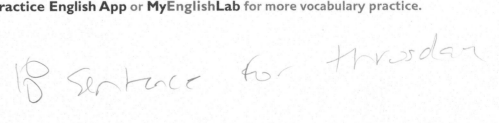

18 sentence for throsday

Taking Notes with Symbols and Abbreviations

Good note takers use symbols—marks that always mean the same thing. They also use abbreviations—short forms of a word or phrase. Symbols and abbreviations help you take notes more quickly.

Look at the list of common symbols and abbreviations. Add any others you know.

Common Symbols	Common Abbreviations
& or **+** and	**e.g.** for example
→ leads to	**etc.** and so on
↗ ↘ increase; decrease	**i.e.** that is
∴ so, therefore	**v.** very
=, ≠ equals, is the same as; doesn't equal	**vs.** versus
♀, ♂ woman; man	**w/** with
X no / not	**w/o** without
~ approximately	

Example

You hear: Getting about 20 to 30 minutes of sunlight first thing in the morning can help you fall asleep earlier.

You write: ~20–30 min. of sunlight in a.m. → help you fall asleep faster

1 Read the notes. What do you think they mean? Discuss your ideas with a partner.

a.
> Not enough sleep → probs. e.g. driving X safe.

b.
> relaxing ≠ sleeping. real rest = bed

c.
> ~33% Americans sleep deprived, i.e. need more

d.
> I went to bed late, ∴ v. tired today

e.
> When parents X sleep, concentration ↘

2 ▶ **Read and listen to the comments. Match the notes in Exercise One with the comments.**

_____ 1. When parents don't get a good night's sleep, their concentration decreases.

_____ 2. I went to bed late last night, so I'm really very tired today.

_____ 3. Relaxing isn't the same as sleeping. If you want to be really rested, you should go to bed.

_____ 4. If people don't sleep enough, it can lead to problems. For example, driving isn't safe if you are sleep deprived.

_____ 5. About one-third of Americans are sleep deprived—that is, they need to sleep more.

Go to **MyEnglishLab** for more note-taking practice.

COMPREHENSION

You will hear a radio interview with Dr. Joyce Walsleben, former director of New York University's Sleep Disorder Center. The show _Satellite Sisters_ is hosted by Lian Dolan and her four sisters.

1 ▶ **Listen to the interview. Create a chart like the one below to take notes. Try to use symbols and abbreviations as you take notes.**

TAKE NOTES **Get Back in Bed!**

Main Ideas	Details

2 **Use your notes to answer the questions. Circle the correct answers.**

1. Host Lian Dolan complains about being constantly tired. What reason does she give?

    a. She can't fall asleep at night.

    b. She has small children.

    c. She wakes up in the middle of the night.

2. According to Dr. Walsleben, how should people combat sleep deprivation?

    a. by making sleep a priority

    b. by not combining careers and parenthood

    c. by making sure their days are active

3. Dr. Walsleben mentions the *Exxon Valdez*, an oil tanker that crashed and spilled 11 million gallons (41.6 million liters) of oil in Alaska. What does she imply about the cause of the accident?

    a. The captain of the ship was sleep deprived.

    b. The mate driving the ship had been working for too many hours.

    c. The crew was sleeping when the accident occurred.

4. How does sleep deprivation affect Lian, the interviewer?

    a. She's too tired to see her parents.

    b. She's too tired to decide what to eat.

    c. She's too tired to make good parenting decisions.

5. How do most people feel about the effects of sleep deprivation?

    a. They don't feel any effects.

    b. They worry about its effects on their health.

    c. They accept that they are sleep deprived.

6. What happens to many workers by the end of the workweek?

    a. They accumulate a large sleep debt.

    b. They often need to take Fridays off.

    c. They can no longer get things done at work.

7. About how many hours of sleep are many people missing by Friday?

    a. four

    b. five

    c. seven

> **USE YOUR NOTES**
>
> Compare your notes with a partner's. How can you improve your notes next time?

1 ▶ **Listen to an excerpt from the interview with Dr. Walsleben. What does she claim sleep deprivation can lead to?**

Recognizing Claims and Evidence

Like writers, speakers use evidence in the form of facts, examples, and statistics to support their claims (main ideas). They sometimes speak in "oral paragraphs," especially when they want to inform or persuade. Effective listeners listen for the claim and the evidence that supports it.

▶ **Read and listen to an excerpt from the interview with Dr. Walsleben. Then answer the questions.**

Example

Host Lian Dolan:	Dr. Walsleben, why are we all so tired?
Dr. Walsleben:	We're probably tired because we don't make sleep a priority. And I think, as a young mother and a career woman, your days are pretty well filled, and I would suspect that you probably think you can do without[1] sleep.

1. What is Dr. Walsleben's claim?

2. What evidence supports her claim? (Here the claim and the evidence are linked by two connecting phrases: *And I think . . .* and *and I would suspect . . .*)

ANSWERS: 1. Her claim is "we don't make sleep a priority."

2. She supports this with four reasons why Lian probably doesn't make sleep a priority: 1) She is a young mother. 2) She is a career woman. 3) Her days are filled. 4) She thinks she can do without sleep.

[1] **do without:** to live without having something

2 ▶ **Listen to excerpts from the interview with Dr. Walsleben. Read the claims and identify the evidence.**

Excerpt One

Claim: Sleep deprivation can be very serious because lack of sleep can affect our performance.

Evidence: Dr. Walsleben supports the claim with examples of two types of accidents. What are they?

1. ___Exxon Valdez / single driver at 2am or 3am.___

2. _____

Excerpt Two

Claim: Sleep deprivation affects us a lot.

Evidence: Lian supports her claim with evidence from her own life. Complete the list:

1. She is tired and cranky.

2. ___Not good parenting decisions / don't give a lot to___

3. ___husband___

4. ___to tired to exercise___

▶ Go to **MyEnglishLab** for more skill practice.

ORGANIZE

What are the characteristics of sleep deprivation? Complete the chart with details from the listenings.

USE YOUR NOTES

APPLY Review your notes from Listening One and Two. Use the information in your notes to complete the chart.

SLEEP DEPRIVATION		
	LISTENING ONE: How Can Teenagers Get Enough Sleep?	LISTENING TWO: Get Back in Bed!
	Teenagers	Parents of Young Children
Causes of sleep deprivation	• teenagers have a natural tendency to go to sleep late	• their children may sleep a little and wake up a lot
Symptoms of sleep deprivation	Fatigue, tired, estress,	
Recommendations from professionals	sleep 8 hours everyday take a nap. Of 20 minutes	Sleep 8 hours take a nap of 20 minutes

SYNTHESIZE

1 **Divide into two groups to discuss a problem.**

GROUP A: Teenagers can't fall asleep at night.

GROUP B: Parents suffer from sleep deprivation.

2 **In your group, list some possible causes of the problem, consequences of the problem, and solutions to the problem.**

3 **Now pair up with a student from the opposite group and share your discussion ideas. Decide whether teenagers or parents have a more serious problem and how to tackle that problem.**

Example

A: We talked about teenagers who can't fall asleep at night. There are several reasons for this . . .

B: The problem with parents is that when they don't get enough sleep, it can be dangerous . . .

🎧 Go to **MyEnglishLab** to check what you learned.

VOCABULARY

REVIEW

Read the article about sleep disorders. Circle the correct words and phrases.

Sleep Disorders: Are You a Victim?

Are you constantly exhausted? You might want to educate yourself about these common sleep disorders. Suffering from **(1) consistency / sleep deprivation** is much more common than you think!

Insomnia
People with insomnia have difficulty falling asleep at night or **(2) have a tendency / make it a priority** to wake up in the middle of the night. Believe it or not, at least 50 percent of people have this problem!

Apnea
This is when your normal breathing gets blocked as you sleep. You may snore or sleep restlessly, and you can feel **(3) cranky / pretty well** easily during the day. If you think you are suffering from apnea, it is **(4) intrinsic / critical** for you to see a doctor.

Restless Legs Syndrome (RLS)
This is a painful feeling in your legs that makes you kick while you are asleep. RLS can lead to fatigue. Fortunately, several treatments for reducing RLS have been **(5) clinically proven / intrinsic**.

Sleepwalking
Although it is not as common as other syndromes, sleepwalking can have a terrible effect on sleepwalkers and their families. If someone in your family gets out of bed and walks around while still asleep, **(6) have a tendency / make it a priority** to send him or her to a doctor for a physical checkup!

Daydreaming
(7) That being said / Over the course of their lives, most people daydream, and daydreaming can be caused by boredom, not just tiredness. In general, be sure to get plenty of sleep, and don't worry if you daydream occasionally!

Nightmares
If your tiredness **(8) accumulates / maintains**, you may find that you have more nightmares. It's not fun to have scary dreams in the middle of the night, but most people **(9) tolerate / recover** quickly from these experiences if they get enough sleep.

EXPAND

Work with a partner. Follow the steps.

1. Read the words and definitions in the box.

2. Complete the conversations with the words and phrases from the box. Use the correct form.

3. Practice the conversations aloud.

> **burn the midnight oil:** to work very late at night
> **demonstrate:** to show a fact clearly
> **drowsy:** tired and almost asleep
> **irritable:** easily annoyed or made angry
> **major concern:** something important that worries or involves you greatly
> **nap** *(n.)*: a short sleep during the day
> **nod off:** to fall asleep by accident
> **power nap** *(n.)*: an extra-short sleep in the middle of the working day
> **run by:** to have someone consider
> **shut-eye:** sleep (informal)

Conversation One: Sleep Pods

MIN-HO: Uh, Mr. Rogers? Could I have a word?

MR. ROGERS: Sure. Come on in. What's up?

MIN-HO: Well, a few of us had an idea that we wanted to _____ you. We've

$\overline{\text{1.}}$

thought of a way you could increase productivity and make your employees

really happy at work. Sleep pods.

MR. ROGERS: Sleep pods? I'm not following you. What are you talking about?

MIN-HO: Well, you know how sometimes people are _____ in the

$\overline{\text{2.}}$

afternoons—some actually have trouble keeping their eyes

open. Sleep pods are private, reclining chairs that allow

people to take _____ . Here, take a

$\overline{\text{3.}}$

look at this brochure . . .

MR. ROGERS: Hm. Sleep pods, huh? They

look expensive.

MIN-HO: But they would practically pay for themselves. Think about it, sir. Everyone would work more productively. Everyone would be nicer, too. You know how some of us get _____ by Friday and start shouting at each other?
4.
Well, that's because we're all so tired.

MR. ROGERS: Well, I'll think it over, but really, are you saying I should pay people to sleep on the job?

MIN-HO: That's not it, sir. It's more like taking a(n) _____ —something
5.
executives do to restore themselves so they can work harder and longer. Just ten minutes and a person can feel refreshed and ready to work again.

MR. ROGERS: Heh, heh. Very clever. Well, as I said, I'll think about it.

Conversation Two: Research on Sleep and Memory

JULIA: Psst, wake up! You've been snoring. Did you _____ for a minute?
6.

NEIL: What? Oh . . . sorry. I guess I did. I got home really late from work last night.

JULIA: You're always _____ . That can't be good for you.
7.

NEIL: Yes, I know. Lately I've been having trouble keeping track of everything I need to do.

JULIA: Well, you'd better take more care. You know, sleep deprivation is a(n) _____ . Some researchers just discovered that when you get
8.
plenty of sleep, your memory improves.

NEIL: Really? How did they _____ that?
9.

JULIA: They took brain images of people while they were sleeping. Apparently, your brain moves your memories from one place to another while you're asleep.

NEIL: That's amazing. I think I'd better go home and get some _____
10.
right away.

CREATE

APPLY **Work with a partner. Take turns asking and answering the questions.**

STUDENT A: Ask one of the questions.

STUDENT B: Answer, beginning with a word or phrase from the box. Try to use the vocabulary in the Answer column. Answer in a few sentences.

| Hm, if I . . . | Well, . . . | I don't know, but . . . | Huh, I've never thought about that before, but . . . |

Question	Answer
1. If you read in bed, does it keep you alert or help you relax? Explain.	*rub my eyes* *make (something) a priority*
2. If you exercise before bed, does it keep you awake or help you sleep? Explain.	*yawn* *snore*
3. If you ride a bus or a train, does it keep you awake or make you sleepy? Explain.	*fatigue* *take a power nap*
4. If you drink tea, coffee, or cola, does it stop you from sleeping? Explain.	*accumulate* *alert*
5. If you take a nap, how does it make you feel? Explain.	*awake* *burn the midnight oil*
6. If you have time on the weekends, do you try to sleep late? Explain.	*do without* *drowsy* *nod off*

Go to the **Pearson Practice English App** or **MyEnglishLab** for more vocabulary practice.

GRAMMAR FOR SPEAKING

1 Work with a partner. Read the conversation aloud. Then answer the questions.

PATIENT: I'm exhausted. I just can't keep my eyes open during the day.

DOCTOR: It seems that you are quite sleep deprived and don't get to bed early enough. If you went to sleep earlier, you would feel a lot better.

PATIENT: That's the problem, doctor. I can't go to bed early. I work the late shift, and I don't get home until 10:00 or 11:00 P.M.

DOCTOR: Well, perhaps you could take naps instead. If you took regular naps, you'd feel less sleepy.

1. What two suggestions does the doctor make?

_____

2. What grammatical structure does the doctor use to make the suggestions?

_____

Using Present Unreal Conditionals

A **present unreal conditional** sentence has two clauses: the *if-clause*, which states the condition, and the **result clause**, which states the outcome. Use the present unreal conditional to talk about something that is untrue, imagined, or possible / desired but will not happen.

To form the present unreal conditional, use the **past form** of the verb in the *if-clause*. Note that the sentence is not in the past, however.	*If I **didn't work** at night, I could go to bed early.* (In reality: I work at night, so I can't go to bed early.)
For the verb *be* **in the** *if-clause*, use **were** for all subjects.	*If they **were working** less, they would have more time to sleep.* (In reality: I am working a lot, so I don't have more time to sleep.)
Use **would** + **base form** of the verb in the main clause to describe the result.	*Lian **would spend** more time asleep if she didn't have such a hectice lifestyle.* *The problem **would not become** so serious if more people paid attention to their sleep habits.*
Use **might** or **could** + **base form** to describe a possible result.	*If people knew more about the dangers of sleep deprivation, they **might treat** their sleep habits more seriously.*
The *if-clause* can come at the beginning or end of the sentence.	*I would feel better if I went to bed earlier.*
If it is at the beginning, use a comma.	*If I went to bed earlier, I would feel better.*
To make a question, use question order in the main clause.	*If you were sleep deprived, how **would you know**?*
The *if-clause* is not needed if the condition is understood by the listener.	*How **would you know**?*

2 Read and complete the interviews using present unreal conditionals. More than one answer may be possible. Then read the interviews aloud with a partner. Use expression.

Interview One: A Sleep Researcher and a Medical Professional

SLEEP RESEARCHER: Thank you for sharing your experience with me. Can you tell me about the sleep problems that medical workers have?

MEDICAL PROFESSIONAL: Well, one of the problems is that medical residents and interns work up to 100 hours a week. They can get really overtired. If they _____worked_____ less, they _____ so tired.
　　　　　　　　　　　　　1. (work)　　　　　　　　　2. (not / get)

(continued on next page)

SLEEP RESEARCHER: And does this fatigue cause serious problems?

MEDICAL PROFESSIONAL: Sure. Just think about your own work. How well ___would you do___ your job if you ___could sleep___ only five
___3. (do)___ ___4. (sleep)___
or six hours a night?

SLEEP RESEARCHER: Aren't there any rules about how much you can work?

MEDICAL PROFESSIONAL: Yes, but they are not strict enough. For example, if interns
___went/would go___ to work from Monday to Saturday,
___5. (go)___
and if they ___worked___ for 16 hours each day, they
___6. (work)___
___might be___ following the regulations—if they
___7. (be)___
___worked___ less the following week.
___8. (work)___

SLEEP RESEARCHER: That's terrible! What can be done?

MEDICAL PROFESSIONAL: We need to raise public awareness. For example, surgeons and
medical technicians are sometimes on call for many nights
week after week. If they ___wouldn't be requir___ to do that, there
___9. (not / be required)___
___might be/could be___ fewer problems.
___10. (be)___

Interview Two: A Sleep Researcher and a Pilots' Association Official

SLEEP RESEARCHER: Hello there. I'd like to ask you about sleep regulations in
the airline industry.

PILOTS' ASSOCIATION OFFICIAL: Well, luckily there have been several studies about the
importance of adequate sleep. Sleep is important for
everyone, but pilots in particular cannot be tired or
distracted. Can you imagine what ___would happen___ if a
___11. (happen)___
pilot ___might fai/fell___ asleep on the job?
___12. (fall)___

SLEEP RESEARCHER: Asleep? I can't imagine that!

PILOTS' ASSOCIATION OFFICIAL: Well, many people take what we call "microsleeps," which
last 5–10 seconds. But if a pilot ___took___ one
___13. (take)___
of these little naps during takeoff or landing, the results
___could be___ disastrous.
___14. (be)___

SLEEP RESEARCHER: I see. So you need to make sure pilots are awake and alert.

PILOTS' ASSOCIATION OFFICIAL: Yes, *alert* is the right word. For example, if you yourself

___couldn't get___ adequate sleep, your reaction
　　15. (not / get)

time ___might be___ affected. The same thing
　　16. (be)

___could happen___ if a pilot ___didn't sleep___ enough.
17. (happen)　　　　　　　　　　 18. (not / sleep)

SLEEP RESEARCHER: Are all pilots made aware of the dangers of sleep

deprivation?

PILOTS' ASSOCIATION OFFICIAL: Certainly. The number of accidents ___would increase___
　　　　　　　　　　　　　　　　　　　　　　　　　19. (increase)

significantly if we ___didn't enforce___ regulations about
　　　　　　　　　　　　　20. (not / enforce)

sufficient sleep.

3 APPLY **Role-play with a partner. Take turns.**

STUDENT A: You are a talk show host. Make suggestions. Use the present unreal conditional.

STUDENT B: You are a caller to the talk show, asking for advice about a sleep problem. Describe a problem from the list.

Example

HOST: Welcome to the show. What's your sleep problem?

CALLER: My schedule changes from day to day. Sometimes I go to bed early, sometimes late, depending on how much homework I have to do. When I finally do go to bed, I can't sleep.

HOST: Why don't you take a bath before going to bed? If you took a warm bath, you would find it easier to go to sleep.

Caller's Problems

- My schedule isn't regular.
- I have trouble sleeping in warm weather. I often wake up feeling really hot and cranky.
- My husband / wife / roommate gets home from work at nine o'clock every evening, so I have dinner very late.
- I get really tired in the evenings. I drink coffee after dinner but then can't sleep.
- I fall asleep in the living room with the TV on. I usually wake up at two or three o'clock in the morning, go to bed, and can't fall asleep again.
- I get home from sports activities at 9:00 P.M. Then I go online and chat with my friends. I usually don't get to bed until after midnight.
- I get a surge of energy late at night, a second wind. I keep remembering things I need to do for the next day, so I stay up until two or three o'clock in the morning taking care of them.

Go to the **Pearson Practice English App** or **MyEnglishLab** for more grammar practice. Check what you learned in **MyEnglishLab.**

Using Contrastive Stress

To contrast words, speakers emphasize the words or syllables in those words. The emphasized words or syllables are said more loudly, more slowly, and with a higher pitch.

▶ **Read and listen. Notice how the speaker contrasts body with brain, and classroom with pillow.**

Example

A: My **BOdy's** in the **CLASSroom,** but my **BRAIN's** still on the **PILlow.**

1. ▶ **Read and listen to the sentences. Underline the contrasted words. Listen again. Then practice saying the sentences to a partner.**

   1. I need to go to bed, but I'm feeling energetic.

   2. Adolescents wake up late, but children wake up early.

   3. Lian is fast asleep, but her children are awake.

   4. My husband has insomnia, but I don't.

   5. I'm sleepy in the morning, but I'm wide awake at night.

2. **Work with a partner. Take turns asking and answering the questions.**

   STUDENT A: Ask a question.

   STUDENT B: Answer, using the information in the Answer column and contrastive stress.

   Example

   A: What is an obvious effect of sleep deprivation? What is a subtle effect?

   B: ABSENTEEISM is an OBVIOUS effect of sleep deprivation, but EMOTIONAL PROBLEMS are a more SUBTLE effect.

Question	Answer
1. What is an obvious effect of sleep deprivation? What is a subtle effect?	(absenteeism / emotional problems)
2. When is melatonin secreted in adults? What about adolescents?	(early evening / late at night)
3. When does melatonin "turn on"? When does it "turn off"?	(evening / morning)
4. According to adults, why do teenagers stay up late? According to teenagers, why do teenagers stay up late?	(because they are having fun / because they are night owls)
5. How do many parents feel on Monday morning? How do they feel by Friday night?	(tired / completely exhausted)

3 APPLY **Complete the survey. Then move around the room asking other students the questions. For each question, find a student who has the opposite or very different answer. Report the differences back to the class using sentences that contrast the information. Use contrastive stress in your comparisons.**

Examples

A: I OFTEN wake up at night, but JOE NEVER does.

B: I take naps in the MORNING, but CELIA takes naps in the AFTERNOON.

Health Survey: Sleep Habits ☾ ⁎ ⁎

OPPOSITE / DIFFERENT
ANSWER

Date: _____ Name: _____ _____

1. Do you never, sometimes, or often wake up at night? _____ _____

2. Do you snore? _____ _____

3. Do you daydream? About what? _____ _____

_____ _____

4. Do you take naps? When? _____ _____

_____ _____

5. Do you use an alarm clock? Why? _____ _____

_____ _____

6. What time do you wake up in the morning? _____ _____

7. How much coffee do you drink? _____ _____

SPEAKING SKILL

Asking for Clarification

Sometimes you may not understand a speaker. Perhaps the person speaks too fast or unclearly, or maybe there is background noise.

To clarify information, especially facts, you can (1) politely interrupt the speaker and ask about what you thought you heard or (2) ask the speaker to repeat what he or she said.

Example

A: Joelle, I heard some horrifying statistics—more than thirty percent of traffic accidents are caused by sleepiness! People should be more careful!

B: Excuse me. What did you say? Thirteen percent?

A: No, I said more than thirty percent. That's a lot, don't you think?

B: Thirty percent! I see what you mean! Wow! That's a very high figure.

(continued on next page)

Here are some expressions you can use when you do not understand something. Use rising intonation for the questions.

Start with . . .	Add . . .
Excuse me? . . .	What did you say?
I'm sorry. . . .	I didn't catch that. Could you say it again?
Sorry. . . .	Could you repeat that?
	I didn't hear you. What was that?
	Could you say that another way?
	Did you say . . . ?
	What? (informal)

Work with a partner. Take turns asking for clarification.

STUDENT A: Read a fact from the list aloud. Consider reading too fast or mispronouncing a number.

STUDENT B: Listen. Ask for clarification. Use expressions from the chart above.

Example

A: I read that 17 percent of Americans are insomniacs!

B: Sorry. Could you repeat that?

Facts:

• Seventeen percent of Americans are insomniacs.

• There are about 1,500 sleep-disorder clinics in the United States, and 40 million Americans suffer from sleep disorders.

• Almost 20 percent of Americans are shift workers and often have different work schedules, working from 7:00 to 3:00, or 3:00 to 11:00.

• During the winter, there are fourteen and a half hours of darkness in some parts of the United States. There's no excuse for not sleeping!

• Even if people are seriously sleep deprived, they can get back on a regular pattern of sleep after only three weeks.

• If rats are completely deprived of sleep for two and a half weeks, they die. In experiments, humans have been known to sustain wakefulness for up to ten days.

• Sleeping pills first became popular in the United States in the 1970s. Today, Americans spend approximately $41 billion annually on sleep aids.

🔘 Go to **MyEnglishLab** for more skill practice and to check what you learned.

In this activity, you will study a situation at the fictional Hilldale General Hospital* and then simulate a meeting between an administrator, a doctor, and a patients' rights activist. The topic of the meeting is how to resolve problems related to sleep deprivation.

PREPARE

1 Read the situation.

Situation

Two weeks ago, a ten-year-old boy was admitted to Hilldale General Hospital for a routine surgery. However, as he was being prepared for the operation, he was accidentally given an overdose of medication. He became very ill and remained so for several days, but fortunately he recovered and was not seriously affected.

Investigations revealed that both the doctor who ordered the medication that night and the nurse who administered it were seriously sleep deprived. They had both been on duty for fifteen hours when the boy received the medication. The doctor had worked ten hours a day for the previous eight days, while the nurse had worked the same shifts for the previous six days. Just before ordering the boy's medication, the doctor and the nurse had spent five hours operating on victims of a car accident.

In addition, HGH is having serious overcrowding and financial problems. The only other hospital in the community of Hilldale closed two years ago due to lack of funding, leaving HGH to cope with too many patients and too little money.

2 Divide into three groups. Each group chooses a different role from the box. (See Student Activities on page 218 for the details about each group.)

Hospital administrators	Doctors	Patients' rights activists

- Read about your group's role in preparation for the meeting.
- Take notes.
- Optional: Do additional research online.

3 Work with your group to clarify your viewpoints.

- Make a list of points you want to discuss. Consider these questions:
  - What are the causes of the crisis at HGH?
  - What are some possible solutions?
  - Who should be responsible for addressing the problems?
- Practice your role with a partner from your group.

---

* The situation is based on real cases at many hospitals.

4 APPLY Consider how to apply the vocabulary, grammar, pronunciation, and speaking skills from the unit. Use the checklist to help you.

☐ **Vocabulary:** Read through the list of vocabulary on page 79. Which words can you include in your role-play to make it clearer and more interesting? Choose at least three words or phrases to use, and add them to your notes.

☐ **Grammar:** Scan your notes for present unreal conditionals. Are you using them correctly?

☐ **Pronunciation:** Record yourself practicing using contrastive stress. Then listen back. Are your ideas clear?

☐ **Speaking Skill:** Think about how you can get clarification about something you didn't hear well or understand. Is it effective?

DISCUSS

Form a new group of three, with each role represented. Simulate a meeting.

- Share your viewpoints.

- Try to reach some solutions that will satisfy everyone.

Example

ADMINISTRATOR: We are seriously understaffed. If we had more staff members, we would not be so concerned about sleep deprivation among the interns.

DOCTOR: I agree that we're seriously understaffed. For example, there are only two of us on the ward at night. If my partner and I didn't show up for work one evening, there would be no one available to help incoming patients.

ACTIVIST: Excuse me? Did you say there were only two people on the ward?

ALTERNATIVE SPEAKING TOPIC

APPLY **Work in a small group. Discuss the questions. Use the vocabulary, grammar, pronunciation, and speaking skills from the unit.**

Most adolescents do not get enough sleep—7–7¼ hours per day. However, experts say that they need 9–9½ hours of sleep. When teenagers get enough sleep, they are in better moods and tend to progress faster in school.

Questions:

– Should schools redesign their schedules to help teenagers sleep more? How?

– What would be some advantages and disadvantages of a school schedule that lets teens sleep later?

CHECK WHAT YOU'VE LEARNED

Check (✔) the outcomes you've met and vocabulary you've learned. Put an X next to the skills and vocabulary you still need to practice.

Learning Outcomes	Vocabulary		Multi-word Units
☐ Infer a speaker's assumptions	☐ accumulate AWL	☐ maintain AWL	☐ clinically proven
☐ Take notes with symbols and abbreviations	☐ consistency AWL	☐ recover AWL	☐ have a tendency
	☐ cranky	☐ reset	☐ make (something) a priority
☐ Recognize claims and evidence	☐ critical	☐ sleep deprivation	☐ over the course of
☐ Use present unreal conditionals	☐ fatigue (n.)	☐ tolerate	☐ pretty well
	☐ intrinsic AWL		☐ that being said
☐ Use contrastive stress			☐ touch on
☐ Ask for clarification			

🢂 Go to **MyEnglishLab** to watch a video about sleep deprivation and health issues, access the Unit Project, and take the Unit 3 Achievement Test.

LEARNING OUTCOMES

> Infer a speaker's attitude
> Avoid non-essential words when taking notes
> Identify parts of oral paragraphs

> Use reported speech
> Use intonation of *yes / no* questions with *or*
> State reasons and give support

🔘 Go to **MyEnglishLab** to check what you know.

Animal Intelligence

1 FOCUS ON THE TOPIC

1. The photo shows dolphins, considered to be one of the most intelligent animals on Earth. In what ways does a dolphin demonstrate intelligence? How might dolphin intelligence be tested?

2. Do *all* animals think? How might the thoughts of animals differ from those of humans?

LISTENING ONE | Who's Smart?

VOCABULARY

1 ▶ **Read and listen to a lecture from an introductory course on animal intelligence. Notice the boldfaced words and phrases. Try to guess their meanings.**

TRANSCRIPT

HOST: Welcome to this month's guest lecture. This morning I'm pleased to introduce Dr. Addison Shanks, visiting scholar from Johnson University. So, without further delay, I'll **give the floor** to Professor Shanks.

DR. SHANKS: Thank you. Good to be here. Today we'll consider whether animals are "intelligent" in the same ways that humans are. Let me begin by asking you how we know humans are intelligent. **Off the top of your head**, would you say it's because we invent language, or use tools? Is it because we **can transfer** knowledge we learn in one **context** to another context? Are we intelligent because we can deceive and intentionally trick others? Or is it because we empathize with others, understanding how they feel? Are other animals capable of these things as well? Let's consider some recent research.

First, humans are conscious beings. When we look into a mirror, for example, we know we are seeing our own image. What about other animals? If you show a chimp his own reflection in a mirror, one might assume that he thinks he's looking at another chimp. But is it true that he just **doesn't get it**? Or would the chimp understand he's looking at himself? Apparently, he would. When some apes look into a mirror for the first time, their reaction is **spontaneous**: They examine their teeth. In some studies, researchers put paint on the faces of sleeping chimps. After waking, the chimps used a mirror to get the paint off. This shows awareness, or knowledge, of self. Dolphins and elephants have also demonstrated self-awareness: They look into mirrors to examine themselves after researchers place marks or objects on their heads.

Dr. Shanks: Second, we've learned some **intriguing** things about the ability of animals to communicate, both with each other and with humans. Of course, most animals aren't able to vocalize—that is, put voice to words. However, a growing number of animals raised in captivity have learned to communicate with humans through computers or gestures, sometimes learning thousands of words. While we could claim that this is just **rote** memorization and not true communication, studies have shown that certain apes can ask and answer questions they have never heard before and even create new "words." For example, a gorilla named Koko saw a picture of a mask for the first time and called it an "eye hat."

What other abilities are unique to humans? We humans show intelligence by putting items into **categories** according to color, size, shape, and so on. Humans also find answers to complex problems and apply the answers in a different context, or new situation. However, many examples show that animals **can figure out** complicated problems and transfer knowledge as well. Crows, for instance, figure out how to steal when fishermen aren't looking, by pulling the fishing line out of the water inch by inch until they get the fish.

Finally, consider emotions. Are humans alone in feeling love, sadness, empathy, compassion? Consider the research gorilla who showed distress and stopped eating when her pet kitten died, or recall that elephants display grief when family members die. Like humans, can animals be **socialized** to help one another? And do animals lie and use deception to trick others? Do animals guess what others are thinking and then take advantage of that knowledge? At this point, you can safely predict yes. Case in point: An elephant secretly learned how to open his cage at a zoo. After the humans had left for the night, the elephant opened all the other elephant cages, releasing his friends for midnight walks.

So we **end up** asking if animal intelligence is really so different from that of humans, and, if so, to what degree? Furthermore, if animals can categorize, perform simple mathematics, intentionally deceive others, make and carry out plans, and communicate with humans, what kind of relationship should we have with them? A growing body of research is pushing the edge of the envelope on what we consider "human" when we think about these questions.

2 Match the words and phrases on the left with the definitions on the right.

<u>H</u>   1. category

<u>C</u>   2. context

<u>D</u>   3. doesn't get it

<u>G</u>   4. end up *(v.)*

<u>B</u>   5. figure out

____   6. give (someone) the floor

<u>A</u>   7. intriguing *(adj.)*

<u>C</u>   8. off the top of (one's) head

<u>I</u>   9. rote

<u>F</u>   10. socialized *(adj.)*

<u>J</u>   11. spontaneous

<u>K</u>   12. transfer *(v.)*

a. interesting because it's unusual or unexpected

b. to understand something after studying it

c. not planned

d. doesn't understand

e. the situation, events, or information related to something

f. trained to behave in a way that is acceptable to others in your group

g. to finish by

h. a group of things with similar qualities

i. habitual, mechanical

j. without thought or planning beforehand

k. to move from one place to another

l. to give somebody else the opportunity to speak

Go to the **Pearson Practice English App** or **MyEnglishLab** for more vocabulary practice.

PREVIEW

Recent research has changed our view of animal emotions and animal intelligence. You will hear a radio interview featuring these psychology professors discussing their experiments:

- Dr. Sally Boysen
- Dr. Irene Pepperberg
- Dr. Stan Kuczaj

Listen to the introduction to the interview. Write the types of animals to be discussed. Talk with a partner and predict what information you might hear about each.

1. _____

2. _____

3. _____

an African grey parrot

LISTEN

1 ▶ **Listen to the whole interview. Create a chart like the one below to take notes.**

> **TAKE NOTES Who's Smart?**
>
> | Main Ideas | Details |
> |---|---|
> | Dr. Boysen:

 Chimp Sara can show compassion, leads Abigail around | – ~ 40 yrs old

 – new chimp, pet ~ 20 yrs = Abigail – difficulty getting around; retinal damage from diabetes

 – Sara was not socialized w/chimps, but helps Abigail |

2 **Compare your notes with a partner's. How can you improve your notes?**

🔖 Go to **MyEnglishLab** to view example notes.

MAIN IDEAS

What does each animal do? Check (✓) the correct pictures. Use your notes to help you.

1.

2.

3.

1 ▶ **Listen again and add to your notes. Then identify the statements as *T* (true) or *F* (false). Correct the false statements. Use your notes to help you. Discuss your answers with a partner.**

_F_ 1. The younger chimp, Abigail, had a hearing disability.

_T_ 2. The behavior of Sara, the older chimp, is remarkable to Dr. Boysen because Sara was not socialized with other chimps.

_F_ 3. Alex, the parrot, uses a computer to communicate.

_T_ 4. Dr. Kuczaj's killer whale uses fish to attract seagulls.

_T_ 5. Dr. Pepperberg says that talking to Alex is like talking to a very young human.

_T_ 6. Dr. Pepperberg calls Alex's talk "two-way communication."

_F_ 7. Alex can answer questions about where he wants to go.

_F_ 8. When Alex answers questions, he doesn't seem to understand the questions; instead, he answers in a rote manner.

2 **With a partner, take turns summarizing your notes. Then discuss how your notes and your answers in Preview helped you understand the listening.**

▶ Go to **MyEnglishLab** for more listening practice.

MAKE INFERENCES 🔍

Inferring a Speaker's Attitude

We can infer a speaker's attitude or feelings toward a subject based on clues such as

– word choice
– word stress
– pausing and hesitation
– exclamations ("oh!" laughter, etc.)

▶ **Read and listen to an excerpt from the interview with Dr. Boysen. Then answer the questions. Check (✓) the clues that helped you.**

Example

HOST ALEX GOODWIN: Dr. Boysen, what about you?

DR. BOYSEN: Oh! You would start with me. I, I guess probably the most remarkable thing I've seen lately is . . .

1. What is Dr. Boysen's attitude toward the host's question?

   a. surprised

   b. pleased

   c. unhappy

Clues

☐ word choice

☐ word stress

☐ pausing and hesitation

☐ exclamation

2. What might she say about her feelings?

   a. "I don't know the answer to that question."

   b. "I wasn't ready to speak first."

ANSWERS: 1. a – "You would start with me" suggests she feels unlucky to be the first. *Guess* and *probably* also suggest surprise. (word choice); Specifically, she stresses *me* to show she wasn't expecting to be the first to speak. (word stress); Her hesitation ("I, I guess . . . ") before giving her example also reflects surprise. (pausing and hesitation); She begins with "Oh!" a expression of surprise. (exclamation); Therefore, all clues could be checked.

2. b

▶ **Listen to the excerpts from the interview with Dr. Boysen and circle the correct answers. Check (✓) the clues.**

Excerpt One

1. What is Dr. Boysen's attitude about Sara's behavior? How does Dr. Boysen communicate her attitude?

   a. She's impressed by it.

   b. She's confused by it.

   c. She's saddened by it.

Clues

☐ word choice

☐ word stress

☐ pausing and hesitation

☐ exclamation

2. What might Dr. Boysen say about what Sara the chimp did?

   a. "This shows that animals can teach each other."

   b. "This shows that animals can be guided by hunger."

   c. "This shows that animals have emotions and feelings."

Excerpt Two

1. What is the host's attitude about Alex's behavior? How does the host communicate his attitude?

   a. He is impressed by what Alex did.

   b. He can't believe the behavior really happened.

   c. He doesn't think the behavior shows intelligence.

Clues

☐ word choice

☐ word stress

☐ pausing and hesitation

☐ exclamation

2. What might the host say about what Alex did?

   a. "He is easily confused by new situations."

   b. "He understood that we were trying to trick him."

   c. "He doesn't fully understand the question."

Work with a partner or in a small group. Discuss the questions.

USE YOUR NOTES

APPLY Find information in your notes to use in your discussion.

1. In the interview, what facts are presented as evidence that each animal is intelligent? Use your notes.

   - Sara, the chimp

   - Alex, the parrot

   - the killer whales

2. Is the evidence convincing? Support your answer.

🖱 Go to **MyEnglishLab** to give your opinion about another question.

LISTENING TWO | What Motivates Animals?

VOCABULARY

1 **Read a news story about a mystery at an aquarium. Notice the boldfaced words and phrases. With a partner or group, try to guess the meanings.**

In the news . . .

Controversy surrounded the disappearance of some crabs at an aquarium in Oregon a few years ago. One morning, workers found crabs missing from their tank and empty crab shells on the floor. New crabs were brought in to replace the dead ones, but the same thing happened several more times. Who was guilty? They installed an overnight camera to find out.

It turns out that a sneaky octopus had learned to **take advantage of** his nighttime privacy. Did he **anticipate** a midnight snack? It looks that way. He waited all day until workers went home. Then he was able to **manipulate** his body, lengthening and narrowing himself to fit into an air tube that led out of his covered tank. He moved across the floor into the crab tank. After enjoying a midnight crab meal, he went back to his own tank the way he had come, looking quite innocent in the morning. Workers were amazed that a seemingly "unintelligent" animal was able to carry out such a trick.

2 Write each boldfaced word or phrase from Exercise One next to its definition.

1. _It turns out_ : something has a particular result
2. _take advantage_ : to profit from
3. _anticipate_ : to expect something to happen
4. _manipulate_ : to skillfully handle or control
5. _controversy_ : a serious disagreement

➤ Go to the **Pearson Practice English App** or **MyEnglishLab** for more vocabulary practice.

NOTE-TAKING SKILL

Avoiding Non-Essential Words When Taking Notes

When taking notes, you might miss important information if you write too many non-essential words. Non-essential words are often adjectives, pronouns, articles, and forms of the verb *be*. To take notes faster, note only key words.

Example

You hear: And **it turns out** that competition for food is what motivates them to perform. So there's been a series of experiments. One of the more recent ones has to do with putting a chimp head-to-head with a human.

You write: *Competition for food motivates*

∴ *experiments: chimp vs. human*

Be sure to review your notes soon after you've taken them, adjusting details to help you remember them.

▶ **Listen to excerpts from an interview with a science writer. Focus on noting key words and avoiding non-essential words.**

Excerpt One

chimp _____ ⟶ _____

Excerpt Two

caching _____ : _____

Excerpt Three

theory of _____ : _____

➤ Go to **MyEnglishLab** for more note-taking practice.

COMPREHENSION

Scientists have added to our knowledge of large-ape and bird intelligence. You will hear a podcast interview with Liz Pennisi, a writer for *Science* magazine who discusses some new research on animal cognition.

1 ▶ **Listen to the interview. Create a chart like the one below to take notes. Try to avoid non-essential words as you take notes.**

TAKE NOTES **What Motivates Animals?**

Main Ideas	Details

2 **Use your notes to answer the questions. Check (✓) Yes or No.**

The speakers say that apes and / or birds can . . .   **Yes**   **No**

1. understand when someone is watching.   ☐   ☐
2. manipulate someone to get what they want.   ☐   ☐
3. operate robots.   ☐   ☐
4. teach their offspring what they've learned.   ☐   ☐
5. remember.   ☐   ☐
6. create works of art.   ☐   ☐
7. plan.   ☐   ☐
8. anticipate the future.   ☐   ☐
9. judge what someone else might be doing.   ☐   ☐
10. deceive others who might steal their food.   ☐   ☐

USE YOUR NOTES

Compare your notes with a partner's. How can you improve your notes next time?

a scrub jay hiding food

1 ▶ **Listen to the deceptive octopus news story from page 88. Notice how the speaker supports her main idea with details and examples.**

Identifying Parts of Oral Paragraphs

In formal contexts, experienced speakers may speak in paragraphs. They often start with a topic sentence, which includes the main idea. They support the main idea with details and examples. Identifying the parts of oral paragraphs can help your comprehension.

▶ **Read and listen to an excerpt from the interview with Liz Pennisi. Then answer the question.**

Example

LIZ PENNISI: A lot of the work is done in chimps and other apes because they're our closest relatives, and the idea is to put the chimps into a situation that they react to. And it turns out that competition for food is what motivates them to perform. So there's been a series of experiments. One of the more recent ones has to do with putting a chimp head to head with a human, and the chimp wants to reach for food and the human has the ability to pull the food away. And what the chimp readily figures out is that if it kind of sneaks around a barrier that the human can't see, it can get the food. What that experiment is showing is that the chimp understands that the human is watching them and understands how to manipulate the situation to get what it wants.

What are the parts of this oral paragraph?

ANSWER: Main idea: *Chimps are capable of manipulation.*

Details / Examples: *In experiment, chimp:*
– wants food
– sneaks around barrier human can't see
– gets food

2 ▶ **Listen to an excerpt from the interview with Liz Pennisi. Complete the notes.**

Main Idea:

Researchers: some ___of the skills___ in chimps / social animals / humans → social birds

Details / Examples:

In experiments:

– uses "caching ___behavior___" = bird (scrub jay / crow) buries food

– knows other bird ___is watching you___: what do you do?

– ___it will go___ behind barrier so onlooker ___can't see what it's doing___

– buries food

– ___Buries the food___ and moves food ___in place___

🔊 Go to **MyEnglishLab** for more skill practice.

ORGANIZE

How do the animals demonstrate intelligence? Complete the chart with details from the listenings.

USE YOUR NOTES

APPLY Review your notes from Listening One and Two. Use the information in your notes to complete the chart.

EVIDENCE OF ANIMAL INTELLIGENCE		
	LISTENING ONE: *Who's Smart?*	**LISTENING TWO:** *What Motivates Animals?*
	Interview with Psychology Professors	*Interview with Science Writer Liz Pennisi*
Chimps	• one chimp understood that another chimp was disabled / helped that chimp	*take advantages of what they call "caching behaviour"*
Birds	Parrot:	Scrub jays and crows: • bury food and hide it from other birds • come back later and change hiding place if they think another bird was watching
Killer whales		

SYNTHESIZE

1 **Work in a small group. Each member will give a short presentation about one of the animals from the unit.**

   • Select chimps, birds, or killer whales.

   • Prepare an oral paragraph: Think of a topic sentence (including main idea) and choose supporting details and examples. (Study the chart for your selected animal.)

   • Give your presentation.

2 **Change groups and repeat your presentation.**

   Example

   A: It's clear from research that chimps are intelligent. We have seen and heard many examples of this. In one case, . . . In another case, . . .

3 **In both listenings, you heard about research that investigates the meaning of intelligence. In your opinion, what is a useful definition of "intelligence"?**

🔎 Go to **MyEnglishLab** to check what you learned.

VOCABULARY

REVIEW

Work with a partner. Say the boldfaced words and phrases aloud. Then underline the two words (or phrases) that are related to the boldfaced word or phrase. Use a dictionary if necessary.

1. **anticipate**	oppose	plan	expect
2. **category**	type	individual	group
3. **context**	knowledge	situation	setting
4. **controversy**	argument	agreement	dispute
5. **doesn't get it**	doesn't understand	doesn't realize	can't imagine
6. **end up**	get behind	finish	result in
7. **figure out**	add	understand	solve
8. **give (someone) the floor**	ask for an opinion	help to walk	allow to speak
9. **intriguing**	irrelevant	fascinating	mysterious
10. **manipulate**	pull	control	use
11. **off the top of (someone's) head**	considered	not researched	quickly
12. **socialized**	tamed	friendly	wild
13. **spontaneous**	thoughtful	unexpected	unplanned

a squirrel

EXPAND

1 ▶ **Work with a partner. Read and listen to a radio talk show. The host and guest are answering calls. Notice the boldfaced words and phrases.**

HOST: Our guest today is Dr. Lara Ruiz, an expert on animal behavior. Welcome, Dr. Ruiz. I've asked our listeners to call in to tell us their stories of smart animals or animals that cause problems. We have calls from all over. Yes, hello, Dodie. You're on the air.

DODIE: Hi, I'm calling about smart squirrels. I have a bird feeder next to my house, and no matter what I do, squirrels always get the food. They climb right up the pole. They're such a nuisance! I put oil on the pole, but the squirrels somehow figured out a solution. And, also, raccoons are getting into my garbage can. They open the lid with their little hands . . .

HOST: Sorry to **butt in** here, Dodie, but I want to stick to one question at a time and get you some answers. Dr. Ruiz, what about Dodie's squirrel problem?

DR. RUIZ: Squirrels enjoy a challenge and are clever at getting food. However, you can anticipate what they'll do. They might be getting at your feeder by jumping from above, so try moving it away from the house and trees. See if that helps.

HOST: Thanks for calling, Dodie. OK, Janek . . . Janek? Are you there? You have the floor.

JANEK: Yes, hello. I'm calling about problems with deer, which are not very intelligent animals. I **make a living** selling garden plants, but deer jump my fence at night and eat everything. It's costing me a fortune. What's more, they're dangerous.

HOST: Dangerous? What do you mean?

JANEK: Deer often run into the street and cause car accidents. I like animals as much as the next person, but at some point we have to admit that humans are more, well, superior to animals. Deer are not **endangered** animals. We just have to **get rid of** them if they become problems.

HOST: You mean kill them? Some people might think killing them is **pushing the envelope** a bit, no? Callers, what do you think? The phone lines are already ringing. Alicia, you're on.

ALICIA: Hi. I just heard your last caller, and I **take issue with** his cruel solution to the deer problem. Animals are helpless next to humans, so it's our responsibility to protect them, not kill them because they're in our way. The **humane** thing to do is stop thinking that wild animals are a nuisance, and learn to live with them.

HOST: Dr. Ruiz, would you like to **weigh in** here?

DR. RUIZ: Both callers have good points. We have to allow for human activity, but we also want to be **ethical** in our treatment of animals. And we want to preserve what we can of the natural world for our children, of course.

HOST: OK, time for one last caller. Kendall, you're on the air.

KENDALL: There's a really smart cat on my local news and on YouTube. He's called the "Cat Burglar" because he sneaks out at night and steals from neighbors. He's on videos taking bathing suits, shoes, toys, all kinds of things, and delivering them to his embarrassed owners. They have tried to **put a stop to** his bad behavior, but they can't keep him in the house all the time. He's taken hundreds of items!

DR. RUIZ: Intriguing case! I'd like to figure out his motivation.

HOST: Maybe he's just having fun! At any rate, we're out of time for today. So thanks for joining us today, Dr. Ruiz!

2 **Match the words on the left with the definitions on the right.**

E 1. butt in   a. compassionate, not cruel

D 2. endangered   b. to remove, throw away

J 3. ethical   c. to give an opinion about something

B 4. get rid of   d. threatened with extinction

A 5. humane   e. to interrupt

G 6. make a living   f. to disagree with

H 7. push the envelope g. to earn enough money to support oneself

I 8. put a stop to   h. to move beyond the limit of what has usually been done

F 9. take issue with   i. to end an activity

C 10. weigh in   j. morally good and correct

CREATE

APPLY **Work with a partner. Take turns asking and answering the questions. Write a few notes to help you speak.**

STUDENT A: Ask one of the questions. You can use your own words.

STUDENT B: Try to use the vocabulary in the Answer column. Answer in a few sentences.

Example:

A: What animals are considered nuisances? Do they pose a danger? Rats

B: Well, I've heard that a lot of deer **end up** getting hit by cars because they're looking for food.

Question	Answer	
1. What animals are considered nuisances? Do they pose a danger?	anticipate butt in	it turns out make a living
2. Are the animals mentioned on the radio show—squirrels, raccoons, deer, cats—intelligent? How?	category context controversy	manipulate off the top of (one's) head
3. What abilities do people and animals share? What abilities do people have that animals don't?	doesn't get it endangered end up	push the envelope put a stop to rote
4. What are some examples of people treating animals inhumanely?	ethical figure out	socialized spontaneous
5. There is debate over whether animals should be used in scientific experiments and whether we should eat meat. Should people stop doing these activities?	get rid of give (someone) the floor humane intriguing	take advantage of take issue with transfer weigh in

Go to the **Pearson Practice English App** or **MyEnglishLab** for more vocabulary practice.

GRAMMAR FOR SPEAKING

1 Work with a partner. Read the conversation and answer the questions.

A: Did you see that documentary about parrots? It **said** some parrots **could recognize** themselves in a mirror.

B: Yeah! It also **reported** that parrots **were able to string** three or four words together. Actually, my professor **told** us that he **was writing** a paper on how parrots learn language. He **said he was going to publish** it next month.

A: What inspired him?

B: He **said he'd been inspired** by seeing parrots in cages at a pet store. That day he realized he **had to raise** awareness about the importance of treating these birds more humanely.

1. Do we know the exact words of the documentary or the professor?

2. Why do you think the speakers choose not to quote the documentary or the professor directly?

Using Reported Speech

Reported speech (also called *indirect speech*) reports what a speaker said but does not use his or her exact words. Use words like *said (that), told, indicated, mentioned, reported, explained,* and *claimed* to show that you are reporting information said by someone or from a source (an article, a documentary, etc.).

	Direct Speech	Reported Speech
When reporting what a speaker or source said, shift the verb in the reported speech back in time. This is called *back-shifting*. Here there is a back-shift from the present progressive to the past progressive. (See more examples on page 97.)	*SCIENTIST: "We **are conducting** some interesting research on endangered whales."*	*The scientist <u>explained</u> that she and her team **were conducting** some interesting research on endangered whales.*
When reporting a person's unchanging beliefs or a general truth rather than an event, back-shifting is optional.	*ZOOLOGIST: "Many animals **are** remarkably intelligent."*	*The zoologist <u>told</u> her students that many animals **are / were** remarkably intelligent.*

Common Verb Changes	Direct Speech	Reported Speech
present → past	**ZOOLOGIST:** "I'**m** a researcher, studying animals' use of tools."	The zoologist said (that) she **was** a researcher, studying animals' use of tools.
present progressive → past progressive	"I'**m conducting** an experiment on crows."	She said (that) she **was conducting** an experiment on crows.
simple past and present perfect → past perfect	**RESEARCHER:** "The crows **made** a hook to get food from a tree."	The researcher reported (that) the crows **had made** a hook to get food from a tree.
	"We **have** never **studied** this behavior before."	She said (that) they **had** never **studied** this behavior before.
will → would	"I **won't** be at the meeting."	She explained (that) she **wouldn't** be at the meeting.
can → could	"I **can** ask my colleague to take notes."	She said (that) she **could** ask her colleague to take notes.
may → might	"I **may** be able to send my assistant."	She mentioned (that) she **might** be able to send her assistant.
must → had to	"I **must** find a way to repeat my experiment."	She said (that) she **had to** find a way to repeat her experiment.
The modals **should, could, might,** and **ought to** do not change.	"I **should** publish my results."	She said (that) she **should** publish her results.
Change the pronouns, possessives, and time words to reflect the original meaning.	**STUDENT:** "I **can't** access **my** computer because it broke down **yesterday**."	The student claimed (that) **she** couldn't access **her** computer because it had broken down **the day before**.

2 Work with a partner. Take turns reading and reporting.

STUDENT A: Read the statement.

STUDENT B: Cover the chart. Report Student A's statement using reported speech. Use a variety of reporting verbs.

STUDENT A: Read the Reported Speech column to check Student B's answer.

Example

A: I'm reading an article about Jane Goodall. She's the world authority on chimpanzees.

B: You said she was the world authority on chimpanzees, right?

A: That's right.

Statement	Reported Speech
1. Jane Goodall **is** the world authority on chimpanzees.	You said she **was** the world authority on chimpanzees.
2. She **has studied** chimpanzees for more than forty-five years.	You said she **had studied** chimpanzees for more than forty-five years.
3. She **discovered** tool-making among chimps.	You explained she **had discovered** tool-making among chimps.
4. Her work **will affect** generations of people.	You told me her work **would affect** generations of people.
5. I**'m reading** about a dolphin research center.	You said you **were reading** about a dolphin research center.
6. I**'m going to visit** the center in August.	You indicated you **were going to visit** the center in August.
7. I**'ve always wanted** to swim with dolphins.	You claimed **you'd always wanted** to swim with dolphins.
8. The dolphins at the center **are used to** interacting with humans.	You reported that the dolphins at the center **were used to** interacting with humans.

3 APPLY Work with a partner. Role-play a conversation between A and B. In your role, support your position with information from the chart on the next page and from the unit. Remember to follow the rules for reported speech.

- A's position is that animals are very intelligent.

- B's position is that animals operate mainly on instinct.

Example

A: My professor said a study showed that an ape had learned to use sign language to communicate.

B: Well, I saw an interview with a zookeeper who said that apes can copy signs, but . . .

Support For A's Position	Support For B's Position
Professor: "A few studies have shown that apes can learn to use sign language to communicate."	**Zookeeper:** "Apes do learn to copy signs, but they don't use grammar or vocabulary as well as humans do."
Radio report: "Crows have been filmed carrying clams high into the air. They drop the clams, and the clamshells break. Then the crows pick up the food."	**Teacher:** "Some animals can be trained to do tricks. That doesn't prove that they are intelligent."
Neighbor: "I have a cat who senses when I'm sick and stays by my side. When I'm well, she usually keeps to herself."	**Parent:** "I love cats, and I've had one for years. Some people say they are smart, and perhaps they are. But they can't understand basic ideas or human emotions."
Friend: "Animals have feelings, too. Whenever I'm away on a short business trip, my family says my dog stops eating."	**Roommate:** "Pets obviously love their owners, but they're also motivated by food or fear. They also get upset when their routine changes."

Go to the **Pearson Practice English App** or **MyEnglishLab** for more grammar practice. Check what you learned in **MyEnglishLab**.

PRONUNCIATION

Using Intonation of *Yes / No* Questions with *Or*

Some *yes / no* questions with *or* ask the listener to make a choice. But some *yes / no* questions that include an *or* phrase are true *yes / no* questions. They are asking the listener to say "Yes" or "No," not to make a choice.

▶ **Read and listen.**

Examples

Choice Questions

A: Did Jane Goodall study chimps or apes?

B: She studied chimps.

- The words joined by *or* are in different thought groups.
- Intonation rises on the first choice and falls on the second.
- The speaker wants the listener to indicate which choice is correct.

True *Yes / No* Questions

A: Did she study plants or birds?

B: No. She concentrated on chimps.

- The *or*-phrase is pronounced as one group.
- Intonation rises smoothly over the *or*-phrase.
- Here the speaker is asking whether Jane Goodall studied those things.

Note that sometimes the answer to a choice question and a true *yes / no* question can be almost the same.

1 ▶ **Read and listen to the questions. Repeat them. The questions are all true *yes / no* questions. Say the words in the *or*-phrase as one thought group. Your voice should rise smoothly over the *or*-phrase.**

    1. Do you have a cat or a dog?

    2. Do you like to visit zoos or parks?

    3. Do chimps communicate with sounds or gestures?

    4. Can your dog shake hands or roll over?

    5. Can that parrot ask or answer questions?

    6. Did the speaker talk about the intelligence of cows or chickens?

    7. Have you read about seagulls or crows?

    8. Do you have a fur coat or a leather jacket?

2 ▶ **Read and listen to the same questions, said differently. Repeat them. This time the speaker is asking choice questions. Say the words in the *or*-phrase in two thought groups. Your voice rises on the first choice and falls on the second.**

3 APPLY **Work with a partner. Follow the steps.**

    1. Read the questions. Some make more sense as choice questions, some make more sense as true *yes / no* questions, and some could be either.

    2. Create short conversations using each question. Group words carefully and use intonation clearly.

       • Can animals manipulate or deceive?

       • Are you a meat-eater or a vegetarian?

       • Do pets prefer human food or pet food?

       • Are you more afraid of snakes or spiders?

       • Would you like to see a tiger or a lion?

       • Should people wear real fur or fake fur?

a chimpanzee

Stating Reasons and Giving Support

To understand a speaker's opinion, listeners often need to hear the support: reasons and details / examples. Read the excerpt from a presentation. Notice the boldfaced expressions.

Example

> **Opinion:** People in cities shouldn't keep dogs.
>
> **Reasons: There are several reasons why.**
>
> **One reason is** space, something most city-dwellers don't have a lot of. A 60-pound (27 kg) dog, **for instance**, needs 100 square feet (9.3 sq. m) of space, at a minimum.
>
> **Another reason is** time, and we don't have much of that in cities, either. **For example**, an adult golden retriever needs an hour of vigorous activity a day.
>
> **One final reason is** money. **Let me explain** the math of owning a dog . . .

State Reasons	Add Details / Examples
There are several reasons why . . .	For example,
One reason is . . .	Here's an example:
Another reason is . . .	For one thing,
One final reason is . . .	For instance,
Here's why . . .	Let me explain . . .
	. . . , such as . . .
	An example that comes to mind is . . .

1 **Complete the conversations. Fill in the blanks with expressions for stating reasons and adding examples or details. More than one correct answer may be possible.**

Conversation One

    A: I just read an interesting article about circuses. A lot of people are happy that most of them no longer use animals.

    B: Why? Kids love to see animals.

    A: One reason that this article gives is that circus animals are often treated badly.

    _____ elephants don't exercise enough, and they have too much
         1.

    stress, so they often get sick. _____ , many develop skin diseases. Also,
             2.

    sometimes trainers hit the elephants.

Conversation Two

A: Did you see that Twitter thread about problems elephants face? People say we need better laws to protect them.

B: Why?

A: Well, _____ elephants are hunted to the point of being endangered.
3.

_____ African elephants are hunted for ivory; hundreds of them are
4.

killed every year. _____ Asian elephants are losing their natural habitat
5.

because of human activity.

Conversation Three

A: I think elephants are extremely intelligent.

B: Why do you say that?

A: _____ female elephants find "babysitters" to help them raise their young.
6.

The babysitters help with all kinds of things.

B: Really?

A: Yes. _____ they protect the young elephants when the group moves from
7.

place to place.

2 APPLY **Work in a group of four. Each person chooses a different topic.**

- Silently read about your topic.
- Begin by sharing with your group an opinion about your topic.
- Then support your position with reasons and details / examples based on the information you read.
- Use reported speech to restate the words of the researcher.

Example

A: Chimps should not be kept in zoos or used in circuses. One reason is because they experience a wide range of emotions, according to research. For example, . . .

Topic A: Expression of Emotions

Research finding: Chimps recognize and express emotions such as happiness and fear.

Researcher statement: "We showed them TV scenes of other chimps playing and fighting. We used thermometers to measure their brain temperature. We found that the chimps had physical reactions to the other chimps' feelings."

Topic B: Self-Recognition

Research finding: Dolphins are able to recognize themselves in mirrors.

Researcher statement: "Our research team used markers to draw lines on the bodies of two captive dolphins. Once the dolphins felt the marker, they swam over to mirrors to inspect various parts of themselves. Then they tried to get rid of the marks by rubbing themselves on the tank."

Topic C: Problem-Solving

Research finding: Crows are creative problem-solvers.

Researcher statement: "I filmed crows in urban Japan. They dropped nuts on the road and waited for cars to run over them and crack the shells. Then the crows went back to eat the nuts."

Topic D: Language

Research finding: Squirrels use their tails to communicate.

Researcher statement: "Tail flashing, or moving the tail in a wave-like motion, is one of the first indications squirrels give when they sense something disturbing. If the threat seems greater, they will add vocalizations—sounds—to the tail flashing."

🔎 Go to **MyEnglishLab** for more skill practice and to check what you learned.

FINAL SPEAKING TASK: Research Presentation 🔍 APPLY

In this activity, you will research an animal ethics issue that interests you. Then you will give a 2–3-minute presentation to the class, supporting your findings.

PREPARE

Homework

1 Work with a partner or in a small group. Choose a topic from the box or think of your own.

> Is it ethical to put animals in zoos?
> Is it humane to raise animals as food for humans?
> Should humans conduct experiments on animals?
> Should we put a stop to hunting for sport or pleasure?
> Should we pass stricter laws to protect endangered species?
> Is it fair to keep animals as pets?

2 Research your topic.

- Go online or to the library. Find an article or video from an academic or otherwise well-respected source (newspaper, magazine, journal).

- As you research, develop the position you want to take.

- Take notes and include supporting reasons and details / examples. Also note the author and website information.

- Use the chart on the next page to organize your notes.

TOPIC:	
Title and Author / Source of Article:	
Your Position:	
Reason 1:	Detail / Example:
Reason 2:	Detail / Example:
Reason 3:	Detail / Example:

3 **APPLY** **Consider how to apply the vocabulary, grammar, pronunciation, and speaking skills from the unit. Use the checklist to help you.**

☐ **Vocabulary:** Read through the list of vocabulary on page 105. Which words can you include in your presentation to make it clearer and more interesting? Choose at least three words or phrases to use, and add them to your notes.

☐ **Grammar:** Scan your notes for direct speech and reported speech. Are you using reporting verbs correctly?

☐ **Pronunciation:** Record yourself practicing using *yes / no* questions with *or*. Then listen back. Are you using correct intonation?

☐ **Speaking Skill:** Be sure to support your point with reasons and details / examples.

PRACTICE

Practice with a partner from your group.

- Practice giving your oral presentation to your partner. Limit your talk to 1–2 minutes.

- Use the chart to give feedback to your partner.

FEEDBACK: 1 Strongly disagree 2 Disagree 3 Agree 4 Strongly agree				
The presenter used interesting direct speech and reported speech.	1	2	3	4
The presenter supported his / her points with reasons and details / examples.	1	2	3	4
What did the presenter do well? How could he / she improve?	Comments:			

PRESENT

1 Present to your group.

2 Create a chart like the one above to give feedback to the other presenters.

ALTERNATIVE SPEAKING TOPIC

APPLY Work in a small group. Read the quotes. Paraphrase each quote. Then choose one that you agree with and explain its meaning to the class. Organize your arguments by stating a main idea and supporting it with details and examples, as in an oral paragraph. Use the vocabulary, grammar, pronunciation, and speaking skills from the unit.

> If an animal does something, we call it instinct; if we do the same thing for the same reason, we call it intelligence.
>
> Will Cuppy, author, 1884–1949

> The greatness of a nation and its moral progress can be judged by the way its animals are treated.
>
> Mahatma Gandhi, statesman and philosopher, 1869–1948

> The soul of man is divided into three parts: intelligence, reason, and passion. Intelligence and passion are possessed by other animals, but reason by man alone.
>
> Pythagoras, mathematician and philosopher, approximately 569–475 BCE

CHECK WHAT YOU'VE LEARNED

Check (✔) the outcomes you've met and vocabulary you've learned. Put an X next to the skills and vocabulary you still need to practice.

Learning Outcomes
- ☐ Infer a speaker's attitude
- ☐ Avoid non-essential words when taking notes
- ☐ Identify parts of oral paragraphs
- ☐ Use reported speech
- ☐ Use intonation of *yes / no* questions with *or*
- ☐ State reasons and give support

Vocabulary
- ☐ anticipate AWL
- ☐ category AWL
- ☐ context AWL
- ☐ controversy AWL
- ☐ intriguing (*adj.*)
- ☐ manipulate AWL
- ☐ rote
- ☐ socialized (*adj.*)
- ☐ spontaneous
- ☐ transfer (*v.*) AWL

Multi-word Units
- ☐ doesn't get it
- ☐ end up
- ☐ figure out
- ☐ give (someone) the floor
- ☐ it turns out
- ☐ off the top of (one's) head
- ☐ take advantage of

🖰 Go to **MyEnglishLab** to watch a video about talking to animals, access the Unit Project, and take the Unit 4 Achievement Test.

LEARNING OUTCOMES

> Infer a speaker's intention
> Take notes with diagrams
> Identify and understand relationships
  between ideas

> Compare past forms
> Use word blends with *you*
> Make suggestions

🔊 Go to **MyEnglishLab** to check what you know.

The Golden Years

1 FOCUS ON THE TOPIC

1. *Longevity* means the length of a person's life. What are some factors that might help a person live a long, happy life?

2. The photo shows an older man running. Is this a good activity for older people? What kinds of activities do senior citizens—older people—enjoy?

3. At what age do people become "elderly," and what problems do people begin to face as they age?

LISTENING ONE | The Longevity Project

VOCABULARY

1 ▶ **Read and listen to a podcast about staying active. Notice the boldfaced words and phrases. Try to guess their meanings.**

TRANSCRIPT

HOST RAUL RASHID: Thanks for joining me today, Elena and Marco. You both live alone and are independent, healthy, and seemingly happy. I want to **delve into** your secret for living long and healthy lives. There have been some scientific **breakthroughs** recently regarding living long and healthy lives. One finding is that we need to stay active. Do you agree?

ELENA: I absolutely agree. Of course, I'm seventy-eight now and I've had to slow down a lot over the years, but I'm pretty active. I stretch and walk a mile every day, take a weekly yoga class, and play basketball every Monday.

RR: Basketball? That seems like **vigorous** exercise for someone who is slowing down.

ELENA: Well, we play a little slowly. But to stay healthy, I have to make a plan and **stick to it**, even if I feel a little stiff at first. I always feel better later.

RR: Marco, what about you?

MARCO: No basketball for me. In fact, I don't do planned exercise or take classes. But I'm pretty **conscientious** about staying active. I live in the city and enjoy walking everywhere I can. That adds up to a few miles every day.

RR: OK, so you're both **persistent** about keeping active. And you certainly look fit. Do you follow strict diets?

MARCO: Not at all. I'm eighty-three years old and never have. I eat out a lot and eat whatever I want. If I kept up with all the news about health, I'd get **overwhelmed** and give up anyway. I eat what I please, just in moderation. I do try to keep my weight down.

ELENA: I try to keep the pounds off, too. I just feel better at my proper weight.

RR: I understand you two have been friends for three **decades**.

ELENA: Thirty-four years, actually. We meet every so often for dinner or a show or something with a group of friends. I do need my alone time, but I also see friends regularly. Some I travel with, too.

MARCO: Yes, so do I.

RR: So friends are a big part of your lives, it seems. What about work?

ELENA: I retired from my part-time job when I was seventy-two, but I still volunteer once a week. Working helps keep me healthy, too.

RR: So at seventy-two, you still had your **nose to the grindstone**. That's impressive.

ELENA: Not really. My work isn't hard, but I really like it. I see lots of people there.

RR: Marco, you've been retired for a long time. Do you agree that work keeps one healthy?

MARCO: Well, when I was a practicing dentist, I liked my work and did my best for my patients. But I was also **prudent** about my time and knew when to relax and when to stop entirely. I probably could have earned more money in my career if I'd worked longer and harder, but why? It's not worth it to **work yourself to death**.

RR: Well, whatever your theories are on the matter, you both seem to **have thrived** as a result. Thanks for sharing your wisdom with us.

MARCO: I don't know if I'm wise. I'd say I just enjoy my life.

ELENA: Absolutely. So do I.

2 Write each word or phrase from the box next to its definition.

breakthrough	have (one's) nose to the grindstone	stick to it
conscientious	overwhelmed *(adj.)*	thrive
decade	persistent	vigorous
delve into	prudent	work (someone) to death

1. _____: to search for more information about someone or something

2. _____: an important new discovery

3. _____: using a lot of energy and strength

4. _____: continuing to say or do something without giving up

5. _____: careful to do everything that is in your job or duty

6. _____: to continue to do something even though it is difficult

7. _____: a feeling that something is too difficult to continue

8. _____: a period of ten years

9. _____: to keep working very hard

10. _____: to work excessively hard and long

11. _____: to become very successful or very strong and healthy

12. _____: sensible and careful

Go to the **Pearson Practice English App** or **MyEnglishLab** for more vocabulary practice.

You will hear an interview about the Longevity Project, an ongoing study that began by following one group of individuals for their entire lives. That original study was expanded by researchers Howard S. Friedman and Leslie Martin and now includes more recent research findings.

▶ **Read and watch an excerpt from the interview (from 0:28 to 0:54). Then answer the questions.**

HOWARD FRIEDMAN: Well, this is really a breakthrough study because it's the first scientific study that followed people from when they were children, back in 1921, throughout their whole lives: when they went through adolescence, as they went through young adulthood, as they got married, had their own children, went into their careers, aged, to see why some people thrived, lived long, stayed healthy. Other people kind of fell off the healthy path and succumbed and died before their time.

Why is the study a breakthrough study? In the study, some people live longer than others. What factors might cause this?

_____

_____

LISTEN

1 ▶ **Watch the whole interview. Create a chart like the one below to take notes.**

TAKE NOTES The Longevity Project	
Main Ideas	**Details**
Project studied aging	– followed 1,500 subjects over 8 decades
Book has info for living long life	

2 **Compare your notes with a partner's. How can you improve your notes?**

↘ Go to **MyEnglishLab** to view example notes.

MAIN IDEAS

Check (✓) the items that are true, according to the interview. Use your notes to help you.

☐ 1. You can live a long life by being dependable and organized.

☐ 2. People who stick to plans live longer.

☐ 3. Stress should be avoided whenever possible.

☐ 4. Carefree people live longer.

☐ 5. Working later into life is linked to a shorter life.

☐ 6. Being active is sufficient physical exercise.

DETAILS

1 ▶ **Watch the interview again and add to your notes. Then use your notes to identify the statements as *T* (true) or *F* (false). Correct the false statements. Use your notes to help you. Discuss your answers with a partner.**

_____ 1. There were 1,500 subjects in the study.

_____ 2. Subjects were followed starting in 1931.

_____ 3. Subjects were followed through their teenage years until they became young adults.

_____ 4. The study produced a large body of information.

_____ 5. People quit exercising because they get overwhelmed.

_____ 6. People who retire early live longest.

_____ 7. Doing an activity consistently is more important than doing it vigorously.

_____ 8. Having close social relationships helps people live longer.

_____ 9. At least forty minutes of vigorous exercise every day improves longevity.

2 **With a partner, take turns summarizing your notes. Then discuss how your notes and your answers in Preview helped you understand the listening.**

🚀 Go to **MyEnglishLab** for more listening practice.

MAKE INFERENCES 🔍

Inferring a Speaker's Intention

Because listeners do not have direct access to a speaker's thoughts, knowing his or her intention—that is, what the person wants to achieve—is not always possible. But understanding the context can help you.

As a listener, you can understand the context by asking questions such as these:

- Who are the participants (speaker, listener, audience)?
- What is the topic and setting (time and place)?
- What type of communication is it (interview, personal conversation, etc.)?
- What is the purpose of the communication?

Recognizing the context can help you make reasonable inferences about a speaker's intention.

Read an excerpt from the Longevity Project interview. Then answer the questions.

Example

> HOST ROBIN ROBERTS: Who doesn't want to live forever? The Longevity Project is an eye-opening book based on a one-of-a-kind study, following 1,500 people over eight decades. This book changes everything we've thought about how to live a long, productive life. We are joined now by doctors Howard Friedman and Leslie Martin.

1. Ask yourself the context questions above.

2. Why does Roberts introduce the segment with the question, "Who doesn't want to live forever?"

   a. to give her upcoming guests a preview of the kind of questions she'll ask

   b. to inspire the audience to think about what it would be like to live forever

   c. to get her audience's attention by appealing to their curiosity

ANSWERS: 1. *Who?* The participants are host Robin Roberts and her large viewing audience. *What?* The topic is a recently released book about longevity, and the setting is a TV studio. *What type of communication?* It is an interview. *What is the purpose?* The purpose of the interview is to promote the findings of the study published in the book. Robin Roberts's purpose is to attract, entertain, and explain information to a large viewing audience.

2. c – From context, we understand that it is part of Roberts's job to "hook" or engage her audience, especially at the start of a segment. Roberts begins with this question (a rhetorical question, which is an attention-getting device) to appeal to her audience (most of whom presumably want to live forever) and to suggest that the key to living forever will be revealed in the segment.

▶ **Read and watch the excerpts from the Longevity Project interview. Think about context. Then circle the correct answers.**

Excerpt One (from 0:25 to 0:28)

ROBIN ROBERTS: Howard, first of all, tell us a bit about the study.

Why does Robin Roberts start the interview this way?

a. to have the guest give an overview of the study to the audience

b. to get background information for herself

c. to show the audience how much her guest knows

Excerpt Two (from 0:58 to 1:03)

ROBIN ROBERTS: And Leslie, is there a best indicator, one thing that really stood out, about why people lived long?

What is Roberts's main reason for asking this question?

a. to keep the interview short

b. to grab the audience's attention

c. to understand Leslie Martin's role in the study

Excerpt Three (from 1:26 to 1:31)

ROBIN ROBERTS: Well, let's have a little true and false here because that will help us get the message across a little bit more.

What is Roberts's primary aim here?

a. to challenge the study's findings

b. to help the audience understand the results of the study

c. to encourage the audience to buy the book online

DISCUSS 🔍

Work with a partner or in a small group. Discuss the questions.

1. What are the most surprising findings from the Longevity Project? What is the most important lesson it teaches us?

2. Are younger people usually interested in advice about living a long and healthy life? What are their most common assumptions?

3. If we want to live for a long time, what factors are under our control, and what is not under our control?

> **USE YOUR NOTES**
>
> **APPLY** Find information in your notes to use in your discussion.

▶ Go to **MyEnglishLab** to give your opinion about another question.

VOCABULARY

1 **Work with a partner. Take turns reading the sentences aloud. Notice the boldfaced words and phrases. Try to guess their meanings.**

1. I didn't get to visit my grandparents last weekend. That thought **has been tugging at me** all week.

2. After my grandmother broke her hip, her life changed **radically**. She could no longer drive, so she learned how to do most of her shopping online, as many seniors do these days.

3. Her injury now **sets the parameters** of what she can and cannot do. She simply has to do less, but she's still witty and fun to be around. She spends more time online than I do.

4. Grandpa says he's too old to learn how to use a computer. But if he were motivated, he **would catch on** easily.

5. After Grandpa retired from a job he loved, he started volunteering at a hospital. He says he's glad he stopped working and **has never looked back**.

2 **Match the words and phrases on the left with the definitions on the right.**

_____ 1. tug at (someone)   a. to determine the boundaries or limits

_____ 2. radically   b. to bother; weigh on one's mind

_____ 3. set the parameters   c. to understand

_____ 4. catch on   d. to have no regrets

_____ 5. never look back   e. extremely; in a significant way

 Go to the **Pearson Practice English App** or **MyEnglishLab** for more vocabulary practice.

Taking Notes with Diagrams

Taking notes in a diagram, such as a flowchart or mind map, can help you understand the relationship between ideas, including chronological order and cause-and-effect. Diagrams can also help you review your notes quickly.

When using a diagram to take notes,

- use shapes (squares, circles) to help you categorize certain kinds of information.
- use arrows to show the order of and relationships between ideas.
- listen for signals.

Order Signals	Cause-and-Effect Signals
First,	As a result,
At the time,	Because . . .
After	. . . , so . . .
After that,	When . . .
When . . .	
Then	
Next,	

Example

You hear: After my mother died, I decided to study to be a physician's assistant. I got my certificate, and then I took a position at a senior living facility.

You write: *mother died → became a PA → got job working w/seniors*

▶ **Listen to a woman tell a story about her parents. Complete the diagram with main ideas and details. Also, write the order and cause-and-effect signal words you hear.**

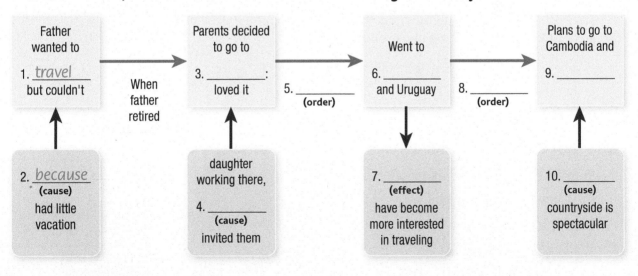

🅺 Go to **MyEnglishLab** for more note-taking practice.

You will hear a report about a woman in her sixties who helps seniors who are less knowledgeable about modern technology.

1 ▶ **Listen to the report. Create a flowchart like the one below to take notes. Try to listen for signal words and add to the chart as you take notes.**

TAKE NOTES Tobey Dichter, Generations Online

☐ → ☐ → ☐ → ☐

2 Use your notes to answer the questions. Circle the correct answers.

1. Tobey Dichter started the program in _____ .

   a. places where seniors live and get together

   b. homes where families meet

   c. hospitals and healthcare centers

2. Dichter knew older people could be witty, wise, and cool. She learned this from _____ .

   a. her grandmother

   b. her mother

   c. her neighbor

3. Before Dichter left her life-long career, she _____ .

   a. wasn't happy with her job

   b. sometimes thought about helping older people

   c. never thought of starting this kind of project

4. Dorothy Gray had _____ .

   a. a difficult time learning to use computers

   b. little trouble learning to use computers

   c. her own computer

5. One motivation for learning about computers that seniors in the report mention is _____ .

   a. to shop and bank online

   b. to be more independent

   c. to email their families

6. Dichter's project _____ .

   a. has changed her a lot

   b. requires a lot of work

   c. is successful for every individual she teaches

USE YOUR NOTES

Compare your notes with a partner's. How can you improve your notes next time?

1 ▶ **Listen to an excerpt from the report about Tobey Dichter and the seniors she helps. Notice what Dichter says about her mother's impact on her life.**

Identifying and Understanding Relationships Between Ideas

Speakers commonly express different relationships between ideas. Some of the most important relationships are

- cause / effect
- comparison / contrast
- term / definition of a term
- concept / explanation of a concept
- problem / solution

▶ **Read and listen to an excerpt from the report about Tobey Dichter and seniors. Then answer the questions.**

Example

WOMAN 2: My daughter and my granddaughter are always the ones doing everything in the computer for me. I would like to be more independent and get my own information, so that way I don't have to bother them.

1. The woman talks about herself versus her daughter and granddaughter. What is the relationship between these ideas?

2. She also talks about her dependence and desire to be less so. What is the relationship between these ideas?

3. What information helped you to answer the questions?

ANSWERS:
1. comparison / contrast
2. problem / solution
3. The woman identifies the problem as having to bother her daughter and granddaughter and the solution as learning how to use the computer.

2 ▶ **Listen to excerpts from the report about Tobey Dichter and seniors. Answer the questions.**

Excerpt One

Is Tobey Dichter providing a term and definition or explaining a problem / solution? What information helped you to answer the question?

_____

Excerpt Two

Is the woman discussing a cause / effect relationship or providing a concept and explanation? What information helped you to answer the question?

_____

🎧 Go to **MyEnglishLab** for more skill practice.

ORGANIZE

How do people live long and happy lives? Complete the chart with details from the listenings.

USE YOUR NOTES

APPLY Review your notes from Listening One and Two. Use the information in your notes to complete the chart.

	A LONG AND HAPPY LIFE	
	LISTENING ONE: The Longevity Project	LISTENING TWO: Tobey Dichter, Generations Online
	Researchers' Advice	Tobey Dichter's Advice
1. What kinds of things can people do to help them live longer and be happier?	• work hard	• stay independent
2. How do people's attitudes or approach to life affect their longevity and happiness?		
3. What kinds of activities are helpful and important?	• activities that you enjoy and will do consistently	

SYNTHESIZE

Work in groups of three to role-play a discussion between a reporter, a Longevity Project researcher, and a volunteer who helps and works with seniors, like Tobey Ditcher, about what factors affect longevity.

STUDENT A: You are a reporter. Use the chart to ask questions about longevity research. Ask for specific examples.

STUDENT B: You are a Longevity Project researcher. Give general trends from the research. Comment on surprising results.

STUDENT C: You are a person with a lot of experience working with and helping seniors. Evaluate the advice the researcher gives. Give examples from your own experience (you can use examples from Tobey Ditcher's story) to illustrate your opinion.

Example

REPORTER: What helps people live long, happy lives?

RESEARCHER: Well, hard work seems to be important. Research shows that . . .

VOLUNTEER: Yes, but doing something you enjoy is more important. For example, . . .

🔊 Go to **MyEnglishLab** to check what you learned.

VOCABULARY

REVIEW

Complete the interview transcript with words and phrases from the box. Use the correct form. Then read the interview aloud with a partner.

have my nose to the grindstone	persistent	stick to it
never look back	prudent	thrive
overwhelmed	radically	vigorous

INTERVIEWER: Welcome to *Business Talks*. Senior employment in the United States has been rising steadily since the 1980s. According to recent government statistics, nearly one-fifth of Americans between sixty-five and seventy-five have paying jobs. And the numbers are rising. By 2020, one-quarter of all workers will be fifty-five and over, a big change from fifteen years ago. These numbers were unheard of in my parents' generation.

My guests today are a business owner, a retired or rehired engineer, and a young engineer. So, guests, is it _____ to work so late in life? Sandy
1.
Han, you were a retired engineer. Why are folks like you who are of retirement age still working?

SANDY HAN: For many of us, being "able" to retire is just a myth—an idea a lot of people like to believe, but which isn't true. When I was near retirement age, my company succumbed to some bad leadership and went out of business. The pension I was counting on suddenly disappeared, and I had very little savings.

INTERVIEWER: A terrible shock for you, I guess.

SH: Absolutely. The company's decline had been a big secret. When we finally learned the truth, I was completely _____. I realized I would
2.
have to _____ much longer than I had planned, or I would run
3.

(continued on next page)

out of money. So, at sixty-seven, here I am working again—part-time. But you

know, a good surprise has been how much I enjoy it and how alive and

_____ working makes me feel. I used to think that at this age,
                4.

I would be a slow old woman.

INTERVIEWER: Miguel Garcia, you own a growing manufacturing company and have hired a

lot of older workers besides Sandy.

MIGUEL GARCIA: Yes, my engineering department ran into some design problems that the

younger workers had never experienced. They were sharp young people, but

when they faced a new challenge, a number of them just couldn't

_____ long enough to solve the problem. Several gave up and
                5.

left us for easier jobs. Our sales began seriously dropping.

INTERVIEWER: So you hired experienced engineers.

MG: Yes. I hired experienced people like Sandy who had actually built the kind of

parts that we make in my plant. They're _____ and don't give
                                                        6.

up when they face a new situation. We were finally able to get that design

problem solved and increase sales again.

INTERVIEWER: What besides experience do older employees offer?

MG: They usually have a terrific work ethic and are very reliable. They call in sick

less often than the younger ones do. They will also work part-time, which

helped a lot when we couldn't afford to hire many full-time employees.

INTERVIEWER: Let me turn to Kyle Stanwicz. Kyle, you're twenty-four with an excellent college

record, but you had trouble finding your first job. Why?

KYLE STANWICZ: Every employer wanted some experience. But how do you get experience if

you can't get hired to begin with? Fortunately, Mr. Garcia took a chance on me.

MG: (laughs) That's right, Kyle, and I _____. You are committed
                                                    7.

and hard-working. No regrets for hiring you, son.

(continued on next page)

INTERVIEWER: Kyle, what's it like working with the senior workers?

KS: It was strange at first. Sandy and the other senior workers are like my grandfather's age. We have _____ different work styles. For
8.
one thing, they don't socialize as much. But now we get along fine. They've helped us younger ones a lot.

INTERVIEWER: Miguel Garcia, what's the final word on hiring retirees?

MG: It works for my business. I hire the best people for the job, young or old. The company has really _____ now that I can hold on to good
9.
employees.

INTERVIEWER: Well, congratulations and good luck, all of you.

Read the magazine article. Then complete the conversations with the boldfaced words and phrases from each box. Use the correct form. Practice the conversations with a partner.

Smart Senior Today:

Gray Divorce: A National Trend for the Over-Fifties

Although divorce rates nationwide have been declining since the 1980s, the divorce rate for the over-fifty crowd has more than doubled. This rate far exceeds that of younger couples. For those sixty-five and older, divorce rates have more than tripled since 1990. Experts predict that those over fifty who are in a second or third marriage have a 150 percent greater chance of divorcing.

Why the Increase?

People in their fifties are more independent and educated than any previous generation, and they're better off financially. If they stayed in unhappy marriages to raise their children, they're able to consider their own dreams and interests after the children leave home. In addition, thanks to technology, it's easier for folks of all ages to connect with people they knew long ago and to make new friends. That means meeting a new spouse isn't the ordeal it might have been years ago.

Divorce is not as frightening as it used to be, so don't despair if it strikes your marriage. Take heart in knowing that many over-fifties who divorce will marry again, and will do so happily.

Conversation One: A Couple in Their Sixties

break (one's) heart: to cause emotional pain
know what (someone) is getting into: to understand the result of someone's action
ordeal: suffering; trouble

TRENT: Did you read that piece about divorce and the over-fifty crowd?

KEIKO: Yes, and I immediately thought of Sue. It _____ when she and Frank split up
1.
after all those years together.

TRENT: It's hard to start over. I hope Sue _____ .
2.

KEIKO: Sue is pretty sharp. And so is Frank, for that matter. I think they'll be fine.

TRENT: I hope this doesn't turn out to be a painful _____ for them. And I sure hope
3.
you don't have similar plans.

KEIKO: After all we've been through together? No thanks! I'm quite happy and have no desire to
start over!

Conversation Two: Teenage Siblings

light a fire under (someone): to make (someone) take action
lose it: to no longer make sense; to lose mental clarity
put up with: to tolerate
set in (one's) ways: resistant to change

YOLANDA: Did you hear that Grandma told Granddad she might want a divorce?

JAVIER: Oh, no. That can't be right! She really must be _____ .
4.

YOLANDA: No, she's still sharp as a tack. I think she doesn't want to _____ Granddad's
5.
stubbornness. He's more _____ than ever. He
6.
barely leaves the house anymore. She thinks he's getting lazy.

JAVIER: But they've been married for forty-eight years. Do you think they'll really divorce?

YOLANDA: No. I think Grandma just wanted to _____ Granddad. And it worked.
7.
They're now planning a vacation to Hawaii.

JAVIER: Those two never stop surprising me.

CREATE

APPLY **Work with a partner. Take turns reading the situations and giving advice.**

STUDENT A: Read one of the situations.

STUDENT B: Give advice beginning with the phrase in the Advice column. Add your own ideas. Try to use the vocabulary in parentheses. Answer in a few sentences.

Situation	Advice
1. My grandmother is ninety-one years old and in good health. She lives alone and still drives. But my sister and I are getting worried. My grandmother can't see as well as she used to, and she's starting to forget. We're worried she'll leave the oven on or something. What do you think I should tell her?	Well, if I were you . . . *(prudent, losing it, radically, set in her ways, set the parameters, overwhelmed)*
2. I'm twenty-seven and work very long hours, but I play hard, too. On my vacations, I love mountain climbing and skydiving. I work out hard at the gym every day and want to live a long life. What else can I do to increase my longevity?	Hm, you could . . . *(conscientious, thrive, work yourself to death, vigorous, have your nose to the grindstone, persistent)*
3. My seventy-nine-year-old grandpa is a widower who has quite a bit of money put aside. He recently started dating a woman fifteen years younger and just told us he is considering marrying her! My siblings and I think it's a terrible idea at his age. Do you have any advice?	Uh, it might be a good idea to . . . *(catch on, light a fire under, put up with, know what he's getting into, break his heart, ordeal)*
4. I have to hire someone at work. I have to choose between an experienced senior and a sharp young person. They have the same qualifications on paper. What would you do?	Hmm, well . . . *(radically, prudent, overwhelmed, persistent, conscientious, set in one's ways, vigorous, breakthrough)*

Go to the **Pearson Practice English App** or **MyEnglishLab** for more vocabulary practice.

GRAMMAR FOR SPEAKING

1 Read the information about aging. Notice the forms of the boldfaced verbs.

The elderly population **has been growing** steadily in the United States over the past century. During the twentieth century, as technology and lifestyles **were changing**, longevity **increased**, growing from an average life expectancy of forty-seven to seventy-six. In 2004, most people **were** under the age of fifty. However, generally, over the last few decades the population **has been aging** dramatically. These changes **have affected** every aspect of society.

Comparing Past Forms

Simple Past and Past Progressive	
The **simple past** is used to describe an action that was completed in the past.	At last month's Global Population conference, experts **discussed** aging and the world population.
The **past progressive** is commonly used with the simple past to describe one action that was interrupted by another action.	They **were sitting** in the conference room when a surprise speaker **arrived**.
These two forms are often interchangeable.	The experts **were investigating / investigated** factors such as lifestyle and diet.
Stative verbs (*be, feel, remember, understand,* etc.) can only be used in the simple form.	I **felt** very honored to be invited to the conference.
Present Perfect and Present Perfect Progressive	
The **present perfect** and **present perfect progressive** are commonly used to talk about things that started in the past, continue to the present, and may continue in the future.	I'm reporting on a follow-up meeting in the Netherlands. Over the last week, experts **have been discussing** several possible explanations for life expectancy increases around the world. For example, governments **have made** many improvements in agriculture and health care.
The **present perfect** is used to talk about things that happened • at an unspecified time in the past; • more than one time in the past.	Most developed countries **have made** access to medical care a priority. They **have focused** on providing better services for the elderly.
The **present perfect progressive** puts greater emphasis on a continuing action (although the present perfect is often simpler).	As a result of their efforts, the average age **has been rising / has risen** gradually over the last century.

2 Complete the conversation. Circle the correct form of the verbs. Then read the interview aloud with a partner.

SCARLET: Dr. Rubio, thank you for helping me with my research paper. My professor **(1) has assigned / was assigning** a report on the elderly population in Chicago.

DR. RUBIO: You're welcome, Scarlet. Well, as you know, I **(2) moved / have moved** to the city in the 1970s, and since then, I **(3) have been working / was working** in the city with an organization called Elderly Matters.

SCARLET: What does the organization do? I mean, I **(4) have been reading / was reading** some of your materials right before I came here, but I'd like to hear more about your work.

DR. RUBIO: Well, our philosophy is that the elderly need both physical and emotional care, so we've established a new program to introduce older people to our younger residents. **(5)** It **was / has been** a big success! Let me give you an example of our work. One of the women we serve—her name is Edna O'Sullivan—is in her nineties. When she was younger, she was a nurse, so obviously she **(6) took care of / has been taking care of** others; that was her job. But now it's hard for her to accept the fact that she herself needs help. We make sure she gets food and medical care, of course, but it's not just that. **(7)** She **was crying / has cried** the other day because she felt so lonely.

SCARLET: That's sad. How do you deal with a situation like that?

DR. RUBIO: Yes, it is sad. We have been talking it over with our team. We **(8) made / have been making** the decision to invite her to the intergenerational program, which takes place every week. She attended the first meeting last week, and she loved it! She **(9) got / has gotten** to meet a lot of young people and tell them about herself.

SCARLET: That was a great idea! What **(10) did she tell / has she told** them about?

DR. RUBIO: Mostly about life when she was a young girl. In that one hour, she **(11) has gotten to know / got to know** several kids, and the whole evening she **(12) didn't stop / hasn't stopped** smiling!

SCARLET: Well, thank you Dr. Rubio. I **(13) have started / have been starting** my report, and I hope to finish soon. I'll be sure to send you a copy when I'm done. Maybe I could even come and meet Mrs. O'Sullivan!

DR. RUBIO: I'm so glad to meet you. You know, I **(14) have done / was doing** a lot of thinking on issues like these over the years. So, if you have any other questions, please don't hesitate to contact me.

3 APPLY **Role-play with a partner. Focus on using past forms correctly.**

STUDENT A: You are Scarlet. Ask about Mrs. O'Sullivan's career as a nurse. Ask about her experience with Elderly Matters.

STUDENT B: You are Edna O'Sullivan. Share your experiences. Ask Scarlet about her studies.

Go to the **Pearson Practice English App** or **MyEnglishLab** for more grammar practice. Check what you learned in **MyEnglishLab**.

PRONUNCIATION

Using Word Blends with *You*

Native speakers often shorten *you* and blend it with other words, especially in informal speech.

Read and listen to the conversation. Notice the boldfaced words.

Example

A: Who **did you** go to the movies with?

B: My eighty-year-old grandmother. **You know,** she's a lot of fun.

BLENDS WITH YOU	
You often has a short, reduced sound in informal speech.	*See **you** later.* *I'll call **you**.* ***You** know, I've been thinking . . .* } = *yə*
When *you* follows a word ending in a /d/ or /t/ sound—for example, *did* or *what*—it is often blended with that word.	***Did you** see the show about the Longevity Project?* = ***Didjə*** *You'll come with me, **won't you?*** = ***wontchə***

You don't have to blend words together when you speak. However, using blends will make your speech smoother. Recognizing blends will also improve your listening comprehension.

1 ▶ **Read and listen to the conversation. Notice how the boldfaced phrases sound. Then practice the conversation with a partner. Blend the words in the boldfaced phrases.**

A: What **(1) did you** do last night?

B: Nothing special. My roommate and I rented a movie. How **(2) about you**?

A: We went to the parade. I called to see **(3) if you** wanted to come, but your cell phone was off.

B: Yeah, I turned it off during the movie. How was the parade? **(4) Did you** see anything interesting?

A: Yeah. There were a bunch of older women wearing some pretty colorful clothes.

B: Oh—the Red Hat Society. You've heard of them, **(5) haven't you**?

A: No. **(6) But you** know, I heard people at the parade talking about the red hats.

B: It's an organization of women who led pretty conservative lives when they were young. The parade gives them a chance to be bold and dress in bright colors.

2 ▶ **Listen to the questions and repeat them. Then listen again and complete them with the phrases from the box.**

can you	How do you	Where did you
can't you	What did you	Where do you
let you	What do you	~~Why did you~~

1. ___Why did you go___ there?

2. _____ see at the parade?

3. You can come, _____ ?

4. They won't _____ in without an ID card.

5. _____ get there?

6. _____ live?

7. You can't come, _____ ?

8. _____ go after class?

9. _____ think about that?

3 APPLY **Work with a partner. Create short conversations with the questions in Exercise Two. Practice shortening and blending *you*.**

SPEAKING SKILL

Making Suggestions

You can politely make suggestions in a variety of ways.

Begin a Suggestion	What if you . . .	You could . . .	If I were him, . . .
	How about . . .	They can . . .	It would be a good idea to . . .
	Why don't you . . .	I think she should . . .	

1 **Work with a partner. Read the conversations. Underline the suggestions.**

1. **A:** I've always wanted to fly an airplane. Too late now, I guess.

   B: What if you took piloting lessons this summer?

2. **A:** I've always wanted to be an actor, but that will never happen.

   B: How about trying out for the local theater production in town? My friend was in a show there last year.

3. **A:** When I was a kid, I wanted to visit every state in the country. Now I can't afford that much time from work.

   B: Don't give up on your dream. If I were you, I'd visit four or five new states every year.

2 APPLY **A "bucket list" is a list of goals people want to reach before they die, or "kick the bucket." Sometimes bucket list goals seem a little impossible, but they are fun to set. Follow the steps:**

1. Create your bucket list. In each category of the chart, write your goals, no matter how "impossible" they seem. Some examples are provided.

2. Read one goal to your partner. Ask your partner to suggest a first step toward reaching it.

3. Switch roles. Use the expressions above when making suggestions to your partner.

My Bucket List	
Travel / Entertainment • Go on a world cruise • Learn to dance tango	**Relationships** • Visit my grandfather's birthplace • "Re-marry" my spouse
Career / Financial • Learn digital design	**Education**
Health / Spiritual • Stop eating meat	**Other**

▶ Go to **MyEnglishLab** for more skill practice and to check what you learned.

In this activity, you will read about a senior's or senior couple's situation. With a partner, you will create and role-play a short conversation about the situation, and then discuss it with the class.

PREPARE

1 Work with a partner. Each pair chooses a senior or senior couple from the box. (See Student Activities on page 219 for each situation.)

- Read about the situation of the senior(s) you chose.

- Take notes about the situation and add your suggestions.

- Prepare a discussion role-play:

STUDENT A: Play the role of the senior.

STUDENT B: Play the role of the senior's partner or another person in the senior's life (friend, daughter, neighbor, etc.). Make suggestions about the person's situation.

> Roman and Betty, senior couple living in Florida
>
> Ho and Sora, senior couple living in New York
>
> Liling, senior living in Chicago
>
> Rafa, senior living in California

2 APPLY Consider how to apply the vocabulary, grammar, pronunciation, and speaking skills from the unit. Use the checklist to help you.

☐ **Vocabulary:** Read through the list of vocabulary on page 131. Which words can you include in your comments to make them clearer and more interesting? Choose at least three words or phrases to use and add them to your notes.

☐ **Grammar:** Scan your notes for verb forms. Are you using them correctly?

☐ **Pronunciation:** Record yourself using word blends with *you*. Then listen back. Are your ideas clear?

☐ **Speaking Skill:** Practice different ways of making suggestions that you have learned in this unit.

DISCUSS

1 Role-play the conversation with your partner.

- Make suggestions. Give reasons. Ask what the other person thinks.

- Come to an agreement on the best suggestions. Give supporting reasons.

2 Share your conversation role-play with the class.

- Describe the situation.

- Role-play your conversation.

- Invite responses and discussion.

ALTERNATIVE SPEAKING TOPIC

APPLY Over the past century, the world's senior population has grown and will continue to grow. Look at the graph and discuss the questions with a partner. Use the vocabulary, grammar, pronunciation, and speaking skills from the unit.

Percentage of People Age 65+

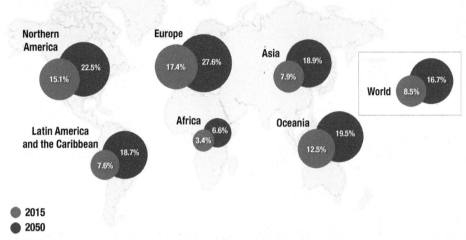

Northern America: 15.1% / 22.5%
Europe: 17.4% / 27.6%
Asia: 7.9% / 18.9%
World: 8.5% / 16.7%
Latin America and the Caribbean: 7.6% / 18.7%
Africa: 3.4% / 6.6%
Oceania: 12.5% / 19.5%

● 2015
● 2050

- Based on what you know, why are people living longer now?
- What are your suggestions for accommodating this growing population?

Examples

A: People used to work hard, which is good for longevity. But they didn't have the medical technology that we have today, so they died younger.

B: As seniors continue to work later into life, it would be a good idea to require employers to do more to accommodate seniors' needs.

CHECK WHAT YOU'VE LEARNED

Check (✔) the outcomes you've met and vocabulary you've learned. Put an X next to the skills and vocabulary you still need to practice.

Learning Outcomes
- ☐ Infer a speaker's intention
- ☐ Take notes with diagrams
- ☐ Identify and understand relationships between ideas
- ☐ Compare past forms
- ☐ Use word blends with *you*
- ☐ Make suggestions

Vocabulary
- ☐ breakthrough (*n.*)
- ☐ conscientious
- ☐ decade AWL
- ☐ overwhelmed (*adj.*)
- ☐ persistent AWL
- ☐ prudent
- ☐ radically AWL
- ☐ thrive
- ☐ vigorous

Multi-word Units
- ☐ catch on
- ☐ delve into
- ☐ have (one's) nose to the grindstone
- ☐ never look back
- ☐ set the parameters
- ☐ stick to it
- ☐ tug at (someone)
- ☐ work (someone) to death

🖱 Go to **MyEnglishLab** to watch a video about the long lives of the residents of Italy's Acciaroli, access the Unit Project, and take the Unit 5 Achievement Test.

LEARNING OUTCOMES

> Infer degree of certainty
> Annotate your notes
> Identify the purpose of direct quotations

> Use relative pronouns in adjective clauses
> Use listing intonation
> Rank ideas

Go to **MyEnglishLab** to check what you know.

Giving to Others: Why Do We Do It?

1 FOCUS ON THE TOPIC

1. The photo shows a line of volunteers unloading supplies for earthquake survivors in Ecuador. Why do people do volunteer work?

2. Philanthropic organizations (sometimes called *nonprofit* or *non-governmental organizations*) collect money to support different social, political, and other activities. Charities collect money to help individuals in need. Why do people donate money to philanthropies and charities?

3. What are some things that people do with money they don't plan to spend while they are alive? What should people with extra wealth do with their money?

LISTENING ONE | Why We Give

VOCABULARY

1 ▶ **Read and listen to an article about philanthropists. Notice the boldfaced words. Try to guess their meanings.**

Pay It Forward*

Bill and Melinda Gates

For Bill Gates, founder of Microsoft, giving to others is a personal **requirement**. Believing that every life has equal value, he and his wife created the Bill & Melinda Gates Foundation, an organization that provides financial assistance to improve health care, reduce poverty, expand educational opportunities, and provide access to information. This powerful foundation places special **emphasis** on developing countries. It is also involved in granting money to other organizations that act in **response** to human needs and are committed to improving living conditions the world over.

Bill and Melinda Gates

Warren Buffett

Warren Buffett is a gifted financial investor and money manager. As a result, he is one of the wealthiest men in the world, but he believes that children should not inherit too much money. So Buffett gave each of his children a gift of $600 million to be used for charity. He also made it clear: If the children ran into financial difficulties and asked him for a loan, he would give them a **definitive** answer: no.

Warren Buffett

Some people might think that Buffett's position is **debatable**. However, his children are thankful. His son Peter and his wife have established their own foundation called NoVo, a nonprofit organization dedicated to empowering women and girls around the world. Warren Buffett is also a notable philanthropist, having pledged to give away 99 percent of his fortune to philanthropic **causes**, primarily via the Gates Foundation.

---

* **pay it forward:** respond to someone's kindness by being kind to someone else

Karen Pittelman

A growing number of young, wealthy Americans believe in some sort of social cause. One such person is Karen Pittelman. Pittelman says that young people need strong **moral** values. She commented, "So many people work equally hard every day, and yet they're struggling to make ends meet. In the meantime, I was given a fortune just for being born." So she founded the Chahara Foundation, an organization to help low-income women. She hopes her actions will motivate other wealthy young people to use their money to benefit others. Young philanthropists consult her organization for advice on how to use their wealth to give back to society.

Phoebe Russell

Phoebe Russell was only five years old when she, too, wanted to make a **contribution** to others. When she saw a homeless man asking for food, she promised to raise $1,000 for the San Francisco Food Bank. Her teacher tried to persuade Phoebe to give more **proportionately** to her age by setting a smaller amount. However, Phoebe was determined to become a **fundraiser**. She began collecting soda cans to return for deposit[1] and asking for small donations so that she could help to provide hot meals for people who did not have enough to eat. Before long, her efforts were successful. Phoebe raised $3,736.30, the equivalent of 17,800 hot meals, for homeless people.

volunteers at a food bank

---

[1] **return for deposit:** In some U.S. states, people who buy drinks in bottles or cans pay a small deposit at the time of purchase. When the empty bottles and cans are returned later, the deposit is refunded.

---

2 **Match the words on the left with the definitions on the right.**

_____ 1. cause *(n.)*   a. not to be doubted or changed

_____ 2. contribution   b. something that is demanded, not voluntary

_____ 3. debatable   c. special importance

_____ 4. definitive   d. related to principles of right or wrong

_____ 5. emphasis   e. a reaction or reply

_____ 6. fundraiser   f. a person seeking financial support for a charity

_____ 7. moral *(adj.)*   g. money, help, or ideas given to others

_____ 8. proportionately   h. having two or more opinions that might be true or right

_____ 9. requirement   i. in balance with

_____ 10. response   j. a principle or aim that people support or fight for

↪ Go to the **Pearson Practice English App** or **MyEnglishLab** for more vocabulary practice.

PREVIEW

You will hear a radio interview by Alex Goodwin, host of the program *The Infinite Mind*. He speaks with Stacy Palmer, editor of the *Chronicle of Philanthropy*, a highly regarded publication for people interested in the world of philanthropy.

 How many people volunteer time or donate money to causes? Check (✓) your predictions. Then listen to an excerpt from the interview to check your prediction.

1. Percentage of Americans who volunteer their time:

   ☐ 25 percent   ☐ 50 percent   ☐ 75 percent

2. Percentage of Americans who donate money to others:

   ☐ 25 percent   ☐ 50 percent   ☐ 75 percent

LISTEN

1 ▶ Listen to the whole interview. Create a chart like the one below to take notes.

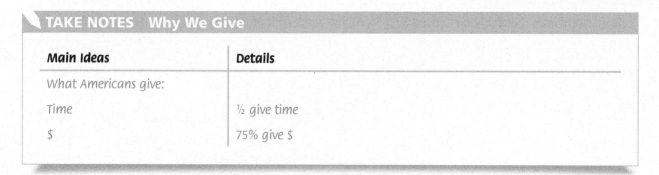

TAKE NOTES Why We Give	
Main Ideas	**Details**
What Americans give:	
Time	½ give time
$	75% give $

2 Compare your notes with a partner's. How can you improve your notes?

↖ Go to **MyEnglishLab** to view example notes.

MAIN IDEAS

Check (✓) the reasons people give their time or money according to the interview. Use your notes to help you.

☐ passion for a cause   ☐ moral or religious beliefs

☐ tax benefits   ☐ family tradition

☐ a desire to repay someone for something   ☐ legal requirements

☐ the need to feel useful   ☐ school requirements

1 ▶ **Listen again and add to your notes. Then circle the correct answers. Use your notes to help you.**

1. Most gestures of everyday generosity are probably _____ .

   a. easy to see   b. spontaneous   c. not recorded

2. When a cause has an enemy or threat, Americans tend to give _____ .

   a. more   b. the same as usual   c. less

3. Most people seem to feel _____ about giving time _____ about giving money.

   a. better . . . than   b. worse . . . than   c. the same . . . as

4. In the United States, cash donations are made to _____ .

   a. relatives   b. religious organizations   c. community projects

5. _____ tend to give anonymously.

   a. Most people   b. Wealthy individuals   c. Less wealthy people

6. When people are asked about what they give, they often _____ .

   a. answer accurately   b. exaggerate their donations   c. don't want to say

7. The group that is most important to educate about giving is _____ .

   a. wealthy people   b. young people   c. influential people

2 **With a partner, take turns summarizing your notes. Then discuss how your notes and your answers in Preview helped you understand the listening.**

🄖 Go to **MyEnglishLab** for more listening practice.

MAKE INFERENCES 🔍

Inferring Degrees of Certainty

Speakers may sound sure and convinced, or they may sound unsure and doubtful.

- One way that they can communicate these degrees of certainty is through voice. When sure, speakers use a quicker pace and greater volume. When unsure, speakers use a slower pace, less volume, and hesitation.
- Another way that speakers communicate degrees of certainty is through word and topic choice.

▶ **Read and listen to an excerpt from the interview with editor Stacy Palmer. Pay attention to her voice and word choice. Then answer the question.**

Example

HOST ALEX GOODWIN: What studies have been done on volunteering and charitable giving?

STACY PALMER: Actually, we don't know all of that much about what really motivates people to give. We know how often they give.

Does Palmer sound sure or unsure?

ANSWER: Palmer sounds unsure at first. Her pace is slow as she admits "we don't know all of that much." Then she changes the topic to something she is very sure about with "We know . . . " Here her pace is faster and voice louder.

▶ Read the questions that host Alex Goodwin asks guest Stacy Palmer. Then listen to excerpts from the interview of Palmer's responses. Circle her degree of certainty on the scale.

Excerpt One

GOODWIN: Do positive appeals work better than negative appeals?

How certain does Palmer sound?

very sure	somewhat sure	unsure
1	2	3

What clues do you hear in her voice and words? _____

_____

Excerpt Two

GOODWIN: Now, what about the difference between volunteering time and volunteering money?

How certain does Palmer sound?

very sure	somewhat sure	unsure
1	2	3

What clues do you hear in her voice and words? _____

_____

Excerpt Three

GOODWIN: What about social class? Is that as predictable as it should be?

How certain does Palmer sound?

very sure	somewhat sure	unsure
1	2	3

What clues do you hear in her voice and words? _____

_____

DISCUSS 🔍

Work with a partner or in a small group. Discuss the questions.

1. According to the listening, how is donating time different from donating money? In your opinion, which is more valuable?

2. According to the listening, what motivates people to donate time or donate money? What might motivate you to give?

3. According to the listening, do contributions from wealthy people differ from those of less wealthy people? Do you think wealthy people should donate more? Explain.

USE YOUR NOTES

APPLY Find information in your notes to use in your discussion.

▶ Go to **MyEnglishLab** to give your opinion about another question.

LISTENING TWO | The Mystery Donor

VOCABULARY

1 Work with a partner. Take turns reading the words and phrases in the box aloud. Try to guess their meanings. Check a dictionary if necessary.

fly under the radar	inspire	think outside the box
have access to	tend to focus on	

2 Complete the sentences with the words and phrases from Exercise One. Use the correct form. Then take turns with a partner reading the sentences aloud.

1. If they want to help others, most people _____ charity organizations in their own community.

2. Luli and Mary created an organization that helps others start organizations. These people are so creative; they always _____ .

3. The mission of the One Laptop per Child (OLPC) project is to see that children in developing countries _____ computers.

4. Omar always participates in a Secret Santa program at work, where the office staff give gifts anonymously to one another. Seeing a co-worker's face brighten when opening even a small gift _____ him to give.

5. Omar has always liked to give anonymously, and this program allows him to _____ as a secret gifter.

▶ Go to the **Pearson Practice English App** or **MyEnglishLab** for more vocabulary practice.

Annotating Your Notes

Taking good notes as you listen is important. But it is just the first step. Reviewing and adding to your notes soon after you've taken them is equally important. Annotating will not only help you recall what you have heard but also make the ideas clearer.

Ways to review and add to your notes:

- Highlight or circle important information.
- Draw arrows to connect related ideas.
- Cross out unimportant information.
- Add your own questions.
- Add your own examples.

Example

You hear: Each year, the woman donates a quarter of her income, which comes from various sources.

You write: *Donates 1/4 of income / yr – from various sources*

Your annotation: *Donates 1/4 of income / yr – from various sources = how much $?*

▶ **Read the notes (in light blue) and annotations (in dark blue). Then listen to an excerpt from a report about donating. Improve the notes with your own annotations.**

Main Ideas	Details
People inspired to give $ at holidays	- ½ all charitable donations: Thanksgiving → New Year's Ex: orgs collect $ outside stores, etc.
Q: Do other countries see increase around holidays?	- guerilla philanthropist = gives year-round, in unusual way

🎧 Go to **MyEnglishLab** for more note-taking practice.

COMPREHENSION

You will hear a radio report about a mystery donor, who explains how and why she gives money to others anonymously.

1 ▶ **Listen to the report. Create a chart like the one below to take notes. Try to improve your notes with annotations after you take notes.**

TAKE NOTES   The Mystery Donor

Main Ideas	Details

2 Use your notes to answer the questions. Circle the correct answers.

1. The Mystery Donor started giving to charity because she _____ .

   a. needed to find meaning in her life

   b. had access to more money than she needed

   c. was encouraged to donate money

2. She donates _____ of her income every year.

   a. 10 percent

   b. 25 percent

   c. 50 percent

3. She gives anonymously because she is _____ .

   a. worried people will think she didn't give enough

   b. embarrassed about how much money she has

   c. unwilling to change her relationship with the receivers

4. One motivation she has for giving to single mothers is that she _____ .

   a. was the child of a single mother

   b. was a poor single mother herself for a while

   c. is most interested in children's causes

5. Philanthropists like the Mystery Donor _____ large foundations.

   a. push their political beliefs on

   b. give most of their donations to

   c. are more flexible and responsive givers than

6. The Mystery Donor _____ if the donation was received.

   a. calls to see

   b. doesn't ask

   c. is always told

USE YOUR NOTES

Compare your notes with a partner's. How can you improve your notes next time?

1 ▶ **Listen again to the report about the Mystery Donor. Besides the announcer at the beginning, how many people (speakers) does the report include? What do you think is the purpose of including more than one person?**

Identifying the Purpose of Direct Quotations

As in written material, audio reports can also include direct quotations from sources.

Reasons for using direct quotations include:

- to explain the reporter's statement in detail
- to provide a specific example
- to engage the listener's emotions by including an anecdote or expressive language
- to give the report credibility, for example, by including an official or key source

▶ **Read and listen to an excerpt from the report about the Mystery Donor. Then answer the question.**

Example

REPORTER AMY RADIL:	Her career as a benefactor really began after she lost her husband.
MYSTERY DONOR:	My husband died about three years ago, and I had access to more money than I needed for expenses. So it was an opportunity to start giving money away.

In your opinion, why does the report include the quotation from the Mystery Donor? Choose two reasons from the list above.

ANSWER: 1) to explain the reporter's statement in detail and 2) to engage the listener's emotions: The donor offers personal details that both help explain the fact introduced by the report and to make it more relatable.

2 ▶ **Read and listen to excerpts from the Mystery Donor report. Why does the report include the Mystery Donor's own words? Circle the correct answers.**

Excerpt One

REPORTER AMY RADIL:	These small personal gifts often go to helping single mothers. Their experience echoes her own years ago. *(The donor's words follow.)*

What is the main reason for including the donor's direct quotation, in your opinion? Check (✓) all that apply and be prepared to explain your answer.

☐ to explain the reporter's statement in detail

☐ to provide a specific example

☐ to engage the listener's emotions

☐ to give the report credibility

REPORTER AMY RADIL: The Mystery Donor says she may create a foundation one day, but right now she enjoys the freedom that comes from giving on her own. *(The donor's words follow.)*

What is the main reason for including the donor's direct quotation, in your opinion? Check (✓) all that apply and be prepared to explain your answer.

☐ to explain the reporter's statement in detail

☐ to provide a specific example

☐ to engage the listener's emotions

☐ to give the report credibility

🔗 Go to **MyEnglishLab** for more skill practice.

> **USE YOUR NOTES**
>
> **APPLY** Review your notes from Listening One and Two. Use the information in your notes to complete the chart.

CONNECT THE LISTENINGS 🔍

ORGANIZE

What are the characteristics of charitable giving? Complete the chart with details from the listenings.

CHARITABLE GIVING		
	LISTENING ONE: *Why We Give*	LISTENING TWO: *The Mystery Donor*
	Typical Donors	*The Mystery Donor*
1. Who volunteers or donates money?	• ½ of all Americans volunteer • 75% of Americans give money	
2. Why do people give?		• because she heard a story on the radio and wanted to help
3. What background factors motivate people to give?	• a worthy need or cause • the amount of money or time they have available • the desire to be recognized for their contributions	
4. Who receives the money or time?		• an unknown single mother • a massage therapist who had broken her leg
5. How does the giver feel?		
6. Does the donor prefer to be public or anonymous?	• wealthier people like to have their names attached to their gift / the less-wealthy prefer anonymity	

SYNTHESIZE

Work with a partner. Choose "Typical Donors" or "Mystery Donor" from the chart on page 143. Study the facts. Then discuss these questions:

1. What are the similarities and differences between the typical donors (L1) and the Mystery Donor (L2)? For example, consider their background, what and how they give, and their motivation for giving.

2. What inferences can you make based on these similarities and differences?

▶ Go to **MyEnglishLab** to check what you learned.

VOCABULARY

REVIEW

1 Complete the chart with the different forms of the words. Then compare answers with a partner.

Noun	Verb	Adjective
	access (have access to)	
cause		
contribution		
		debatable
		definitive
emphasis		
	focus (tend to focus on)	
fundraiser		
		inspiring
		moral
requirement		
response		

2 Complete the transcript of a speech given by the chief executive officer (CEO) of a philanthropic organization. Use the words and phrases from the box. Use the correct form. Then take turns with a partner practicing the speech.

cause	focus	inspire	required
contribution	have access to	moralize	response

Tsunami Relief Fund — Helping others in times of crisis

HAL HADI: Good evening. I'm Hal Hadi, CEO of VINTEL, and tonight I'd like to talk to you about a worthy charity. The film clips you have just seen of tsunami disasters speak for themselves. We all know that people around the world suffer from such terrible events every year. Their futures depend on other people's quick _____ to their situation.
1.

Tonight, I'm not here to _____; I'm here to tell you that my involvement with
2.
the Tsunami Relief Fund has enriched my own life.

You and I are among the fortunate. No one in this room is struggling to survive every day. Each one of us _____ to wealth, either because we've had work that has paid us well
3.
or because we inherited it from our parents. So let's be honest: We all have enough to take care of our own families and still be generous to others. No one is _____ to help others,
4.
but there comes a time when we should give back to society. Even a small donation will help so many others.

The volunteers of Tsunami Relief Fund are working people, using their time and skills to rebuild homes, feed the hungry, and treat the sick. Look, it's easy to _____ on our
5.
own problems instead of the broader world outside us, but these volunteers are very motivated to help the victims and are _____ by the power of relief work. They donate their
6.
time far from home at great expense to themselves, but they can't continue without your help.

Let me be brief: Charity work is life changing. Please make a generous _____
7.
tonight. Contribute at our website right now. Or help with our next volunteer project. You will be listed in our donor directory. Or if you prefer, donate anonymously to this worthy

_____. Either way, I know you won't regret it.
8.
Thank you.

EXPAND

Read an email from a friend to the speaker, Hal Hadi. Complete the email with the words and phrases from the box.

have your back	make a difference	put our weight into it	year-round
in a big way	pay off	turn you down	

Subject: Nice Job!

From: Daniel Zabala

To: Hal Hadi

Hey Hal,

Marja and I were impressed by your speech last night. It affected us _____, and
1.
we're sure your efforts will _____ in the form of many donations.
2.

You were so persuasive that we can't _____: We just made a contribution on your
3.
website. We had thought about going anonymous so that we could fly under the radar, but we

decided against it because we want others to know that this work is important to us. If they see us

give, maybe they'll do the same.

Since it's holiday time, people will probably be generous, but a(n) _____ solution is
4.
needed. You're right that if we think outside the box, we'll find creative solutions. Look, Hal, I

_____ here and support you 100 percent. Let's get our two companies together on
5.
this and really _____ in the world. How about each of us asking our staff for
6.
volunteers to think of a joint charity project? If they come up with a good idea, you and I can both

_____ and make it happen.
7.

Let's talk about it when the four of us get together next week.

Daniel

CREATE

APPLY **Work with a partner or in a small group. Follow the steps.**

1. Read about the nonprofit organizations.

2. Imagine that you have $1 million to give away. Discuss each organization and decide which one(s) to contribute to and how much to give. You can give all the money to one organization or spread it across the organizations.[1] Then share with the class how you spent the money and why.

3. Try to use vocabulary from Review and Expand.

The Nature Conservancy

The mission of The Nature Conservancy (NC) is to preserve the plants, animals, and natural environment of life on Earth by protecting the lands and waters. The Nature Conservancy works with corporations, traditional communities, and other partners to develop ways for people to live and work without hurting the natural world around them. The Nature Conservancy also buys fragile land to protect it from development.

The International Committee of the Red Cross

The International Committee of the Red Cross (ICRC) is an independent, non-political organization that protects human life. The ICRC does not support or oppose governments. Instead, it tries to protect the lives of people who are victims of war and internal violence. It provides medical aid and other assistance.

Habitat for Humanity International

Habitat for Humanity International (HHI) helps reduce poverty and homelessness throughout the world. Habitat invites people of all backgrounds, races, and religions to build houses together with families who need them. Volunteers give money, materials, or their own work to build simple but good houses, working side by side with the new owners.

Amnesty International

Amnesty International (AI) is a worldwide movement of people who work toward human rights around the world. AI does not support or oppose any government or political system. It tries to work with governments to protect the basic human rights of all individuals by helping to prevent discrimination, and physical and mental abuse.

The Union of Concerned Scientists

The Union of Concerned Scientists (UCS) uses science to work toward solving our planet's most pressing problems. Scientists and citizens work together to create solutions for a "healthy, safe, and sustainable future."

---

[1] In the United States, the government does not directly support these particular efforts; in other countries, however, such organizations do receive government support.

🔎 Go to the **Pearson Practice English App** or **MyEnglishLab** for more vocabulary practice.

1 Work with a partner. Read the profile aloud and answer the questions.

Sting, **who is a popular British musician**, is actively involved with humanitarian and environmental causes. With the support of his wife and a local leader, Sting established the Rainforest Foundation, an organization **whose goal is to help save the world's rainforests**. Although at first it operated only in Brazil, **where it was founded**, the organization now operates in other countries, too. In fact, a frog **that is native to Colombia** has been named after Sting to honor the musician's contributions to the environment.

1. Which nouns do the boldfaced phrases describe?

2. Which word in each boldfaced phrase indicates which noun is being described?

Using Relative Pronouns in Adjective Clauses

Adjective clauses (also called *relative clauses*) are used to add information about nouns. Usually, the adjective clause directly follows the noun it refers to. These clauses are introduced by a relative pronoun, such as *who, that, which, whose, where,* or *when*.

An **identifying adjective clause,** or *restrictive clause,* gives essential information about the noun it refers to. No commas surround the identifying adjective clause.	*Sting is the singer **who helped establish the Rainforest Foundation**.* *The foundation **that Sting established** is involved with conservation.*
A **non-identifying adjective clause,** or *nonrestrictive clause,* gives extra information about the noun it refers to. It is set off in a written sentence by commas. Pronunciation note: In speaking, people often pause and lower their tone of voice to say the words in a non-identifying relative clause.	*The Rainforest Foundation**, which was founded in 1989,** is working to protect forests around the world.*
Who refers to people. It can be the subject or the object of an adjective clause.	Subject: *Sting is a musician **who is concerned about the environment**.* Subject: *Musicians **who are concerned about the environment** sometimes donate the proceeds of their concerts to charity.*
In spoken English, even when ***who*** is the object of an adjective clause, ***who*** is usually used instead of the more formal ***whom***.	Object: *There are many hundreds of young people **who (or whom) Sting has inspired**.*
That and ***which*** refer to places and things. They can be the subject or object of an adjective clause. ***That*** cannot be used in a non-identifying adjective clause or after a preposition. You must use ***which***. In identifying adjective clauses, speakers often omit the relative pronoun when it is the object of the verb.	*The Rainforest Foundation is a group **that / which** he founded to protect the world's natural resources.* *This foundation, **which** is working with human rights groups, raises money to protect tropical rainforests.* *This is an organization **(that)** many young people are interested in.*
Whose refers to people's possessions. It can be the subject or object of an adjective clause.	Subject: *That's the woman **whose** organization raised millions of dollars.* Object: *That's the man **whose** organization I want to work for.*
Where refers to a place; ***when*** refers to a time. They can be the object of an adjective clause.	*Brazil is one of the countries **where** the foundation's efforts have been successful.* *The foundation was started at a time **when** many people were unaware of the environmental problems we face.*

2 **The three organizations in the blog post have been helping others for a long time. Work with a partner. Complete the post with the relative pronouns *who*, *that*, *which*, *whose*, *when*, and *where*. Then take turns reading the post aloud.**

The Hole in the Wall (HIWEL) is a project _____ began several years ago in New
1.
Delhi, India. Dr. Sugata Mitra was a computer scientist _____ had the innovative idea
2.
of helping the children in the neighborhood _____ he worked. In the wall outside his
3.
office, he installed a computer _____ was connected to the internet and available for
4.
neighborhood children to play with. Within minutes, children began to touch the computer, a
machine _____ many of them had never seen before. Now there are many children,
5.
both boys and girls, _____ lives have been touched by Mitra's generosity and
6.
_____ have gained a high level of computer literacy. Since its founding, HIWEL has
7.
established more than 100 learning stations for children.

_____

Orbis International, _____ is an innovative humanitarian organization, operates out of
8.
an airplane. The plane is equipped as a flying eye hospital, a kind of hospital and training facility
_____ flies all over the world to deliver medical assistance and training to local doctors.
9.
Bangladesh, China, Ethiopia, India, and Vietnam, _____ are the priority nations for the
10.
project, employ local health professionals _____ receive special training and support
11.
from the Orbis group. The approximately 285 million people _____ have been helped in
12.
more than ninety-two nations of the world include both adults and children. The world surgeons
_____ donate their time and the volunteers _____ form the backbone of
13.   14.
the organization share a single goal: to save people's sight worldwide.

_____

CAMFED, _____ stands for the Campaign for Female Education, was launched in 1993
15.
with the goal of fighting poverty and disease in rural Africa. That was a time _____
16.
families _____ could not afford to educate all their children gave priority to boys. But
17.
the group's founders knew that women _____ are educated are more likely to become
18.
leaders in their communities by encouraging others to get jobs and raise healthy children. Now, more
than 500,000 young women _____ lives were transformed by the campaign are giving
19.
back to the organization by making their own contributions. CAMFED has won many international
awards to continue its work. The small program _____ was first developed nearly thirty
20.
years ago has now expanded to numerous countries and helped 2.4 million children.

3 Work with a partner. Take turns asking and answering the questions.

STUDENT A: Ask one of the questions.

STUDENT B: Answer, using relative pronouns. Use a variety of adjective clauses.

Example

A: Who is Karen Pittelman?

B: Let me see . . . I think she's a woman who inherited a lot of money when she was young.

Question	Answer
	Use identifying clauses.
1. Who is Karen Pittelman?	Let me see . . . I think she's a woman who _____ . . .
2. What's a philanthropist?	Well, a philanthropist is _____ . . .
3. Do people feel better when they volunteer or donate and why?	If I remember correctly, people . . .
4. What's a charity?	Well, a charity is an organization _____ . . .
5. Why is it important to teach young people about philanthropy?	I guess one reason might be that young kids, _____ experiences . . .
	Use non-identifying clauses.
6. What is Camfed?	Oh, yes. Camfed, _____ was established in 1993, fights poverty in . . .
7. Who's Phoebe Russell, and what did she do?	As far as I can remember, Phoebe Russell, _____ was five years old at the time, started . . .
8. What is Orbis International, and what countries does it help?	Oh, Orbis, _____ . . .
9. Who's Sting?	I think Sting, _____ is a successful musician and performer, also . . .

Go to the **Pearson Practice English App** or **MyEnglishLab** for more grammar practice. Check what you learned in **MyEnglishLab**.

Using Listing Intonation

When we list items or talk about a series of items, we use special intonation, depending on whether the list is finished (everything has been listed) or unfinished (there are more items in the list that aren't mentioned).

A finished list: The speaker's voice rises on every item except the last one. The speaker's voice falls on the last item. Falling intonation tells the listener the list is finished. The word *and* is usually used in closed lists.

An unfinished list: The speaker's voice rises on every item, including the last item. This tells the listener that the speaker is still thinking or that there are other possibilities. The conjunction *and* is not usually used in closed lists but can be.

▶ **Read and listen.**

Examples

• Notice the speaker's intonation.

A: The Nature Conservancy works with **corporations, communities,** and

nonprofit organizations.

B: People who volunteer with the Nature Conservancy include **students,**

local businesspeople, nature lovers . . .

1 ▶ **Read and listen to the conversation. Underline the words or ideas that are in lists. Draw intonation lines over those items. Then practice the conversation with a classmate.**

Hana and Mondi are college students who live in the same dormitory. They are discussing the upcoming Thanksgiving Day holiday.

HANA: Are you having Thanksgiving dinner at your house?

MONDI: Actually, every year we spend Thanksgiving at a homeless shelter. We decorate the shelter, help with the cooking, serve the guests, and talk to them. Would you like to come?

HANA: Yes, I really would. For a long time, I've been thinking about volunteering somewhere—at a school, the library, a retirement home. This sounds so interesting.

MONDI: Great. We can pick you up here Thursday morning. Just bring your hands, your energy, and a smile. The shelter supplies everything else.

2 **APPLY Work in a small group. Think of at least three things that ordinary people could do to help your school, community, or country. Describe them to members of your group. Speak clearly and use listing intonation.**

Ranking Ideas

When discussing ideas, it helps to rank them, from most important to least important (or the opposite). Here are some useful expressions:

Most Important	*Our top priority is . . .*
	First of all, . . .
	First and foremost, . . .
	Above all, . . .
Important	*It's also important . . .*
	In addition, . . .
	Another consideration is . . .
	Aside from that, . . .
Least Important	*The least important thing is . . .*
	Of least concern is . . .
	The lowest priority is . . .

Work with a partner. Read the conversation between two students who are working on a project together. Pay attention to the boldfaced expressions.

Example

A: OK, so let's get started and get this philanthropy research paper finished. **Our top priority** is selecting the right topic, don't you think?

B: Yeah. But **it's also important** to make sure we can get the information we need for the research. **In addition**, there's the writing and then the editing . . .

A: Well, I think **the least important thing** right now is the writing. We can only do that when we have everything else we need first.

1 Read the ads for volunteer positions with nonprofit organizations.

WANTED

Volunteer for neighborhood animal shelter

Help find owners of lost pets. Show homeless animals to potential adoptive families.

Help with feeding, walking, and taking care of homeless animals. Some contact with the public and record-keeping necessary.

Volunteers needed at least four hours per week:
daily 8 A.M. to 10 P.M.

POSITION

Volunteers needed at local environmental organization.

Help clean up city park and riverbank. Meet with other volunteers on monthly clean-up days. Organization will provide all equipment. Roll up your sleeves and get involved in keeping the community park and riverbank lovely for all.

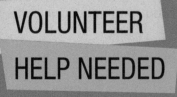

Hospital helper

Volunteer needed to be a companion to ill patients.

Read aloud to patients, take them for walks, offer a shoulder to lean on. Our motto: "A friend when you need one." Call 555-5863 or email us at **www.we-care.org**.

VOLUNTEERS NEEDED

Telephone workers

Public, commercial-free radio station needs volunteer telephone representatives for one week during our Phone-a-thon Appeal.

Answer calls, encourage donations, and take payment information We will train you. Your time will be spent on a good cause.

2 APPLY **Work with a partner. Read the chart listing important qualities for job candidates. Which qualities does each volunteer position in Exercise One require? Add your own ideas. Then rank the qualities for each position. Imagine you are choosing volunteers for each job in Exercise One. Write a conversation about the skills and attitudes required. Perform the conversation for classmates.**

Important Qualities for Job Candidates		
be able to:	• finish tasks • work long hours • get along with people	
be:	• flexible • cheerful • clean	• assertive • patient
have:	• good listening skills • good communication skills • good office skills • compassion	• emotional strength • experience (with ____) • a sense of humor • a stylish appearance

Example

A: **First and foremost**, volunteers at the animal shelter must love animals.

B: Of course. But **it's also important** for them to have good communication skills, don't you think?

A: Yes, you're right. And **aside from that**, I think the animal shelter will want a person who has good office skills for the administrative work.

➤ Go to **MyEnglishLab** for more skill practice and to check what you learned.

FINAL SPEAKING TASK: Public Service Announcement 🔍 APPLY

In this activity, you and a partner will create and present a public service announcement (PSA). A PSA is a short announcement aired on the radio, TV, or internet that educates people about an important cause or encourages them to donate money or volunteer time.

PREPARE

1 ▶ **Listen to the PSA. Then discuss the questions with a partner.**

1. What is the PSA encouraging people to do?

2. Do you think the PSA is persuasive? Why or why not?

2 With your partner, choose a nonprofit organization from the list, find one of your own on the internet, or use one of the organizations you learned about in this unit.

Amnesty International

Brooklyn Academy of Music

Doctors Without Borders

Habitat for Humanity International

National Association of Latino Arts and Cultures (NALAC)

The Nature Conservancy

The Red Cross

UNICEF

The Union of Concerned Scientists

World Wildlife Fund

Other: _____

3 Plan your PSA with your partner. Complete the chart. Then write a script for your one-minute PSA.

	Notes
Audience: Is the PSA directed to any particular group, such as college students, parents, specialists, etc.?	
Method: Is your ad for radio? TV? The internet?	
Request: What exactly do you want people to do?	

4 APPLY Consider how to apply the vocabulary, grammar, pronunciation, and speaking skills from the unit. Use the checklist to help you.

☐ **Vocabulary:** Read through the list of vocabulary on page 159. Which words can you include in your PSA to make it clearer and more interesting? Choose at least three words or phrases to use and add them to your notes.

☐ **Grammar:** Scan your PSA script for relative pronouns. Are you using them correctly?

☐ **Pronunciation:** Record yourself practicing listing intonation. Then listen back. Are your ideas clear?

☐ **Speaking Skill:** Think about ranking ideas and how that can help your audience understand your message.

PRACTICE

Practice with another pair.

- Practice delivering your PSA to another pair.
- Use the chart to give feedback to that pair.

FEEDBACK: 1 Strongly disagree 2 Disagree 3 Agree 4 Strongly agree				
The presentation was clear and persuasive.	1	2	3	4
The presenters organized the information well.	1	2	3	4
The presenters engaged the audience.	1	2	3	4
What did the presenters do well? How could they improve?	Comments:			

PRESENT

1 **Present to the class.**

2 **Create a chart like the one above to give feedback to the other presenters.**

ALTERNATIVE SPEAKING TOPIC

APPLY **Work in a small group. Read each student's point of view and the questions. Discuss your ideas. Use the vocabulary, grammar, pronunciation, and speaking skills from the unit.**

A: High schools should require community service in order for students to graduate. It's just as important for students to learn to be good citizens as it is for them to learn math, history, and science. Even students who didn't like the idea at first would probably change their minds after they spent some time volunteering.

B: Service opportunities should be available for students who are interested, but they shouldn't be required. Students should have some choice about what they want to do in high school, but I think it would be great if volunteering could be part of that choice. They could get credit for service the same way they do for art, music, or gym class.

1. Which student's viewpoint is most like your own?

2. For high school students, what are some benefits of volunteering? What are some drawbacks?

3. How many hours a week should students volunteer?

4. Should teenagers be required or encouraged to volunteer when they are not in school? (for example, after school or on weekends, or during vacations) Why or why not?

5. What kinds of organizations would be best suited for teenage volunteers?

CHECK WHAT YOU'VE LEARNED

Check (✔) the outcomes you've met and vocabulary you've learned. Put an X next to the skills and vocabulary you still need to practice.

Learning Outcomes	Vocabulary		Multi-word Units
☐ Infer degree of certainty	☐ cause (*n.*)	☐ inspire	☐ fly under the radar
☐ Annotate your notes	☐ contribution AWL	☐ moral (*adj.*)	☐ have access to
☐ Identify the purpose of direct quotations	☐ debatable AWL	☐ proportionately AWL	☐ tend to focus on
	☐ definitive AWL	☐ requirement AWL	
☐ Use relative pronouns in adjective clauses	☐ emphasis AWL	☐ response AWL	☐ think outside the box
☐ Use listing intonation	☐ fundraiser		
☐ Rank ideas			

Go to **MyEnglishLab** to watch a video about philanthropy, access the Unit Project, and take the Unit 6 Achievement Test.

LEARNING OUTCOMES

> Infer the purpose of questions
> Take notes with handouts
> Listen for multiple details

> Use causal verbs
> Pronounce stressed and unstressed vowels
> Refer to a visual aid

Go to **MyEnglishLab** to check what you know.

Water, Water, Everywhere?

1 FOCUS ON THE TOPIC

1. Water has been called our most precious resource. Why do we need water so badly?

2. The photo shows a man in southeast India fetching water. What issues do countries and communities face when there is a water shortage?

3. What should be done to protect our water supplies?

LISTENING ONE | Water Shortage: Past the Tipping Point?

VOCABULARY

1 ▶ **Read and listen to the conversation. Notice the boldfaced words and phrases. Try to guess their meanings.**

ANNIE: Ying, I got to the lecture late this morning, and I didn't pick up the handout about aquifers. Let me see your copy. Why are aquifers so important?

YING: OK, look at this. See that layer of rock where the rainfall accumulates? That's an aquifer, and that's where more than a third of our drinking water comes from. It's the water we use every day to wash, to brush our teeth, and to keep our cities clean. It's also the water that's used to **irrigate** crops.

ANNIE: I see. But Professor Dinkins was saying that the world's aquifers are being **depleted.**

YING: That's right. Some of the world's aquifers are thousands of years old, but as people continue to use more and more water from them, and the rate of **withdrawal** rises, there will be serious problems. Basically, our aquifers **are in rough shape.** They're not getting refilled as fast as they are being used, meaning they're not getting the **replenishment** they need.

ANNIE: Huh. I don't really understand that.

YING: Let's see . . . well, think about climate change. Many parts of the world are facing **droughts,** so the water levels in lakes and **reservoirs** are dropping to dangerous levels **at an alarming rate.** At least that's what recent studies are showing.

ANNIE: Oh, that sounds really bad.

YING: It is. You should see some of the **findings** from the studies Professor Dinkins was talking about. More than a billion people don't even have access to clean drinking water. Billions more run out of water at least one month every year. It's a **grim** situation.

ANNIE: Yeah? What does your note here on the handout say? Water **sustainability?** What's that about?

YING: Well, I wrote that down because the professor was talking about having enough water for the foreseeable future. See, the world population is growing, and our modern lifestyle is increasingly dependent on water. We need to find ways to conserve it.

ANNIE: Hmm. It was frightening to hear Professor Dinkins say that we may have already reached the **tipping point.** Did she mean it's too late for us to find a solution?

YING: Well, that's what we need to find out. I'd like to know what we can do to help conserve water.

2 Match the words and phrases on the left with the definitions on the right.

_____ 1. at an alarming rate   a. being maintained at a certain rate

_____ 2. be in rough shape   b. to be in bad condition

_____ 3. deplete   c. extremely quickly

_____ 4. drought   d. extremely serious and depressing

_____ 5. finding (n.)   e. a large natural or artificial lake

_____ 6. grim   f. to supply water to crops

_____ 7. irrigate   g. a long period without rain

_____ 8. replenishment   h. the moment when small changes become serious

_____ 9. reservoir   i. to use up a supply of something

_____ 10. sustainability   j. the act of taking (something) out

_____ 11. tipping point   k. the process of filling up again

_____ 12. withdrawal   l. a conclusion reached by a study

🔎 Go to the **Pearson Practice English App** or **MyEnglishLab** for more vocabulary practice.

PREVIEW

You will hear an interview about the water crisis affecting many parts of the globe.

▶ **Listen to the introduction to the interview. Then answer the questions.**

1. What problem have two new studies identified? _____

2. Which countries do these studies mention? _____

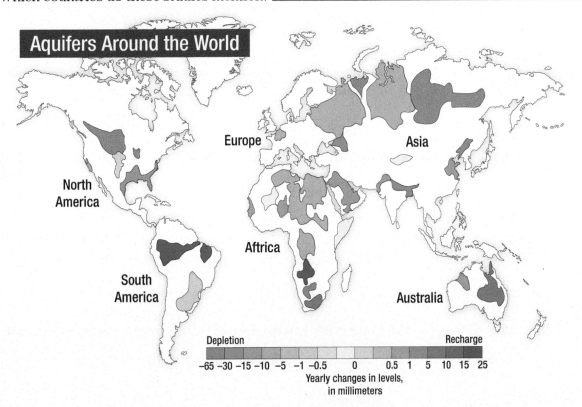

Aquifers Around the World

Europe   Asia

North America

Aftrica

South America

Australia

Depletion   Recharge

−65 −30 −15 −10 −5 −1 −0.5   0   0.5 1 5 10 15 25

Yearly changes in levels, in millimeters

LISTEN

1 ▶ **Listen to the whole interview. Create a chart like the one below to take notes.**

> **TAKE NOTES   Water Shortage: Past the Tipping Point?**
>
> | Main Ideas | Details |
> |---|---|
> | New studies: Aquifers in danger | – 21 of 37 largest losing water faster than being replaced |
> | | – Countries affected: China, Russia, Australia, India, and the U.S. |

2 **Compare your notes with a partner's. How can you improve your notes?**

↘ Go to **MyEnglishLab** to view example notes.

MAIN IDEAS

Identify the statements as *T* (true) or *F* (false). Then correct the false statements. Use your notes to help you.

_____ 1. A few of the world's aquifers are no longer sustainable.

_____ 2. Water resources are being managed well.

_____ 3. The problem affects every continent in the world.

_____ 4. During periods of drought, people rely on the groundwater in aquifers.

_____ 5. Recent studies have shown how little water is left in our aquifers.

DETAILS

1 ▶ **Listen again and add to your notes. Then complete the conversation with the correct numbers. Use your notes to help you.**

JACK: Hey there, Enid. You were just in that lecture, weren't you? Alarming, right? What was it the professor said—that 17 of the world's aquifers are in danger?

ENID: No, Jack, it's even worse than that. He said _____ are no longer
1.
sustainable.

JACK: Wait, what? Aren't there only _____ major aquifers worldwide?
2.

ENID: Yes, as far as we know, anyway. So it's a really serious problem.

JACK: Plus, you know, that water is not just for drinking. The professor also said that the aquifers provide _____ percent of the water we use for agriculture.
3.

ENID: Uh, and there's been a drought in California for _____ years.
4.

Apparently, they've been losing about _____ trillion gallons of
5.

groundwater for the past four years.

JACK: I couldn't believe what I was hearing. We need to protect the world's aquifers. He

said that _____ billion people rely on this water to live.
6.

ENID: Listen, I couldn't agree more. Let's talk about what we can do as individuals.

2 With a partner, take turns summarizing your notes. Then discuss how your notes and your answers in Preview helped you understand the listening.

🔊 Go to **MyEnglishLab** for more listening practice.

MAKE INFERENCES 🔍

Inferring the Purpose of Questions

Interviews are often guided by interviewers' questions. These questions can have different purposes, including the need for these kinds of information:

- a definition of a concept so that listeners understand it better

- a request for additional information, or an explanation

- a *yes / no* answer

▶ **Read and listen to an excerpt from the interview about the water crisis.**

Example

INTERVIEWER JUDY WOODRUFF: Welcome, Mr. Famiglietti. Remind us: What is an aquifer and how does it produce the clean water?

JAY FAMIGLIETTI: An aquifer is an underground soil or rock unit that contains, contains water in its, in its pore spaces, and the way we get at that water is by drilling wells and pumping it up from the subsurface.

Why does the interviewer ask this question?

a. to ask for a definition of a key concept

b. to request additional information or an explanation

c. to get a *yes / no* answer

ANSWER: a – The interviewer is asking for a definition. She wants Famiglietti to tell listeners what an aquifer is.

▶ **Listen to excerpts from the interview about the water crisis. Circle the correct answers.**

Excerpt One

Why does the interviewer ask this question?

a. to ask for a definition of a key concept

b. to request additional information

c. to get a *yes / no* answer

Excerpt Two

Why does the interviewer ask this question?

a. to ask for a definition of a key concept

b. to request additional information

c. to get a *yes / no* answer

Excerpt Three

Why does the interviewer ask this question?

a. to ask for a definition of a key concept

b. to request additional information

c. to get a *yes / no* answer

DISCUSS 🔍

Work with a partner. Discuss the questions.

1. According to the interview, how serious is the issue of aquifer depletion? Which areas of the world are in the most danger, and why?

2. In your view, what was most shocking about the information in this interview? Do solutions exist to tackle the problem?

3. Is access to water a problem where you live? Give details.

▶ Go to **MyEnglishLab** to give your opinion about another question.

> **USE YOUR NOTES**
>
> APPLY Find information in your notes to use in your discussion.

LISTENING TWO | Putting Water to Work

1 **Work with a partner. Take turns reading the words in the box aloud. Try to guess their meanings. Check a dictionary if necessary.**

| affordable | contaminate | key | multi-purpose | scarcity |

2 **Complete the student presentation with the words from Exercise One. Use the correct form. Then take turns with a partner reading the presentation aloud.**

STUDENT: Hello, everyone. Today I'm going to talk about simple, _____

1.

steps we can all take in our lives to save water. We need to do this in our own

homes, but the _____ question is *how*?

2.

I know what you might be thinking: Water-saving mechanisms are not in

everyone's price range. But you're wrong: There are many innovative ways to

save water.

For example, consider the _____ containers in your house,

3.

like buckets and bowls, that could be used to collect "greywater." That is the

relatively clear water created after you run the dishwasher, take a shower, or

brush your teeth. Before our reservoirs run out, we should think about using

this greywater for our needs: We could collect it and use it to flush toilets or

water gardens. After all, we're not _____ this water, so we can

4.

reuse it before draining it away. Some places already use greywater in different

ways, in fact.

Listen, unless we cut down on our water use and learn to think creatively,

the world is headed for disaster. Our current wasteful lifestyle just isn't

sustainable—that's why we must all take action. There is a growing

_____ of clean water. Let's get together and come up with ways to

5.

conserve it!

 Go to the **Pearson Practice English App** or **MyEnglishLab** for more vocabulary practice.

Taking Notes with Handouts

Reports with a lot of technical information (specialized vocabulary and discussion of processes) often rely on the use of handouts. Handouts often feature illustrations or photos. Examine this information not only to see what information it provides but also to help you anticipate what you will hear.

Example

You see: *(see handout)*

You hear: Right now an average family of four in the United States uses more than 250 gallons of clean water per day. Most of it—including the greywater—goes right back out to the sewer. Greywater, you may recall, is the relatively clean wastewater from sources like the bathtub, shower, sink, washing machine, and so on.

You write: Avg. family of 4 uses 250+ gal of clean water / day. Most → to sewer

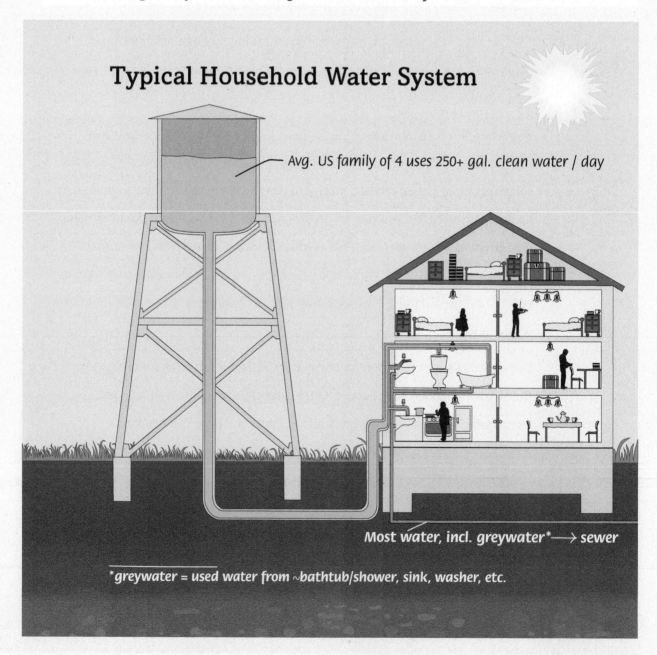

Typical Household Water System

Avg. US family of 4 uses 250+ gal. clean water / day

Most water, incl. greywater* ⟶ sewer

*greywater = used water from ~bathtub/shower, sink, washer, etc.

▶ **Work with a partner. Examine the handout on page 168. Then listen to excerpts from a report about greywater. Complete the statements with the information you hear.**

Excerpt One

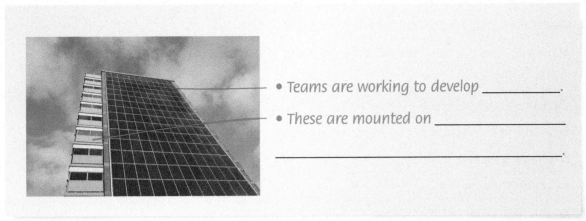

- Teams are working to develop _____.
- These are mounted on _____
  _____.

Excerpt Two

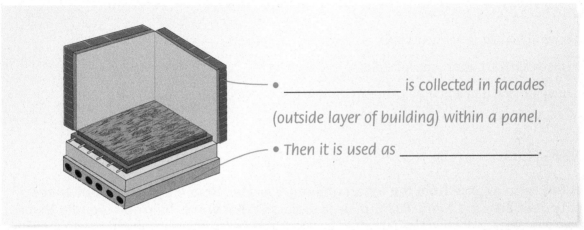

- _____ is collected in facades
  (outside layer of building) within a panel.
- Then it is used as _____.

↖ Go to **MyEnglishLab** for more note-taking practice.

COMPREHENSION

You will hear a report about a team of engineers who are working on one possible way we can reduce our water use.

1 ▶ **Listen to the report. Create a chart like the one below to take notes. Try to identify key words as you take notes.**

TAKE NOTES Putting Water to Work

Main Ideas	Details

2 Use your notes to answer the questions. Then compare your answers with a partner.

1. What does Maria Paz Gutierrez aim to do?

   a. mentor (guide) a new generation of engineers

   b. design more affordable building technologies

2. Which issue does she describe as being "very key"?

   a. water scarcity

   b. environmental pollution

3. What solution do she and her colleagues propose?

   a. reusing greywater

   b. using thermal power

4. What is a main goal of the engineers?

   a. to make water as important as oil

   b. to have people use water twice

5. Who will benefit from their ideas, according to the report?

   a. researchers, businesspeople, environmentalists

   b. consumers, municipalities, the environment

> **USE YOUR NOTES**
>
> Compare your notes with a partner's. How can you improve your notes next time?

LISTENING SKILL

1 ▶ Listen to an excerpt from the report about greywater. How many aspects of water scarcity does architect Maria Paz Gutierrez discuss? What words help you identify them?

Listening for Multiple Details

When speakers are listing ideas, they sometimes pause between each one. Often, they also link the ideas using words such as *and, also, too, not only . . . but also,* and *plus*. Listen carefully for these markers to help you identify the details.

▶ Read and listen to an excerpt from the greywater report. Then answer the questions.

Example

REPORTER MILES O'BRIEN: This team is working to develop solar panels like these, designed to mount on the side of a building and take greywater recycling to a new level. And they're designed to be multi-purpose, too.

1. How many benefits of solar panels does the reporter mention?

   a. one

   b. two

   c. three

2. What words, if any, does he use to link these benefits?

ANSWERS: 1. b They can recycle greywater and are also designed for additional purposes.

2. He uses *and* and *too*.

2 ▶ **Listen to excerpts from the report about greywater. Circle the correct answers.**

Excerpt One

1. According to the engineer, how many benefits are there of using water more than once?

   a. three

   b. four

   c. five

2. What words, if any, does he use to list these benefits?

Excerpt Two

1. According to Maria Paz Gutierrez, how many groups will benefit from the building project?

   a. two

   b. three

   c. four

2. What words, if any, does she use to list these groups?

↖ Go to **MyEnglishLab** for more skill practice.

CONNECT THE LISTENINGS 🔍

ORGANIZE

What problems does water scarcity pose? What are the solutions? Complete the chart with details from the listenings.

USE YOUR NOTES

APPLY Review your notes from Listening One and Two. Use the information in your notes to complete the chart.

	WATER SCARCITY	
	LISTENING ONE: *Water Shortage: Past the Tipping Point?*	LISTENING TWO: *Putting Water to Work*
	Global	*Local*
Problems	– depleted aquifers worldwide	– waste of water
Solutions	– better management of water	– new building technologies

SYNTHESIZE

Work in a group of four. Create a role-play of a city planning committee meeting. Follow the steps.

STUDENT A: You are an environmental consultant and environmental studies lecturer. You've been invited to be a guest speaker at the local city planning meeting. Share your knowledge about global water scarcity.

STUDENTS B, C, D: You are members of the city planning committee. You are focused on reducing water waste in your community. You want to know specifically about greywater recycling and how it could be applied locally. Ask the guest speaker questions.

Go to **MyEnglishLab** to check what you learned.

VOCABULARY

REVIEW

1 Complete the chart with different forms of the words. Then compare answers with a partner. Check a dictionary or ask your instructor.

Noun	Verb	Adjective
		affordable
	irrigate	
replenishment		
	deplete	
withdrawal		
		sustainable

2 Work with a partner. Complete the conversation with the words and phrases from the box. Use the correct form. Then take turns reading the conversation aloud.

at an alarming rate	depletion	contaminate	tipping point
deplete	~~finding~~	sustainability	

NANCY: So guys, we all read the research articles. Let's decide on our topic. I vote for the

_____findings_____ on golf courses. They use water __at an alarming rate__
       1.   **2.**

CLAUDE: Yeah, I know. Golf courses use 25–60 inches (63–152 cm) of water every year,

depending on the climate. That's more than the rain some places get in years. And

we know that there are plenty of golf courses in arid areas all over the world that

__Deplete__ water resources like crazy.
     3.

JAKE: Hold on. I didn't get to read that article, but I love to play golf. Let's not attack it.

CLAUDE: I like to golf, too, Jake. And no one is attacking golf, but it *is* just a sport, and we *are*

focusing on a probable crisis for clean drinking water. Besides, a lot of golf courses

are moving toward __sustainability__ , as the article said.
                               4.

JAKE: How? I'm very aware that aquifer __Depletion__ in most arid areas has already
                                            5.

reached a(n) __tipping point__ . And, yes, most golf courses are fertilized and
               6.

treated to keep the grass green, which __contaminates__ the water. But still, golf is
                                                    7.

such a great sport. We can't eliminate it.

grim = bad news

| affordable | irrigate | replenishment | scarcity |
| grim | multi-purpose | reservoir | |

NANCY: (laughs) I know you love golf, but the future isn't so _grim_ (8.) for golfers. There are ways golf courses can save clean water.

JAKE: Probably costs a fortune . . .

NANCY: No. Evidently, golf courses are already moving toward _multi-purpose_ (9.) water use with new methods that are actually _affordable_ (10.).

CLAUDE: Right. They don't have to use as much fresh water from _reservoir_ (11.) and aquifers. For example, a lot of golf courses include water retention ponds to catch the water that runs off from grass-watering and from rooftops of buildings when it rains. Then they pump the water back out to _replenish_ (12.) all that grass again. These attempts at water _irrigation_ (13.) at a local level help to reduce water _scarcity_ (14.) on a larger scale.

EXPAND

Work in a small group. Follow the steps.

1. Read the article.

2. Look closely at the boldfaced words. Match them to their synonyms on the next page.

3. Guess what letters A–J refer to. You can find the solutions on the next page.

Taking Responsibility for Our Water Use

Our modern lifestyle involves a lot of water, and we need to **make people think about** their water use. This is a problem that won't disappear overnight: We need to **come up with solutions** to address it. For example, did you know that the food we eat makes up more than two thirds of our total **water use**? Take this quiz to find out how much water it takes to make your favorite food.

QUIZ

Drinks
The beverages we consume each day use a lot of water. Do you drink tea or coffee? Well, **incredibly**, one of these drinks (A) uses ten times as much water as the other (B).

Meat
Do you eat more chicken or beef? One of these meats (C) requires more than three times as much water as the other (D), and most meat requires a lot of water. So you might consider **reducing your consumption of** meat.

Non-meat options
If you're a vegetarian, your food uses up much less water. So this lifestyle is better yet. Should you have tofu or a lentil burger for dinner? Well, although (E) takes only 302 gallons (1,143 liters) per pound (almost 1/2 kg), (F) takes even less. Therefore, (F) is a good **choice**.

Grains
What about rice and pasta? Trick question. Rice and pasta need about the same amount of water. So whichever option you choose is good. **You decide!**

Fruit
Which needs more water to produce, peaches or oranges? This one's **obvious**. (G) is a much better choice if you are concerned about saving water. This type of fruit requires less water to grow than the other one (H).

Oil
If you like to cook, should you use olive oil (I) or sunflower oil (J)? That's every cook's **dilemma**. Well, it takes 1,729 gallons of water per pound to produce (I), whereas it only takes 814 gallons (3,081 liters) to produce (J). So think about this before you get that skillet on the fire.

To sum up, you can consume less water by avoiding too much meat, dairy, and processed food. Other foods have a much smaller water footprint.

1. _____: believe it or not
2. _____: clear-cut
3. _____: cutting down on
4. _____: difficult decision
5. _____: In short

6. _____: It's up to you!
7. _____: find answers
8. _____: option
9. _____: raise awareness of
10. _____: water footprint

CREATE

APPLY **Work in a group. Follow the steps.**

1. Choose an image from below.

2. Describe it to the group. Talk about the problem it shows and any possible solutions. Tell how it relates to what you have studied in this unit.

3. Try to use the vocabulary from the box.

affordable	deplete	grim	replenishment	sustainability
at an alarming rate	depletion	irrigate	reservoir	tipping point
contaminate	finding	multi-purpose	scarcity	

🔵 Go to the **Pearson Practice English App** or **MyEnglishLab** for more vocabulary practice.

GRAMMAR FOR SPEAKING

1 Work with a partner. Read the conversation. Then explain what the boldfaced phrases mean.

A: Why do hotels always post a sign saying they won't change the guests' towels every day?

B: Well, they are trying to **get** people **to reuse** their towels so that they can save water! It makes sense.

A: I know, but you can't **make** people **use** the same towels over and over again, can you?

B: I don't see why not. After all, most people don't change their towels every day when they're at home. The sign just **helps** people **remember** that we are all responsible for conserving water.

Using Causal Verbs

Make, Have, Let	
To **make someone do something** = to force someone to do something	*The hotel manager **makes** the employees **read** statistics about water use in hotels.*
To **have someone do something** = to ask or pay someone to do something	*She **has** them **take** training sessions to learn how to conserve water.*
To **let someone do something** = to allow or permit to do something	*She also **lets** them **contribute** their own ideas about how to save water.*
Use **make**, **have**, and **let** + object + base form of the verb to talk about things that someone can **require, cause,** or **allow** another person to do.	

Help	
Use **help** object + base form of the verb to talk about something someone assisted another person with.	*The manager **helped** me **understand** the problem better.*
Help can also be followed by an **object** + **infinitive**. The meaning is the same.	*The manager **helped** me **to understand** the problem better.*

Get	
To **get someone to do something** = to coax or indirectly force someone to do something	*The manager **got** us **to attend** a training session.*
Get has a similar meaning to **make**, although it is not as strong.	
It is always followed by an **object + infinitive**, not the base form of the verb.	NOT: *The manager **got** us **attend** a training session.*

2 Complete the conversations. Use the verbs provided. Choose the correct causal verb: *make, get, have,* or *let.* More than one correct answer may be possible.

Conversation One: Mother and Father

A: I'm trying to get Halim to use water more carefully. He just doesn't seem to understand that he's behaving irresponsibly.

B: Irresponsibly? What do you mean?

A: Well, for example, he wastes a lot of water. When he's brushing his teeth, I can't

_____get_____ him ____to turn off____ the faucet.
                                1. (turn off)

B: I'll speak to him tonight, but can't you ~~make~~ get him to pay more attention?
                                                                      2. (pay more attention)

Conversation Two: College Roommates

A: You know how you can check for leaks in the toilet? You just put food coloring into the tank.

B: Really? I don't know how to do that.

A: Well, you don't have to do it yourself. ____let____ your landlord

~~✱~~ ____do____ it.
     3. (do)

B: I can't. He's on vacation this week.

A: So ____~~get~~ Have____ someone else ____show____ you. It's pretty easy. You just
                                                  4. (show)

remove the lid of the tank and drop it in. If color still appears after fifteen minutes,

it means there's a leak. This really _makes_ the toilet _work_
                                                              5. (work)

more efficiently. You could save 100 gallons (378.5 liters) of water per week!

B: Wow, that's a lot. OK, I'll definitely give it a try.

Conversation Three: Neighbors

A: Cape Town, South Africa, has been facing a huge water crisis. So the city came up with all kinds of ways to have residents save water.

B: What did they do?

A: They distributed brochures with a list of tips, and they also ____Have____

people ____attend____ educational meetings. They wouldn't ____let____
        6. (attend)

people ____water____ their lawns, and they ____help____ them
        7. (water)

____to recycle____ the greywater from their homes.
8. (recycle)

B: Well, were they successful?

A: Well, they did make progress, but they had to take extreme measures. They only _____Make_____ residents ____Use____ 13 gallons (49 liters) of water per

9. (use)

day. That's the minimum an individual needs to survive.

Conversation Four: Mayor and Citizen

A: Mayor, I'm here today to help raise awareness of the water crisis. Why doesn't the government _____let_____ people _____conserve_____ water? It's ridiculous to

10. (conserve)

think that we are facing a water shortage, but nobody seems to be taking a stand.

B: Look, I agree with you 100 percent. But you have to _____like_____ people _____live_____ their own lives and make their own decisions. But I have

11. (live)

some good news for you. My office is putting out a series of brochures to try to

_____giv_____ citizens _____watr_____ their lawns less frequently and to

12. (water)

take fewer showers. That's a difficult thing to do, but we can't _____let_____ this

problem _____get_____ out of control.

13. (get)

A: I think we can all agree on that. Thank you, Mayor.

---

3 [APPLY] **Work in a small group. Follow the steps.**

1. A person from the group reads a problem from the box aloud.
2. The other members of the group offer solutions using *make, have, let, help,* or *get*.
3. As a group, think of 3 more problems and solutions connected to water use.

Example

A: My roommate takes forever in the shower.

B: You should **have** her read about preserving water and **help** her monitor her water use. We all have to work together to protect our water resources.

a. My roommate takes forever in the shower. She spends at least half an hour in there!

b. My parents leave the faucet running while they are brushing their teeth. It drives me crazy.

c. My kids buy a lot of food wrapped in plastic, and I know that wastes water resources.

d. My niece has beautiful flowers behind her house. She waters them three or four times a week.

e. My husband runs the dishwasher when it's half full because he likes to keep the kitchen clean.

f. There's a leaky faucet in the bathroom, and I'm not sure how to fix it myself.

Go to the **Pearson Practice English App** or **MyEnglishLab** for more grammar practice.
Check what you learned in **MyEnglishLab**.

PRONUNCIATION

Pronouncing Stressed and Unstressed Vowels

Stressed vowels in English are longer, louder, and higher in pitch. Unstressed vowels are short. They are usually pronounced /ə/, regardless of how they are spelled.

▶ **Read and listen.**

Examples

Stressed vowels:	report	water
Unstressed vowels:	support	tomorrow

The unstressed /ə/ sound has a special name: *schwa*. It is the sound of the hesitation word that native speakers use when they need time to think: *uh . . . uh*. Schwa is the most common vowel sound in English.

ago: əgo

support: səport

Unstressed vowels spelled with the letters *i* or *e* can be pronounced /ə/ or /ɪ/.

decide: dəcide or dɪcide

because: bəcause or bɪcause

The unstressed endings *-ow* and *-y* are not pronounced /ə/.

tomorrow: təmorroʊ

ready: readɪ

1 ▶ **The phonetic spellings show how the unstressed vowels are pronounced. Follow the steps.**

1. Listen to each word and repeat. Then write the correct spelling. Check your answers with a partner.

2. Listen again. Draw a line over the stressed vowel in each word.

3. With a partner, practice saying the words. Make the stressed vowels longer, louder, and higher in pitch.

1. əffordəbl   *affōrdable*
2. əround
3. cəllect
4. cultərəl
5. manəge

6. probləm
7. prəduce
8. rəmind
9. səpport
10. səstainəbility

2 ▶ **Listen to each question and repeat. Use the boldfaced phonetic spellings to guide your pronunciation.**

1. Do you **əgree** that we are all **rəsponsəble** for water scarcity?

2. Do you **manəge** to reuse water? What **methəds** do you use?

3. In your opinion, are most people **əware** of this **probləm**?

3 APPLY Work with a partner. Write a short conversation. Use one of the questions in Exercise Two to begin. Draw a line through the unstressed vowels. Then practice saying the conversation. Practice pronouncing stressed and unstressed vowels.

SPEAKING SKILL

Referring to a Visual Aid

When you speak using a visual aid, be sure to use it effectively to illustrate what you are saying. Follow these guidelines:

- Look carefully at your visual aid and decide what you want to say.
- Speak before you show your visual aid, making sure you clearly state your main point.
- Stand to the side so you do not block any part of your visual aid.
- Look at and speak to your audience, not the visual aid.
- Introduce the visual aid and draw attention to it by using phrases like these:

Examples

Now take a look at . . .

If you look carefully at X, you will notice that . . .

Let me show you X . . .

X illustrates my point by . . .

- Link the specific item you focused on to your larger point or main idea.

APPLY Work in a small group. Choose a visual aid from below or anywhere in the unit that interests you. Follow the steps outlined above and tell your group about your visual aid.

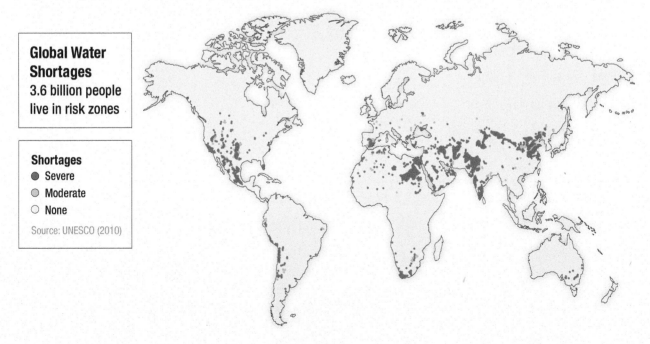

Global Water Shortages
3.6 billion people live in risk zones

Shortages
- ● Severe
- ◐ Moderate
- ○ None

Source: UNESCO (2010)

Water Shortage: Causes and Effects

Average Water Use Per Person Per Day, by Country, in Liters (Gallons)

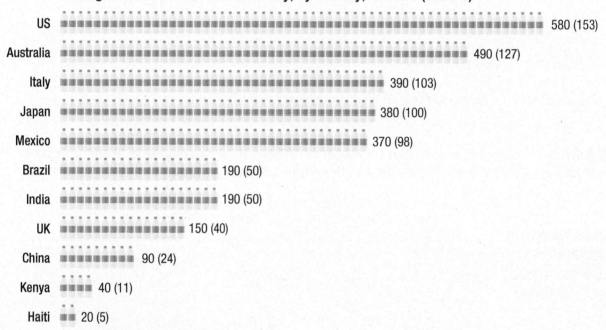

Country	Liters (Gallons)
US	580 (153)
Australia	490 (127)
Italy	390 (103)
Japan	380 (100)
Mexico	370 (98)
Brazil	190 (50)
India	190 (50)
UK	150 (40)
China	90 (24)
Kenya	40 (11)
Haiti	20 (5)

Go to **MyEnglishLab** for more skill practice and to check what you learned.

In this activity, you will work in a group to explain a problem and solution relating to water. You will create a 3-minute presentation using visual aids.

PREPARE

1 Divide into small groups. Follow the steps.

1. As a group, choose a question from the box.

2. Each member researches the question online.

3. Together, organize the information using a problem / solution diagram.

4. Draft an outline of your presentation. Include an introduction, a middle with key information, and an end that summarizes. Divide up the presentation so that each member has a turn speaking. (You may want to format the presentation like a short panel discussion or simply one presentation, divided up.)

Questions

- Why is water becoming more scarce?

- Which countries or cities are facing water scarcity and why?

- About 20 percent of the world's population faces water scarcity. Which groups are most affected by water scarcity problems?

- What solutions have been proposed to address the problem of water scarcity?

- Which solutions have been tried, and were they successful?

- How is water wasted or saved in your own home, community, school, or workplace?

- What are some ways that individuals can conserve water?

2 Find or prepare your own visual aid to help explain the problem or answer the question. Use a poster, handout, Powerpoint, large chart or graph, Prezi, etc. Use these guidelines to help you:

- Visual aids should be used sparingly—too many can be overwhelming. For this presentation, use no more than three.

- If using slides, use bullet points.

- Each slide should contain minimal information and minimal text (no more than three words per slide) in large format.

- Posters, charts, and graphs should also be easy to read.

- Use visual aids to clarify your point, not prolong your presentation.

- Do not read aloud from your visual aid. Make sure you speak to the audience, making eye contact.

- If you use photos from the internet, be sure to credit the source.

3 APPLY **Consider how to apply the vocabulary, grammar, pronunciation, and speaking skills from the unit. Use the checklist to help you.**

☐ **Vocabulary:** Read through the list of vocabulary on page 185. Can you include four or more terms in your presentation to make it clearer and more interesting? Add them to your notes.

☐ **Grammar:** Scan your notes for structures with *make*, *have*, *let*, *help*, or *get*. Are you using them correctly? Make any corrections to your notes.

☐ **Pronunciation:** Practice your delivery, focusing on stressing words correctly.

☐ **Speaking Skill:** Make sure you are clear when referring to your visual aids.

PRACTICE

Practice with your group.

• Practice giving your presentation to your group.

• Use the chart to give feedback to another presenter.

FEEDBACK: 1 *Strongly disagree* 2 *Disagree* 3 *Agree* 4 *Strongly agree*				
The presentation contained interesting research.	1	2	3	4
The presenters organized the information well.	1	2	3	4
The presenters used a visual aid effectively.	1	2	3	4
What did the presenters do well? How could they improve?	Comments:			

PRESENT

1 Present to the class.

2 Create a chart like the one above to give feedback to the other presenters.

ALTERNATIVE SPEAKING TOPIC

APPLY Divide the class into three groups. Choose one of the quotes. Tell your group how the quote you chose relates to what you have learned in this unit. Then form a new group with one person from each of the other two groups. Explain what your original group discussed. Use the vocabulary, grammar, pronunciation, and speaking skills from the unit.

> **Water is life, and clean water means health.**
>
> Audrey Hepburn, Belgian actress, 1929–1993

> **For many of us, clean water is so plentiful and readily available that we rarely, if ever, pause to consider what life would be without it.**
>
> Marcus Samuelsson, Ethiopian chef, 1971–

> **Without regard to whether some place is wealthy or poor, everybody should have the chance at clean air and clean water.**
>
> Barack Obama, former U.S. president, 1961–

> **When the well is dry, we will know the worth of water.**
>
> Benjamin Franklin, U.S. founding father, 1706–1790

> **The wars of the twenty-first century will be fought over water.**
>
> Ismail Serageldin, Egyptian economist, 1944–

CHECK WHAT YOU'VE LEARNED

Check (✔) the outcomes you've met and vocabulary you've learned. Put an X next to the skills and vocabulary you still need to practice.

Learning Outcomes
- ☐ Infer the purpose of questions
- ☐ Take notes with handouts
- ☐ Listen for multiple details
- ☐ Use causal verbs
- ☐ Pronounce stressed and unstressed vowels
- ☐ Refer to a visual aid

Vocabulary
- ☐ affordable
- ☐ contaminate
- ☐ deplete
- ☐ drought
- ☐ finding (*n.*)
- ☐ grim
- ☐ irrigate
- ☐ key (*adj.*)
- ☐ multi-purpose
- ☐ replenishment
- ☐ reservoir
- ☐ scarcity
- ☐ sustainability AWL
- ☐ withdrawal

Multi-word Units
- ☐ at an alarming rate
- ☐ be in rough shape
- ☐ tipping point

🔊 Go to **MyEnglishLab** to watch a video about water conservation in college dormitories, access the Unit Project, and take the Unit 7 Achievement Test.

LEARNING OUTCOMES

> Infer contrasting information
> Take notes with an outline
> Identify counterarguments

> Use phrasal verbs
> Use stress with adverbial particles
> Make concessions

Go to **MyEnglishLab** to check what you know.

8

Video Games: Friend or Foe?

1 FOCUS ON THE TOPIC

1. What are some benefits and drawbacks of playing video games?

2. What is a reasonable daily amount of screen time for teens? What about adults?

FOCUS ON LISTENING

LISTENING ONE | The Darker Side of Video Games

VOCABULARY

1 ▶ **Read and listen to an interview about investing money in video game companies. Notice the boldfaced words and phrases. Try to guess their meanings.**

The Ethical Investor   **Investing in Game Companies: Should you?**

TRANSCRIPT

REPORTER: *Video gaming has become wildly popular in recent years. Global sales are expected to reach $120 billion in the next two years, with at least 25 percent of those sales in China alone. I recently spoke to Todd Rudamill, an investment specialist.*

Todd, I remember when video games were was played only by nerds[1], the kids who were not popular or athletic. It seemed kids played video games to **substitute** for playing with other kids. But now computer gaming has totally **shed its** nerdy **image** and become popular worldwide with people of all ages.

TODD RUDAMILL: That's right: Both kids and adults of all ages are big gamers now. Games are **interactive**, and people play against others around the world, meeting people **randomly** through playing games. This industry offers tempting investment opportunities and huge profits.

REPORTER: But there must be a downside. What do new investors need to consider?

TR: Well, the gaming industry is controversial. In some cases, too much gaming can be addictive. It's well known that some **features** of online games are psychological **reinforcements** designed to keep players playing—for example, they reward players for the number of hours they spend playing and for the number of levels they complete.

REPORTER: Would you really call it an addiction, though?

TR: Yes. Gaming addicts display all the symptoms of other addicts: They **lose contact with** family and friends, they sleep less, they miss school, and they lose jobs. They can even **go berserk** when their gaming is somehow stopped. Some can quit—many **go cold turkey**. But others remain **obsessive** about playing. This might scare some investors away.

REPORTER: In that case, it seems risky to invest. Public opinion could turn against gaming then?

TR: Well, it's not a **compulsion** for all players, only some. There are many benefits for people who aren't compulsive. Gaming is used for educational and medical purposes with great success. It can be effective in treating and even diagnosing some mental illnesses. There are games for almost anything: getting kids to take their medicine; teaching young parents to care for babies; helping people learn to do things like read, do math, compensate for disabilities, and speak other languages. Games are used to train pilots, astronauts, surgeons, and many others. The possibilities are endless, so investment is very tempting. But it can be risky, as you say.

REPORTER: So, a note to potential investors: **Keep an eye on** this industry. Gaming is still in its youth, with lots of room to grow.

---

[1] **nerd:** someone who is awkward in social situations and has only intellectual interests

2 Match the words and phrases on the left with the definitions on the right.

_____ 1. substitute *(v.)*

_____ 2. shed its image

_____ 3. interactive

_____ 4. feature *(n.)*

_____ 5. reinforcement

_____ 6. randomly

_____ 7. lose contact with

_____ 8. go cold turkey

_____ 9. go berserk

_____ 10. obsessive

_____ 11. compulsion

_____ 12. keep an eye on

a. thinking so much about something that you neglect things

b. to use something new or different in place of something else

c. involving people working or talking together

d. a strong desire to do something that is wrong

e. to pay very close attention to

f. to change, leaving behind a popular idea

g. to become uncontrollably angry and violent

h. a reward designed to encourage certain behavior

i. to suddenly stop an activity or give up a substance that you are addicted to

j. to stop communicating with

k. an important, interesting, or typical part of something

l. without any definite plan, aim, or pattern

Go to the **Pearson Practice English App** or **MyEnglishLab** for more vocabulary practice.

PREVIEW

Video games are played on a variety of devices, by all ages, and around the world. You will hear a BBC radio report about gaming addiction among teens.

- In Part 1, you will hear an interview with two gamers, Leo and Chris, and Chris's mother, Allison Dando.

- In Part 2, you will hear comments from Professor Mark Griffiths, a world authority on gaming, and Adrian Hon, an award-winning games designer.

▶ **Think about the title of the listening (The Darker Side of Video Games) and the title of this unit (Video Games: Friend or Foe?). What issues do you think you will hear about? Circle your predictions. Then listen to the excerpt from the report to check your predictions.**

In the United Kingdom, people spend **more / less** money on video gaming than they do on movies and **more / less** money than they do on music. In fact, they spend more than **£ 1 billion / £ 3 billion / £ 5 billion** a year.

£ 1 (pound) = $1.32 (U.S. dollars)

LISTEN

▶ **Listen to the whole report, presented in two parts. Create a chart like the one below to take notes.**

TAKE NOTES   The Darker Side of Video Games

Main Ideas	Details
I. Video gaming is popular = big business	£ 3 billion / year on gaming
	more than on film or music
	essential part of youth culture

2 Compare your notes with a partner's. How can you improve your notes?

◉ Go to **MyEnglishLab** to view example notes.

MAIN IDEAS

Circle the correct answers. Use your notes to help you.

Part 1:

1. Video gaming _____ .

   a. does not cause problems for teens

   b. is a huge industry

   c. can lead to drug addiction

2. Gaming addiction _____ .

   a. mostly affects the parents of children and teens

   b. occurs especially when gamers play alone

   c. is similar to other addictions

Part 2:

3. Video game designers use techniques to _____ .

   a. encourage gambling

   b. keep people playing

   c. prevent addiction

4. People continue playing ____ .

    a. to ease pain

    b. only if they become skillful

    c. because of unanticipated rewards

5. The best way to get people to play video games more is to reward them ____ .

    a. frequently

    b. at predictable times

    c. randomly

DETAILS

1 ▶ **Listen again and add to your notes. Then circle the correct answers. Use your notes to help you.**

    1. How much time was Leo playing games each day?

        a. 2 hours

        b. 12 hours

        c. 20 hours

    2. Which was NOT an effect of Leo's gaming?

        a. His schoolwork suffered.

        b. He lost contact with friends.

        c. He didn't get enough sleep.

    3. What does Leo compare video games to?

        a. having a disease

        b. gambling

        c. surfing the internet

    4. Where did the teenagers in Chris's family play computer games?

        a. at their friends' houses

        b. in their bedrooms

        c. both at school and at home

    5. What sent Chris into a violent rage?

        a. He lost an important game.

        b. His parents told him to stop playing.

        c. He lost internet service.

6. According to Professor Mark Griffiths, a world authority on the psychological impact of computer games, how does gaming compare to other addictions?

   a. Gaming is more addictive than tobacco or alcohol.

   b. Gaming addicts are usually also gambling addicts.

   c. Gaming addicts have the same symptoms as other addicts.

7. Which category of games causes the most problems?

   a. off-line

   b. online

   c. board

8. How was the "variable rate of reinforcement" theory first developed?

   a. by studying rats and food

   b. by studying athletes and sports

   c. by studying people and gambling

2 With a partner, take turns summarizing your notes. Then discuss how your notes and your answers in Preview helped you understand the listening.

Go to **MyEnglishLab** for more listening practice.

MAKE INFERENCES 🔍

Inferring Contrasting Information

To highlight contrasting information, speakers emphasize words by saying them louder or with a higher pitch. They may also speak more slowly or pause before certain ideas. Lastly, they may use vocabulary that introduces contrast, such as *but*.

▶ **Read and listen to an excerpt from the report about video games. Notice the words that receive emphasis. Then answer the questions.**

Example

> PROF. MARK GRIFFITHS: The good news is that, for the vast majority of people, video games are something that's very positive in their life. But we have to take on board that there is a growing literature that suggests for a small but significant minority, things like gaming can be potentially problematic.

1. In each item (a, b, c), circle the word(s) that receive(s) emphasis.

   a. *The good news is that . . .*

   b. *. . . But we have to take on board . . .*

   c. *. . . gaming can be potentially problematic.*

2. Professor Griffiths delivers the first half of the statement at a normal pace because it is _____ information. He delivers the second half more slowly and in a higher pitch because it is _____ information.

   a. known / contrasting

   b. contrasting / known

ANSWERS: 1. a - *good*; b - *have to* and *take on board*; c - *gaming* and *potentially problematic*. These words are said both louder and at a higher pitch.

2. a. Professor Griffiths concedes or indicates that although gaming is fine for most people, we must also recognize that it is a problem for others.

▶ **Listen to the excerpts from the report about video games and circle the correct answers.**

Excerpt One

1. Which boldfaced words does Leo emphasize?

   LEO: It was **fun** while you're **playing**. But then when you think about the **derogatory effect** it's having on your **life**, then, then obviously, you **don't** feel so **good**.

2. What is Leo contrasting?

   _____

   _____

Excerpt Two

1. Which boldfaced words does Professor Mark Griffiths emphasize?

   PROF. GRIFFITHS: People put **money** into **alcohol and tobacco addiction**, maybe even into **gambling addiction**. But in **gaming addiction**, it's kind of so new, people **don't** see it as an important research area to look into.

2. What is Professor Griffiths contrasting?

   _____

   _____

USE YOUR NOTES

APPLY Find information in your notes to use in your discussion.

Work with a partner or in a small group. Discuss the questions.

1. According to the listening, how are Leo's and Chris's situations similar and different?

2. According to the listening, in what ways is video gaming a serious problem? How convincing is this information?

3. According to the listening, who takes responsibility for video game addiction: gamers, parents, teachers, game developers, others? In your view, who should take responsibility?

🔘 Go to **MyEnglishLab** to give your opinion about another question.

LISTENING TWO | Truths and Myths in Gaming

VOCABULARY

1 Notice the boldfaced words and phrases as you read the sentences about gaming. Circle the correct definitions.

1. I'm not **capable of** winning this video game. I just can't do it!

   a. able to (do something)

   b. motivated to (do something)

2. Video games where players work together can teach the valuable skill of **cooperation**.

   a. working with other people

   b. solving problems alone

3. When they play games, gamers **crave** rewards, such as earning points.

   a. lose interest in

   b. want very badly

4. Watching a movie is an **escapist** opportunity—it lets us enter an imaginary world.

   a. getting away from real life

   b. experiencing real life

5. Games often involve using a **strategy** to solve a complex problem.

   a. luck or chance

   b. a plan or method

2 **Complete the parent-doctor conversation with the boldfaced words and phrases from Exercise One. Then take turns with a partner reading the conversation aloud.**

PARENT: Hi, Dr. Marsden. Listen, I'm worried about my son. He spends hours and hours playing games online. He seems to _____ the stimulation.
1.

DOCTOR: Well, I wouldn't worry too much. He's a teenager, right? Does he have any other problems? Are you worried about things like discipline or _____ with you on daily chores, like cleaning the house or helping with meals?
2.

PARENT: No, not really. He's a great kid. I'm just concerned that he's wasting his time. He's _____ doing so well in school, but his grades have slipped. Is he
3.
avoiding schoolwork or something? Shouldn't he be hanging out with his friends instead? Aren't games just _____—you know, a way to avoid reality?
4.

DOCTOR: Well, kids who play these games are often interacting with other kids who are online, sometimes even in other countries. It's a great _____ for communicating
5.
with others, actually, and for improving computer skills, and that in turn can help with your son's schoolwork. Keep paying attention, though, and let me know if he displays signs of actual addiction.

↖ Go to the **Pearson Practice English App** or **MyEnglishLab** for more vocabulary practice.

Taking Notes with an Outline

Using an outline can help you organize and understand what you hear. An outline is more detailed than the Cornell Method chart (the style of chart used in most of the Listen sections throughout the book, including page 6, for example). It is an organizational tool that lets you note in detail the topic, main ideas, supporting details, and examples. Use numbers, letters, and indentation (the setting of text in from the left) to show the relationship between ideas.

Example

You hear: There are a couple of concerns that come up when we talk about video games. The first is addiction, and that's definitely a real problem.

You write: Topic: Concerns About Video Games

I. Addiction –real problem, but: A.

B.

C.

Leave space for adding details later and be sure to review your notes soon after listening, revising and annotating your notes to improve your comprehension of the material.

▶ **Listen to excerpts from a report about video game concerns. Complete the outline. Remember to use numbers and letters for each additional bit of information.**

Excerpt One

Listen and add to the outline.

Excerpt Two

Listen and complete the outline.

Topic: Addressing Concerns About Video Games

I. Addiction –real problem, but games do a good job

    A. Games provide things _____.

       1. Satisfying _____.

      _____ Chance _____.

      _____ Sense of _____.

    _____ Games offer things that _____ does not

    _____ Take from games and transfer _____.

▶ Go to **MyEnglishLab** for more note-taking practice.

COMPREHENSION

You will hear an interview with Jane McGonigal, an award-winning game designer. After a brain injury, she made a video game to help herself recover.

1 ▶ **Listen to the interview. Create a chart like the one below to take notes. Try to organize the ideas in outline form as you take notes.**

TAKE NOTES Truths and Myths in Gaming

Main Ideas	Details
I.	
	A.
	1.

2 Use your notes to answer the questions. Circle the correct answers.

1. Jane McGonigal acknowledges that video games can be addictive because _____ .

   a. many games are poorly designed

   b. they provide the things we crave most

   c. some gamers have poor self-control

2. According to McGonigal, games allow us to _____ .

   a. learn something important about ourselves

   b. apply skills from our daily lives to game playing

   c. start out unskilled at something and then improve

3. McGonigal argues that playing games _____ .

   a. increases cooperation because gamers solve problems together

   b. is not as bad as watching violent movies

   c. has no connection to violent behavior

4. McGonigal says that games are escapist _____ .

   a. yet not dangerous, even if played for long hours

   b. but help develop skills that players can use in their real lives

   c. and provide relaxation for stressed people

5. McGonigal's conclusion is that playing games _____ .

   a. can help people solve problems and world issues

   b. is a harmless way to relax and have fun

   c. can potentially cause problems, so should be monitored

USE YOUR NOTES

Compare your notes with a partner's. How can you improve your notes next time?

1 ▶ **Listen to an excerpt from the interview with Jane McGonigal. What counterargument is she making? When and how does she signal it?**

Identifying Counterarguments

When speakers want to persuade others, they sometimes point out an opposing point of view. They may even acknowledge that some aspect of that point of view is valid. This is called making a *concession*. Typically, they go on to explain why they do not agree. This is an effective strategy and is called a *counterargument*.

Speakers may introduce counterarguments with a contrast in tone and with expressions like these:

But . . . / However, . . .   *In fact, . . .*

On the other hand, . . .   *You know, . . .*

Nevertheless, . . .   *Actually, / Really, . . .*

There's no evidence of this.

▶ **Read and listen to an excerpt from the interview with Jane McGonigal. Then answer the questions.**

Example

JANE MCGONIGAL: There are a couple of concerns that come up often when we talk about video games. The first is addiction, and that's definitely a real problem. You know, what I've discovered is that games do a better job, in many ways, of providing things we crave most.

1. McGonigal says that addiction is a concern when we talk about video games. Then she begins a counterargument. What is it?

2. What phrase does she use to introduce the counterargument?

ANSWER: 1. Her counterargument is that video games provide things we want. This weakens or provides a counterargument to the opinion that games are addictive and bad for us.

2. "You know, what I've discovered is . . . "

2 ▶ **Listen to excerpts from the interview with Jane McGonigal. Answer the questions.**

1. McGonigal agrees that violence is a big concern, and then she offers a counterargument. What is it?

   _____

2. What phrases does she use to introduce the counterargument?

   _____

1. McGonigal concedes that games can be addictive. Then she offers a counterargument. What is it?

   _____

2. What phrase does she use to introduce the counterargument?

   _____

🔗 Go to **MyEnglishLab** for more skill practice.

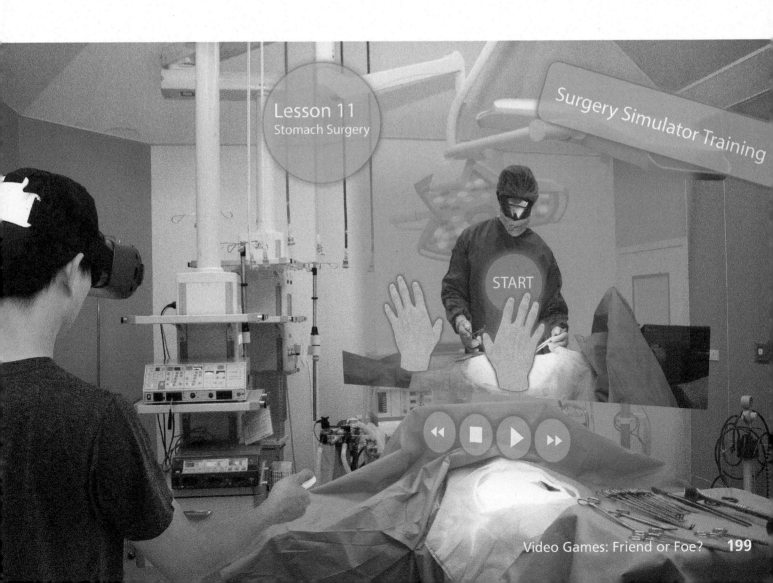

Lesson 11
Stomach Surgery

Surgery Simulator Training

START

CONNECT THE LISTENINGS 🔍

ORGANIZE

What are the benefits and drawbacks of gaming? Complete the chart with details from the listenings.

USE YOUR NOTES

APPLY Review your notes from Listening One and Two. Use the information in your notes to complete the chart.

Benefits and Drawbacks of Gaming		
	LISTENING ONE: The Darker Side of Video Games	LISTENING TWO: Truths and Myths in Gaming
	Report by BBC Reporter Rafael Rose	Interview with Game Developer Jane McGonigal
Benefits	• gaming is immersive, interactive, cinematic / positive for most people	• games provide a sense of hands-on work
Drawbacks	• gaming can be addictive	• games can be addictive / escapist

SYNTHESIZE

1 **Divide into two groups. One group will prepare a short presentation on the benefits of gaming. The other group will prepare a short presentation on the drawbacks.**

- Use the information from the chart. Include supporting details and examples from the listenings.

2 **Now pair up with a student from the opposite group.**

- Present your ideas to your partner.

- Listen carefully to the information your partner presents. Use the chart to check what your partner has included.

🔘 Go to **MyEnglishLab** to check what you learned.

VOCABULARY

REVIEW

Games are not just for entertainment anymore. Complete each conversation with words and phrases from each box. Use the correct form.

Conversation One

The moderator and Panelist 1 are at a health and wellness conference, discussing how health care professionals can improve results at their hospitals.

capable of	interactive	reinforcement	substitute (*v.*)
escapist	obsessive	strategy	

MODERATOR: Thanks for being on our panel. So what are some health benefits of gaming for medical patients?

PANELIST 1: First, it seems that video games can provide relief from pain by allowing patients to _____ a virtual world for their real world of pain. Seriously injured

1.

soldiers who played games required less medication and recovered more quickly than those who didn't play.

M: Interesting. Now, some of the research also relates to stress.

P1: That's right. Stress levels and levels of depression improved for those who played. We believe that games are _____ and, therefore, allow patients to

2.

escape from worry and give them time to relax.

M: Earlier, we spoke about the elderly playing online games.

P1: Yes, interesting findings there. Elderly patients showed improved vision when the games they played required hitting a target. Also, seniors who play video games report higher degrees of happiness than those who don't play. And they aren't _____ about playing. Most play only occasionally.

3.

M: And what about young children? I understand there are specific benefits for them.

P1: Right. Studies show that chronically ill children who play games have better attitudes. We believe the _____ they practice in the games act as a(n)

4.

_____ for their feelings of control. They're more emotionally flexible,

5.

have more confidence, and become more motivated to get better. It seems that gaming helps the brain produce positive emotions.

M: Are there other benefits for young patients?

P1: Yes, we found that young children who play video games are _____
6.
performing better on tests of motor skills than non-gamers. Of course, it's possible the manipulation required makes these games intrinsically attractive to kids with better motor skills.

M: And what about meeting other players online? Does that help patients?

P1: Yes, of course. It's normal for patients to feel a little lonely. But when they do _____ activities with other people, they feel much better.
7.

M: Seems that video gaming would be helpful for our doctors and health workers, as well as our patients.

P1: I fully agree, yes.

Conversation Two

The moderator and Panelist 2 are discussing how video games can develop useful skills.

| compulsion | crave | go cold turkey | randomly |
| cooperation | feature (*n.*) | lose contact with | |

MODERATOR: Tell us some of the reasons why gaming seems to help people. What is it about video games that makes them so compelling?

PANELIST 2: Well, the most obvious benefit is that when people are playing, they're focusing on the tasks in the game, not on their illness. The games stop them from worrying so much. Many of the games have _____ like bright colors and
8.
beautiful scenes that simply make people feel happier. Perhaps that's why people _____ playing these games so much. They're great fun!
9.

M: Yes, I can see that.

P2: And this focus keeps people's minds sharp. For example, gamers can detect new information more easily than non-gamers. For instance, say you're playing a game and a new obstacle _____ appears. You will use all your skills to try to
10.
overcome it and, when you do, that brings a sense of satisfaction.

M: We all need that feeling, and I can see how it can help people in the hospital, where it's easy to feel quite isolated.

P2: Exactly. I work with patients all the time, and it's common for them to feel a little depressed. They sometimes think they _____ the outside
11.
world. But look at the benefits of playing online. Suddenly you're working in _____ with other players. They may not be in the same room as you,
12.
but you're working together toward a goal, and that feels good.

M: This all sounds wonderful, but isn't gaming just as risky for patients as it is for everyone else? We know people can become addicted to gaming. They develop a(n) _____ to play.
13.

P2: Well, of course that's true. I guess that if that happens and they need to stop playing, they have to _____ , like other players! But that risk is small compared
14.
to the great benefits gaming has brought to patients.

EXPAND

1 Complete the chart with the correct forms of the words. Then compare answers with a partner. (The boldfaced words are from Listening One or Two.)

Noun	Verb	Adjective	Adverb
• adaptability • adaptation			
• addiction •			.
anxiety			
compulsion		• •	• compellingly •
cooperation			
	crave		
• escape •		**escapist**	
			initially
• interactivity •		**interactive**	
		moderate	
		obsessive	
			randomly
reinforcement			
strategy			
• •	**substitute**		

204   UNIT 8

2 Some high school students prepared short presentations for class. Complete each presentation. Use the correct form of the boldfaced words. Then practice reading the presentations aloud with a partner.

SEBASTIAN: I'm Sebastian, I'm seventeen, and I'm a gamer. For years, I've heard people tell me that gaming is harmful. Games will make me _____ ! They
1. (anxiety)
are powerfully addictive! I've been playing games all through high school, and I disagree. I have first-hand evidence: myself. I'm an honors student, I have an active social life and belong to two clubs, plus I'm on the track team. In fact, I think video games have helped make me a better student and a better person. I'm more flexible with problem solving because I'm used to figuring things out quickly. My social life has improved because I play games with other friends. In fact, my level of play has increased from my middle school years.

NINA: My name is Nina, and I love the _____ of video games. After
2. (interactive)
all, when you are playing online, you're never alone. In fact, you're talking to
_____ people from all over the world! My mother says that I'm
3. (randomly)
using games as a(n) _____ for quality time with my family. My
4. (substitute)
father is also worried that I'm using games as a form of _____ .
5. (escapist)
OK, I understand that their friend became totally _____ to
6. (addiction)
gaming, and she felt a(n) _____ to play all day long. But I'm not
7. (compulsion)
like that. Gaming is a great activity for teenagers.

SEAN: I'm Sean, and I also want to stress the way that games teach people to
_____ with each other. Of course, like anything else, you have
8. (cooperation)
to play in _____—you can't be on the computer all day. But
9. (moderate)
the joy of online games is that you can play at any time, so you have a lot of flexibility. I also think that games teach people useful skills, like how to strategize and how to _____ to new scenarios.
10. (adaptability)

CREATE

APPLY **Work with a partner. Take turns asking and answering the questions.**

STUDENT A: Ask one of the questions.

STUDENT B: Answer, beginning with the response in the Answer column. Try to use the
vocabulary in parentheses. Answer in a few sentences.

Question	Answer
1. Do you really think gamers learn anything useful?	Sure. Gamers learn strategy and cooperation from all those hours of play. In addition, they're capable of ____ . . . (*strategy, cooperation*)
2. I've heard that pilots and astronauts train with games. Is that true?	Absolutely. ____ . . . (*substitute, feature*)
3. How can playing video games help surgeons to become better at what they do?	Oh, they can help in several ways. ____ . . . (*capable of, keep an eye on*)
4. Engineering students are often trained using games. What skills do they learn that help them become better engineers?	Well, there are several different skills they learn. ____ . . . (*interactive, reinforcement*)
5. I've read that air traffic controllers are trained to do their jobs by using video games. Why do you think that happens?	Think about it. They have to deal with all kinds of different situations. ____ . . . (*randomly, escape*)
6. How could playing games help truck drivers deal with their long hours on the job?	Driving a truck is a hard job because you have to maintain your concentration. ____ . . . (*obsessive, crave*)

➤ Go to the **Pearson Practice English App** or **MyEnglishLab** for more vocabulary practice.

A flight simulator

GRAMMAR FOR SPEAKING

1 Work with a partner. Read the conversation and notice the boldfaced phrases. How is A's boldfaced phrase different from B's?

A: I love my new laptop, but I can't **turn it off** without getting an error message.

B: Take it right back to the store. The tech people can **look into it**.

Using Phrasal Verbs

Phrasal Verbs	
A **phrasal verb** is a verb with a particle (usually a preposition). Together they have a different meaning from either word alone. **point out:** to call attention to **fill in:** to complete to inform of	*Our son said it was early, but we **pointed out** that it was past noon.* *I **filled in** the blanks on the application.* *She **filled** me **in** on the details.*
Separable Phrasal Verbs	
Most phrasal verbs are separable and can take an object. If the object is a noun, it can go between the verb and particle or after the particle. Object pronouns can go only between the verb and particle. **shut down:** to turn off **check out:** to look at	*I always **shut down** <u>my laptop</u> when I finish.* *When the computer freezes, just **shut** <u>it</u> **down** for a few seconds.* *Did you **check out** <u>this new screen</u>?* *I saw a new game. Let's **check** <u>it</u> **out**!*
Inseparable Phrasal Verbs	
Some phrasal verbs are inseparable. The verb and particle must stay together. If there is an object, it follows the particle. **look into:** to try to understand **come up:** occur	*This problem **has come up** before; it's not new to them.* *There's a problem with my phone. The tech people **are looking into** <u>it</u>.*

2 **Work with a partner. Complete the blogs with the phrasal verbs and objects. Use the correct form. Put the objects between the verb and particle when possible. Use the chart below to see if a phrasal verb is separable or inseparable. Circle other phrasal verbs in the blogs. Then take turns reading each blog aloud.**

Separable

bring up: to mention a new idea in a conversation

figure out: to find an answer

give out: to give something to each person in a group

iron out: to solve a small problem

show off: to do things to try to impress people

Inseparable

look up to: to admire and respect someone

miss out on: to not have a chance to do something you enjoy

take part in: to participate in something

Jacob's Blog

As a college soccer player, I have to

_____ some issues
  1. (bring up / some issues)
I have with e-sports. When the National

Association of Collegiate E-Sports was

formed, I thought this ridiculous idea

would never take off. Wrong! Suddenly

colleges are creating varsity gaming

teams and _____
  2. (give out / scholarships)
to kids who were really good. I can't

_____: why something that requires no strength or real physical training
  3. (figure out / it)
has become a thing. I even had a huge fight about it with my girlfriend, who is a gamer. I agree

with her that gaming can be exciting, but is it a sport? I mean, come on! My teammates and I

had to work really hard at soccer for years so that we wouldn't _____.
                                                                    4. (miss out on / scholarships)
And here are these nerdy kids who never seem to go outside, getting full rides to college for

gaming skills! It's fun, but this stuff isn't academic or athletic. My girlfriend and I

_____, of course, but I still can't believe e-sports have been accepted
  5. (iron out / everything)
as real sports.

Yun's Blog

My boyfriend and I had an argument about gaming. We didn't break up or anything, but we had to calm down and listen to each other's views. We both like video games, but he's right: I am a little hooked on them. For me, video games are exciting and totally fun. My best friend and I love to _____ to each other, although she's better than I am. I

6. (show off / our skills)

_____ for practicing every day—and for winning her first competition

7. (look up to / my friend)

last month. She won money and a chance to _____ next year for

8. (take part in / a huge competition)

$2 million in prizes! Since she hasn't found a summer job this year, all this gaming practice might turn out really well for her.

---

3 **APPLY** Work with a partner or in a small group. Read the statements and make notes saying if you agree or disagree and why. Try to use three phrasal verbs (both separable and inseparable) from the box. Then discuss the statements.

1. E-sports are appropriate as Olympic events.

2. PC gaming is better than console gaming.

3. Video gaming promotes communication and friendships.

4. Video games can cause bad behavior in children.

5. Psychological techniques used in game design should be listed as warnings on games.

6. Learning from games is better than learning from books.

Separable	Inseparable
break down: to analyze (an argument or opinion)	**add up:** to seem true or reasonable (evidence)
cut off: to interrupt (speech)	**butt in:** to interrupt
lay out: to explain (a plan, argument)	**cut in:** to interrupt
pass up: to decline	**get back:** to return to (a topic)
put off: to postpone	**get through:** to succeed in, finish
sum up: to conclude	**keep up with:** to go as fast as
tear down: to destroy	**log on / off:** to start (computer, game, account)
turn over: to give to someone	**run through:** to rehearse
use up: to finish the supply (time)	**stick to:** to continue with (a topic)
work out: to be successful	

➤ Go to the **Pearson Practice English App** or **MyEnglishLab** for more grammar practice.
Check what you learned in **MyEnglishLab**.

Using Stress with Adverbial Particles

Adverbial particles such as *up, down, off, on, back,* and *out* are part of phrasal verbs and usually stressed:

> I'm fed **UP**.

- Stress them when they follow the verb:

> Log **OFF**.

- Stress them when they follow the object:

> Turn <u>it</u> **DOWN**.

- Do not stress them when they are used as prepositions or are part of an infinitive:

> Turn left ~~on~~ the next street.

> I want ~~to~~ move!

- Link them to the consonant sound of the preceding word when they begin with vowel sounds, like *up, on, in, out,* and *off*:

> Come **ON**.

> Hurry **UP**.

> Get **OUT**.

▶ **Read and listen.**

- Notice how the boldfaced word is stressed when it is part of a phrasal verb: *hand in, try on, pick up.*

   Examples

> Hand the paper **in** to the teacher.
> The chair is **in** the corner.
>
> Let's go shopping **on** Sunday.
> Do you like this jacket? Then try it **on**.
>
> She lives **up** the block.
> I'll pick you **up** at four o'clock.

1 ▶ **Read and listen to the sentences. Circle the particles that are stressed.**

1. I tried to follow the instructions, but then I gave up.

2. I asked him to turn it down, but he said he didn't want to.

3. Come in and sit down. Looks like work really wore you out.

4. I want to buy a game console. This one keeps breaking down.

5. I'm taking this new tablet back. I can't get it to work right, and I'm really fed up.

2 Work with a partner. Match the comments on the left with the responses on the right.

_____ 1. When did your friend show up?

_____ 2. Do you want to go out tonight?

_____ 3. I got the new download of that game, but the app keeps shutting down.

_____ 4. I'm fed up with this new monitor.

_____ 5. Ugh! I have six new messages and no time to reply.

a. I can't. I have to get up early.

b. The same thing happened to me. The new version is always freezing up.

c. Why don't you take it back to the store?

d. But they're probably new customers. You have to text them back.

e. Forty minutes after I called him up.

3 **APPLY** **With your partner, use the comments and responses from the conversations in Exercise Two to create short conversations. Stress the particles when appropriate.**

SPEAKING SKILL

Making Concessions

When presenting an opposing argument, you don't want to sound too strong. To make it softer, first agree with the other person's point before giving your counterargument. This strategy is called *conceding a point* or *making a concession*. It's effective not only because it softens your counterargument but also because it shows that you have both an open mind and your own point of view. People will listen more closely to hear your point of view.

Introduce a Concession	Present the Counterargument	
It's true that . . . *I agree that . . .* *You're correct in saying that . . .*	*But / However, . . .* *On the other hand, . . .* *Nevertheless, . . .*	***It's true that*** *teenagers spend a lot of time texting.* ***However,*** *texting can be valuable communication.* ***I agree that*** *many video games are violent.* ***Nevertheless,*** *research hasn't shown a link between playing violent games and actual violent behavior.*
Although / Even though . . . *While . . .* *Despite / In spite of . . .*		***Even though*** *some video games are expensive, they can be played many times.* ***While*** *that is an interesting anecdote, actual research is in our favor.*

NOTE: No counterargument expression is needed with concessions that use *although, even though, while, despite,* or *in spite of.*

APPLY Work with a partner. Read and practice the example. Then choose one of the situations (1–3). Have a conversation using the concession and counterargument.

Situation

- **STUDENT A:** a training video game vendor (salesperson)
- **STUDENT B:** an airline manager

The vendor is selling a video game that trains pilots to navigate in poor weather. The manager is concerned about the expense.

VENDOR:	This is our most effective game. Your trainees will learn quickly with it.
MANAGER:	**Concession:** The game seems effective. **Counterargument:** The company can't spend extra money on games. Although your game is effective for training, we can't spend the extra money.
VENDOR:	**Concession:** The game is expensive. **Counterargument:** You can save the money you now pay to trainers. It's true that this game is expensive. However, it costs less than paying trainers.

Situation One

- **STUDENT A:** a statistics professor
- **STUDENT B:** the statistics department dean

The professor wants to use gaming in the classroom to get students engaged in learning. The dean is concerned that computers will replace good professors.

PROFESSOR:	We should introduce some games in class. They can be very effective, and our students are having difficulty with math.
DEAN:	**Concession:** The students are having difficulty with math. **Counterargument:** Games can't replace a good professor's knowledge.
PROFESSOR:	**Concession:** Games can't replace a good professor's knowledge. **Counterargument:** Professors can use games as an additional tool.

Situation Two

- **STUDENT A:** a video game salesperson
- **STUDENT B:** an instructor from a driving school

The salesperson wants the driver's education school to purchase a video game that helps teens learn to drive. An instructor is concerned: Will teenagers take responsibility for driving safely?

SALESPERSON:	It's very motivating. Kids love playing games!
INSTRUCTOR:	**Concession:** All kids love video games. **Counterargument:** Teens might not drive responsibly if they learn on a game.
SALESPERSON:	**Concession:** Games cannot force teens to drive responsibly. **Counterargument:** It's safer to learn to drive on a game than on the road.

Situation Three

- **STUDENT A:** Heart surgeon A

- **STUDENT B:** Heart surgeon B

There's a new computer game for training in new surgical techniques. Surgeon A likes the idea, believing it's safer for patients. Surgeon B feels the only way to get better at surgery is to work on real patients.

SURGEON A: **Argument:** Practicing on a game is safer than practicing on real patients.

SURGEON B: **Concession:** Yes, it's safer.
Counterargument: The only way to learn is to practice on real patients.

SURGEON A: **Concession:** Practicing on real patients is more effective.
Counterargument: It's also more dangerous. New doctors can use the game first and then practice on real patients later.

Go to **MyEnglishLab** for more skill practice and to check what you learned.

FINAL SPEAKING TASK: Debate

In this activity, you will participate in a small-group debate about whether playing violent video games can cause violent behavior.

PREPARE

1 Work with a partner.

- Eventually, the class will divide into two teams: Team Yes and Team No.

- Team Yes will argue that violent games are harmful. Team No will argue that they are not.

2 With your partner, choose a side and make speaking notes supporting your argument.

- Use information from this unit and the chart. Make a list of your own ideas.

CAN PLAYING VIOLENT VIDEO GAMES CAUSE VIOLENT BEHAVIOR?	
Team Yes	**Team No**
Violent video games . . .	**Violent video games . . .**
• teach young people that violence is a good way to solve problems and reach goals. • contribute to bullying. In one study, 60 percent of middle school boys who played mature-rated games hit or had fights with other boys, compared to 39 percent of boys that did not play such games. • reward players for simulated violence, which increases aggressive behavior and thinking. • make children of all ages less sensitive to the problem of violence in society.	• have not led to an increase in crime and have not been shown to cause violent behavior. • don't cause violence, although they may have more appeal for young people who are already violent. • are a safe way for people to get rid of the angry or violent feelings that they experience. • have lots of benefits for the brain and teach valuable skills and strategies that can be applied to real life.

3 Practice.

- Debate with your partner. Use your notes, as needed.

  Follow this process:

  - Team Yes presents its arguments.

  - Team No presents its arguments.

  - Team Yes responds to Team No's arguments and makes a conclusion.

  - Team No responds to Team Yes's argument and makes a conclusion.

- Join another pair and debate. Choose three vocabulary words you want to use.

4 [APPLY] Consider how to apply the vocabulary, grammar, pronunciation, and speaking skills from the unit. Use the checklist to help you.

- ☐ **Vocabulary:** Read through the list of vocabulary on page 215. Which words can you include in your debate to make it clearer and more interesting? Choose at least three words or phrases to use, and add them to your notes.

- ☐ **Grammar:** Scan your notes for phrasal verbs. Are you using them correctly?

- ☐ **Pronunciation:** Record yourself using adverbial particles. Then listen back. Are your ideas clear?

- ☐ **Speaking Skill:** Think about making concessions and counterarguments. How can you use each to engage your audience?

DISCUSS

1 As a class, divide into two teams (Yes and No) and debate. Use counterarguments to strengthen your points.

2 Discuss the questions as a class.

- Did you change your initial opinion? Which arguments for each side were the most convincing? Why?

- Considering all the information: Do violent video games cause violent behavior? If so, what are some ideas for solving this problem?

ALTERNATIVE SPEAKING TOPIC

APPLY Work in a group of three. Read the advertisement for a computer game that features historical events. Then role-play a discussion between a professor who wants to use the game in class, a student who doesn't, and an administrator who isn't sure. Use the ideas in the chart and your own. Use the vocabulary, grammar, pronunciation, and speaking skills from the unit.

Get Students Addicted to Learning—Play *Civilizations Through the Ages*!

In this highly interactive game, different players choose and build a civilization. They make choices about whether to develop agriculture or manufacturing or commerce, how many cities to build and where, and whether to invade neighboring countries. The computer program gives them information about the historical times, and they react to that information.

Can be played individually or cooperatively.

Professor	Student	Administrator
Game . . . • is highly motivating. • gives students experience making decisions. • allows students' decisions to be compared to actual historical events. • helps students understand why historical events happened the way they did.	• Games can be played at home; students come to class for something different. • Games aren't real life. • Professors should be teaching information directly.	• Games are fun; but do students really learn anything? • What does research show about using games in class? • How can games be used effectively? • The best method to use in class is one that gets results.

CHECK WHAT YOU'VE LEARNED

Check (✔) the outcomes you've met and vocabulary you've learned. Put an X next to the skills and vocabulary you still need to practice.

Learning Outcomes
- ☐ **Infer contrasting information**
- ☐ **Take notes with an outline**
- ☐ **Identify counterarguments**
- ☐ **Use phrasal verbs**
- ☐ **Use stress with adverbial particles**
- ☐ **Make concessions**

Vocabulary
- ☐ **compulsion**
- ☐ **cooperation** AWL
- ☐ **crave**
- ☐ **escapist**
- ☐ **feature** (*n.*) AWL
- ☐ **interactive** AWL
- ☐ **obsessive**
- ☐ **randomly** AWL
- ☐ **reinforcement** AWL
- ☐ **strategy** AWL
- ☐ **substitute** (*v.*) AWL

Multi-word Units
- ☐ **capable of**
- ☐ **go berserk**
- ☐ **go cold turkey**
- ☐ **keep an eye on**
- ☐ **lose contact with**
- ☐ **shed its image**

▶ Go to **MyEnglishLab** to watch a video about a video game, access the Unit Project, and take the Unit 8 Achievement Test.

STUDENT ACTIVITIES

Case study 1: The Young Tennis Dynamo

Born in Slovakia, Martina Hingis (1980–) began playing tennis at the age of two. Her parents, both professional tennis players, entered her in her first tournament when she was four. She went on to become the youngest person to win a Grand Slam tournament when she won Wimbledon in 1996 at the age of fifteen. She announced her retirement from tennis in 2003 at the age of twenty-two, due to injuries. But she returned two years later and continues to play professionally today.

Case study 2: The Math Whiz

At the age of six, Indian math whiz Priyanshi Somani (1998–) began tackling difficult math problems. Six years later, she won the Mental Calculation World Cup by taking just 2 minutes and 43 seconds to figure out the square root of ten six-digit numbers. For Somani, it's a family affair, receiving support from her parents and brother.

Case study 3: The Promising Violinist

German child prodigy Akim Camara (2000–) began taking violin lessons before he had learned to talk. With an impressive memory, he was able to learn music by ear, giving his first performance at the age of three. A famous Dutch violist who heard about Camara began paying for and overseeing the boy's lessons. Camara also plays piano and sings.

Case study 4: The Chess Master

The son of a chemical engineer and an IT consultant, Norwegian chess prodigy Magnus Carlsen (1990–) learned to play chess at the age of five and entered his first tournament at the age of eight. As a teen Carlsen received the guidance of a chess grandmaster and today is a grandmaster himself.

Jim Abbott – American baseball player (1967–)
- Born without a right hand
- Became a talented pitcher
- Developed a special technique of slipping his glove on and off
- Helped the United States win a gold medal at the 1988 Olympics
- Encourages businesses to hire people with disabilities

Javid Abidi – Indian journalist and activist (1965–2018)
- Born with a birth defect that led to spinal damage
- Earned a degree in journalism in the United States
- Prompted Parliament to pass the Persons with Disabilities Act
- Is credited with improving wheelchair accessibility to buildings throughout India
- Was the director of a national organization that promotes employment opportunities for the disabled

Frida Kahlo – Mexican surrealist artist (1907–1954)
- Was badly injured in a traffic accident at the age of 18
- Gave up her dream of medical school
- Pursued her passion to paint
- Known as a highly innovative portrait artist
- Is an internationally famous feminist icon

Millie Knight – British skier (1999–)
- Had a childhood illness that left her with less than 10% vision
- Took ski lessons with her family from the age of 6
- Descends mountains at up to 115 km/h (71 mph) with the help of a guide
- After two major crashes, she has overcome her fear and returned to skiing

Marlee Beth Matlin – American actress and writer (1965–)
- Had a serious infection as a baby that destroyed her hearing
- Began acting as a child
- Earned a degree in criminal justice
- Won an Academy Award for best actress; she is the only deaf performer to do so
- Has published four books

Marla Runyan – American track and field athlete (1969–)
- Has been legally blind since childhood
- Encouraged by her parents to excel
- Accomplished in high jump, long jump, cycling, and 5,000- and 800-meter run
- Is an Olympic medalist and one of the fastest women to run a marathon
- Teaches at the school that Helen Keller attended

Justin Skeesuck – American adventurist and motivational speaker (1975–)
- Has gradually lost the ability to move arms and legs
- Pushed in his wheelchair by best friend Patrick on a 500-mile trip across Spain
- Featured in the memoir and movie *I'll Push You*
- As a motivational speaker, shares his belief that life is not defined by limitations but by accomplishments

UNIT 3: FINAL SPEAKING TASK: Simulation

Roles

Hospital administrators: You are worried. HGH is facing a number of problems:
- There is little money to operate the hospital.
- You have a serious lack of staff.
- Because of patient demand and staff shortage, the staff works long hours (sixteen hours a day maximum).
- You need to cover all the shifts and keep the emergency room open twenty-four hours a day.

Doctors: You are dedicated professionals committed to helping the community, but you have many challenges:
- You work very long, hard hours for average pay.
- You sometimes work eighty hours a week, the legal limit, which is really exhausting.
- You know that sometimes you don't perform well because you are sleep deprived.
- You don't feel you have a choice. There is no one else to take your place.

Patients' rights activists: You are concerned about the patients. You fear that someone will be hurt because the hospital staff is overworked and sleep deprived. You want the administration to take action.
- You want the hospital to explore innovative solutions.
- You propose using cameras to assess staff performance.
- You think computers could be used to regulate doses of medicine.

Roman and Betty, senior couple
- Live in a small home in Miami, Florida
- Are retired and enjoy a quiet life
- Have a small dog and enjoy gardening
- Have a married daughter with a new baby; money is tight for the daughter's family; the daughter's husband lost his tech job a year ago and is now studying for an MBA
- Are considering two options: a) selling their home, moving to a small apartment, and lending their daughter's family a large amount of money, or b) staying in their home and inviting their daughter's family to move in

Ho and Sora, senior couple
- Live in an apartment in Queens, New York, where they have lots of Korean friends
- Moved from Seoul thirty years ago and mostly speak Korean; they know a little English
- Sold the restaurant they owned but still help out on occasion
- Are active and in good health
- Have a married son with two young kids who is soon moving his family 200 miles (322 km) away for a new job and to be near his wife's parents
- Are thinking of selling their home to follow their son's family

Liling, senior
- Lives in a house in Chicago, Illinois
- Moved from Beijing 45 years ago; speaks Mandarin and English well
- Works part-time as a translator and is financially comfortable
- Is in good health but newly widowed; is now the only single person in her friend group and feels out of place although the friends are kind
- Has a single son in graduate school in Florida
- Has a daughter who lives in Denmark who has invited Liling to move in with her family

Rafa, senior
- Lives in a condo in Sacramento, California
- Is retired from an accounting firm, but does friends' and neighbors' taxes each year
- Became widowed one year ago; was very active because of his wife; he feels lost now
- Has grown children and grandchildren in Chicago and Boston; he sees them three or four times a year

EXPAND VOCABULARY LISTS

UNIT 1
Vocabulary
common sense
complex (*adj.*) `AWL`
inherit
innate
instinctive
motivate `AWL`
predisposed

Multi-word Units
be in favor of
in actual fact
on their own
out of the blue
take into account

UNIT 2
Multi-word Units
another level
open (one's) eyes
reach a high point
reach deep down
reach a new heights

UNIT 3
Vocabulary
demonstrate `AWL`
drowsy
irritable
nap (*n.*)
power nap (*n.*)
shut-eye

Multi-word Units
burn the midnight oil
major concern
nod off
run by

UNIT 4
Vocabulary
endangered (*adj.*)
ethical `AWL`
humane

Multi-word Units
butt in
get rid of
make a living
push the envelope
put a stop to
take issue with
weigh in

UNIT 5
Vocabulary
ordeal

Multi-word Units
break (one's) heart
know what (someone)
    is getting into
lose it
put up with
set in (one's) ways

UNIT 6
Vocabulary
year-round

Multi-word Units
have (one's) back
in a big way
make a difference
pay off
put (one's) weight
    into (something)
turn (someone) down

UNIT 7
Vocabulary
choice
dilemma
incredibly
obvious `AWL`
water use

Multi-word Units
come up with
    solutions
make people think
    about (something)
reduce (one's)
    consumption of
to sum up
You decide!

UNIT 8
Vocabulary
adaptability `AWL`
adaptation `AWL`
addiction
anxiety
initially `AWL`
moderate

ACADEMIC WORD LIST VOCABULARY AWL

Words with an * are target vocabulary in the unit. The remainder of the words appear in context in the listening texts.

access
accumulate*
accurate
accurately
achieve*
achievement
adaptability*
adaptation*
adulthood
adults
affect (v.)
anticipate*
appreciate
approach
area
aspect
assess
assistance
attach
attitude
author
authority
aware
awareness*
benefit (n.)
benefit (v.)
capability
capable
category*
challenge (n.)
chemically
committed (adj.)
communicate
communication
community
complex* (adj.)
computer

concentration
conduct
consistency*
consistent
consistently
consult
contact (n.)
context*
contribute
contribution*
controversy*
cooperation*
cooperative
create
creatively
cultural
culture
data
debatable*
debate
decade*
decline
define
definitely
definition
definitive*
demonstrate*
design
designed
designer
differentiate
display (v.)
economist
edit
emphasis*
energy
environment

environmental
equip
equivalent
establish
ethical*
evidence
evolutionary
exceed
expand
expert
expose
facility
factor (n.)
feature* (n.)
final
finally
flexible
focused (adj.)
foundation
founder
fund (n.)
fundamentally
generate
generation
global
globe
goal
grade (n.)
identical
identify
image
impact (n.)
incident
income
inconclusive*
indication
indicator

individual
infrastructure
initially*
institution
intelligence
intelligent
interact*
interactive*
intrinsic*
involve
issue (n.)
item
job
layer (n.)
locate
located (adj.)
maintain*
major (adj.)
majority
manipulate*
mentally
minority (n.)
motivate*
negative
networking (n.)
norm (n.)
objective* (adj.)
obvious*
obviously
occur
outcome
panel
parameters
percent
percentage
period
persistent*

physical

physically

positive

potential* (n.)

potentially

predictable

primary

prior

priority

process (n.)

processed (adj.)

professional

project (n.)

proportionately*

psychological

radically*

random

randomly*

react

recover*

region

reinforcement*

rely

require

requirement*

research (n.)

researcher

resident

resource

respond

response*

responsive

revise*

section

series

shift (v.)

significant

similarity

so-called

source (n.)

specific

specifically

sphere

strategy*

stress (v.)

structure

substitute* (v.)

supplement

sustainability*

sustainable

task (n.)

team (n.)

team (v.)

technique

technology

theory

topic

tradition

traditional

transfer* (v.)

transition (n.)

transition* (v.)

variable

volunteer (v.)

GRAMMAR BOOK REFERENCES

NorthStar: Listening and Speaking Level 4, Fifth Edition	*Focus on Grammar, Level 4*, Fifth Edition	*Azar's Understanding and Using English Grammar*, Fifth Edition
Unit 1 Passive Voice	**Unit 17** The Passive: Overview	**Chapter 11** The Passive: 11-1, 11-2, 11-3, 11-4
Unit 2 Gerunds and Infinitives	**Unit 9** Gerunds and Infinitives: Review and Expansion	**Chapter 14** Gerunds and Infinitives, Part 1 **Chapter 15** Gerunds and Infinitives, Part 2: 15-2
Unit 3 Present Unreal Conditionals	**Unit 22** Present and Future Unreal Conditional Sentences	**Chapter 20** Conditional Sentences and Wishes: 20-1, 20-3
Unit 4 Reported Speech	**Unit 24** Direct and Indirect Speech **Unit 25** Tense Changes in Indirect Speech	**Chapter 12** Noun Clauses: 12-6, 12-7, 12-8
Unit 5 Comparing Past Forms	**Unit 2** Simple Past and Past Progressive **Unit 3** Simple Past, Present Perfect, and Present Perfect Progressive	**Chapter 1** Present and Past; Simple and Progressive: 1-4, 1-5 **Chapter 2** Perfect and Perfect Progressive Tenses: 2-3, 2-4, 2-7
Unit 6 *Will* and *If*-clauses	**Unit 12** Adjective Clauses with Subject Relative Pronouns **Unit 13** Adjective Clauses with Object Relative Pronouns	**Chapter 13** Adjective Clauses: 13-1, 13-2, 13-4, 13-5, 13-6, 13-7, 13-8
Unit 7 Causal Verbs	**Unit 10** *Make, Have, Let, Help,* and *Get*	**Chapter 15** Gerunds and Infinitives, Part 2: 15-8, 15-9
Unit 8 Phrasal Verbs	**Unit 11** Phrasal Verbs: Review and Expansion	**Chapter 14** Gerunds and Infinitives, Part 1: 14-2

AUDIO SCRIPT

Listening One, Page 5, Preview

Scott Pelley: There's a composer studying at New York's renowned Juilliard School who some say is the greatest talent to come along in 200 years. He's written five full-length symphonies, and listen to this: He's 12 years old.

Page 6, Listen

Scott Pelley: There's a composer studying at New York's renowned Juilliard School who some say is the greatest talent to come along in 200 years. He's written five full-length symphonies, and listen to this: He's 12 years old. He's a kid named Jay Greenberg, although he likes to sign his work "Bluejay" because, as he told us, blue jays are small and they make a lot of noise. Jay says that the music just fills his head, and he has to write it down to get it out. What's going on in Bluejay's head? Have a listen: [music] A 12-year-old wrote this. He wrote every note for each and every instrument. And the really amazing part is, he wrote it in just a few hours. And when the last note sailed into the night, Jay Greenberg navigated an unfamiliar stage, past musicians who'd been playing longer than he'd been alive. And Bluejay took his bow. We haven't seen his like in how long?

Sam Zyman: Hundreds of years, probably 200 years. We are talking about a prodigy of the level of the greatest prodigies in history when it comes to composition.

SP: Sam Zyman is a composer. He teaches music theory to Jay at Juilliard in New York City, where he's been teaching for 17 years.

SZ: This is an absolute fact. This is objective. This is not a subjective opinion. Jay could be sitting right here, and he could be composing right now. He could finish a piano sonata before our very eyes in probably 25 minutes. And it would be a great piece.

SP: How's that possible? Well, Jay told us that he doesn't know where the music comes from, but it comes fully written—playing like an orchestra in his head.

SP: As you hear it playing, can you change it as it goes along? Can you say to yourself, "Oh, let's bring the oboes in here or let's bring the string section in here?"

Jay Greenberg: No, they seem to come in by themselves if they need to.

SP: It's not something you're trying to do.

JG: Yeah, because, it's like the unconscious mind is giving orders at the speed of light. You know, I mean, so I just hear it as if it were a smooth performance of a work already written, when it isn't.

SP: It's involuntary.

JG: I suppose so, yeah.

SP: Like the beating of the heart. You don't have to think about it.

JG: Uh-uh.

SP: It seems all the kids are downloading music these days. It's just that Jay, with his composing program, is downloading it from his mind. The program records his notes and plays them back—that is, when the computer is up and running. Jay composes so rapidly that he often crashes the computer.

SZ: It is as if he's looking at a picture of the score, and he's just taking it from the picture, basically.

SP: Jay's parents are as surprised as anyone. Neither is a professional musician. His father, Robert, is a linguist, a scholar in Slavic language, who lost his sight at the age of 36 to retinitis pigmentosa. His mother, Orna, is an Israeli-born painter.

Orna Greenberg: I think, around two, when he started writing and actually drawing instruments, we knew that he was fascinated with it.

SP: Started writing? At the age of two?

OG: Yeah, I'm afraid so. He managed to draw a cello and ask for a cello, and wrote the word cello. And I was surprised because neither of us have anything to do with string instruments. And I didn't expect him to know what it was.

SP: What a cello was.

OG: Right.

SP: You didn't have a cello?

OG: No, we had no cello in the house.

SP: Had he seen a cello?

OG: No.

SP: But he knew he wanted one, so his mother brought him to a music store, where he was shown a miniature cello.

OG: And he just sat there, put the cello, and he started playing on it. And I was like, "How do you know how to do this?"

SP: By age three, Jay was still drawing cellos, but he had turned them into notes on a scale. He was beginning to compose. Jay's parents watched the notes come faster and faster. He was writing anytime, anywhere. By elementary school, his teachers had no idea how to handle a boy whose hero wasn't Batman, but Beethoven. There's one thing about Jay: When the music comes up in his head, he has a lot of confidence about what he puts down on paper.

SP: Do you ever go back and say, "No, no, that's not right. This should be this way instead of that way."

JG: No, I don't really ever do that.

SP: You don't go back and edit and revise?

JG: No. Don't need to.

SP: Why not?

JG: Because, just, usually it comes, it comes right the first time.

Page 8, Make Inferences

Excerpt One

Scott Pelley: We haven't seen his like in how long?

Sam Zyman: Hundreds of years, probably 200 years. We are talking about a prodigy of the level of the greatest prodigies in history when it comes to composition.

Excerpt Two

Orna Greenberg: He managed to draw a cello and ask for a cello and wrote the word

cello. And I was surprised, because neither of us have anything to do with string instruments. And I didn't expect him to know what it was.

Page 10, Note-taking Skill

Excerpt One

Dr. Grainne McLoughlin: It does seem to be the case that prodigies run in families, so if there is one prodigy in the family, it's more likely that there will be another one—it could be a sibling, parent, or even a cousin.

Excerpt Two

Dr. GM: A great deal of research has been done on abilities in different areas, for example: art, sports, and science.

Listening Two, Page 11, Comprehension

Interviewer: Dr. McLoughlin, everyone is fascinated by prodigies, aren't they? What do we know about their abilities?

Dr. Grainne McLoughlin: Yes, prodigies *are* fascinating because to see a young child display a skill that usually takes years of practice is unusual. Actually, prodigies are quite *rare:* It's not often, for example, that you can see young children play complicated pieces of music, or even compose their own music. And a great deal of research has been conducted on this topic. It does seem to be the case that prodigies run in families, so if there is one prodigy in the family, it's more likely that there will be another one—it could be a sibling, parent, or even a cousin.

When we study the brains of prodigies using neuro-imaging scans, we can see that their brain activity works *differently.* The main way that this is different from the rest of the population is that they use an area called the cerebellum, located at the back of the brain, more efficiently. This means that their brains work faster, particularly when it comes to learning. The skill called "working memory," which can be measured simply by seeing how many items you can remember during a task, is also faster and better in prodigies.

INTERVIEWER: Interesting. You are an expert in twin studies. How can twins help us understand prodigies?

DR. GM: Twins are especially useful for understanding questions about nature and nurture. We can think of twins as a natural experiment, as there are both identical twins—who are genetically identical, essentially genetic clones of each other—and fraternal twins, who share half their genes, just like other siblings. The study of twins has allowed us to understand the influence of nature and nurture on many different behaviors and abilities. Again, a great deal of research has been done on abilities in different areas, for example: art, sports, and science. But the results are often inconclusive. It could even depend on what specific abilities we are talking about. In a twin study of mathematical ability, for example, genes were found to be more influential than family environment. But in a different twin study—this one on musical ability—the researchers found that although genes did have a substantial effect on achieving success, family environment had an even larger effect. Having a natural ability is clearly very important, but having parents or siblings who encourage you to develop your musical talent is even more important.

INTERVIEWER: In the end, what's more important—your genes or your environment?

DR. GM: This question has been debated extensively. A few years ago, a child in the UK was found to have exceptional ability in math. His parents had no special mathematical ability, and in fact took little interest in their son's achievements. But this boy went on to graduate from Cambridge University at the age of 17. This suggests that he was *born* a genius. However, there are many other examples of children whose parents started training them in a particular area from a young age, and they, too, became very accomplished. Tiger Woods is one such example. His father started training him in golf at the age of two. He then went on to achieve great success in the golfing world. Would he have developed this exceptional ability if his father had not supported him? Perhaps not. His experience suggests that a person can be *made* a genius.

In the end, the *potential* for being a prodigy is likely to be something children are born with. But whether or not they become a prodigy may depend on what happens in their early lives shortly afterwards. It could even be that we *all* have the potential for genius in a certain ability, but it depends on how we interact with the world. As our understanding grows about how genes work, and how we are influenced by our environment, we will understand more about whether geniuses are born or made. But for now, we can safely say it is a bit of both.

Page 12, Listening Skill

Exercise 1

DR. GRAINNE MCLOUGHLIN: When we study the brains of prodigies using neuro-imaging scans, we can see that their brain activity works *differently.*

Exercise 2

Excerpt One

DR. GM: His experience suggests that a person can be *made* a genius.

Excerpt Two

DR. GM: It could even be that we *all* have the potential for genius in a certain ability, but it depends on how we interact with the world.

UNIT 2: PUSHING THE BOUNDARIES

Listening One, Page 32, Preview

CAROL SAYLOR: My name is Carol Saylor. I am 73 years old. I am a sculptor and an art teacher. . . . *And you slam it down! Punch it some more.* . . . And I happen to be blind and deaf.

Page 32, Listen

CAROL SAYLOR: My name is Carol Saylor. I am 73 years old. I am a sculptor and an art teacher. . . . *And you slam it down! Punch it some more.* . . . And I happen to be blind and deaf. . . . When I first got the diagnosis, I was devastated. I thought that this was it. I had this stereotypical picture of blindness that the sighted world has. One of the misconceptions is, is that you see black, which I don't. I see all kinds of colors and shapes and vibrating spots, and it's quite beautiful.

KATE WHITMAN: *Sammy is right here, over to your right . . .*

KW: My name is Kate Whitman, and I teach art at Heritan High School. Today, I brought my 3-D multimedia sculpture class to see Carol Saylor's work. . . . For me, her story is just as important as the work itself. She's been through so much hardship, and she's found a way to always overcome and find a way to be positive and keep persevering.

CS: Today we're talking to about 12 students. I want them to close their eyes and touch my work. . . . *Do you have your eyes closed?*

BOY: Yeah.

CS: I want them to think about their mind's eye. I want them not to be afraid of blindness.

BOY: I didn't really think about what it would be like to be an artist while being blind and deaf. It's a crazy thing to think about. She's really good with touching things, and she can really make the form of the body look cool when she can't even see it.

CS: My favorite subject is the female form. And I like sensuous shapes, and I like faces. The things that I have learned about art go far beyond, I think, what the average sighted person knows. And that's really what my art is all about. I'm trying to demonstrate to the sighted community that there is another level to art.

GIRL: My name's Ofelia Castalito, and I'm in 9th grade, and I'm here on a field trip with my school. I thought that she was an amazing artist. She opened my eyes to that everything isn't just about what you see. It's also about what you feel.

CS: My art expresses these feelings of grief and loss and also hope. But it is definitely not art therapy. It is way beyond art therapy: It is . . . it's, it's an expression of my inner "gut" (laughs). . . . It's just . . . it's part of me. I would hate to not be able to do it because that's what keeps me going, I think.

Page 34, Make Inferences

Excerpt One

GIRL: She opened my eyes to that everything isn't just about what you see. It's also about what you feel.

Excerpt Two

CAROL SAYLOR: It is definitely not art therapy. It is way beyond art therapy: It is . . . it's, it's an expression of my inner "gut" (laughs). . . . It's just . . . it's part of me. I would hate to not be able to do it because that's what keeps me going, I think.

Page 35, Note-taking Skill

Excerpt One

HOST: I should mention that Ryan is involved with an organization called Stay Focused, which teaches young people with disabilities how to develop confidence and leadership skills.

NATALIE ESCALANTE: Right. They do that by encouraging kids to stay focused on what they want to achieve. To persevere. To not give up.

Excerpt Two

NE: With Ryan and the Push Across America project, he wasn't just physically fit. He was mentally fit. Once he set off, it was just him and the road, for weeks on end. He had a support team with him, of course. But the trip required a lot of drive and concentration. I think it's actually good training for life.

HOST: I totally agree: Whether you're rebounding from a difficult experience, or trying to reach a goal, or working through any issue, really: You have to be mentally strong.

Listening Two, Page 36, Comprehension

HOST: Our final story this evening is about a 23-year-old man by the name of Ryan Chalmers, who was born with spina bifida, but it has not slowed him down. He set off to race across the United States—an epic journey that took him from Los Angeles to New York. His trip lasted a total of 71 days, during which time he raised awareness and funds for disabled teens and adults for a project called "Push Across America." This is the kind of thing we in the news business should talk about more often.

You're probably wondering how he did it, and that's the most incredible thing of all. He *pushed* himself across the country in a wheelchair, more specifically a racing chair, which was equipped for the purpose. In all, he traveled 3,000 miles, across 18 states and through dozens of towns and cities, including the hometown of our guest, Natalie Escalante. Watching Chalmers race and following his journey has changed her life. Welcome Natalie.

NATALIE ESCALANTE: Thanks. It's great to be here.

HOST: So tell us about seeing Ryan Chalmers race and what that experience has meant for you.

NE: Well, like Ryan, I was born with a condition known as spina bifida, which affects the backbone and spinal cord and sometimes the use of your legs. For me, what's been so inspiring is that it hasn't held Ryan Chalmers back. He's played wheelchair sports like basketball and track since he was eight. He's also competed at the London Paralympic Games in 2012. He's completed marathons. And, most importantly, in my opinion, he's encouraged people with disabilities to get involved in sports.

HOST: Which is where you come in.

NE: Right. After that day, after seeing him race through my town, I had a big realization. I realized that disabled athletes aren't really any different from athletes who are able-bodied: Both put their heart and soul into their sport. Both work hard. Both try to challenge themselves. Both want to reach their goals.

HOST: And you, what's your goal now?

NE: Well, after seeing Ryan race, I started competing in wheelchair tennis. I'm not great, yet, but I'll get there. That's my hope anyway. But that's not my goal. Like Ryan, I want to help others make the transition that I did. That's my goal. You know, a lot of young people don't have anyone to look up to. We need more role models like Ryan Chalmers.

HOST: I should mention that Ryan is involved with an organization called Stay Focused, which teaches young people with disabilities how to develop confidence and leadership skills.

NE: Right. They do that by encouraging kids to stay focused on what they want to achieve. To persevere. To not give up.

HOST: That raises a great point. Many people don't understand that it's not just about the physical challenge.

NE: Absolutely. With Ryan and the Push Across America project, he wasn't just physically fit. He was mentally fit. Once he set off, it was just him and the road, for weeks on end. He had a support team with him, of course. But the trip required a lot of drive and concentration. I think it's actually good training for life.

HOST: I totally agree: Whether you're rebounding from a difficult experience, or trying to reach a goal, or working through any issue, really: You have to be mentally strong.

NE: Yeah. It's something I work on. Being focused. Being confident. Like Ryan, I believe you can do anything if you set your mind to it!

HOST: Well said. Well, thank you, Natalie, for sharing *your* journey with us. And if you want to know more about Chalmers's journey, just search online for "Push Across America."

Page 37, Listening Skill

Exercise 1

HOST: Our final story this evening is about a 23-year-old man by the name of Ryan Chalmers, who was born with spina bifida, but it has not slowed him down. He set off to race across the United States—an epic journey that took him from Los Angeles to New York.

Exercise 2

Excerpt One

NE: For me, what's been so inspiring is that it hasn't held Ryan Chalmers back. He's played wheelchair sports like basketball and track since he was eight. He's also competed at the London Paralympic Games in 2012. He's completed marathons. And, most importantly, in my opinion, he's encouraged people with disabilities to get involved in sports.

Excerpt Two

NE: After that day, after seeing him race through my town, I had a big realization. I realized that disabled athletes aren't really any different from athletes who are able-bodied: Both put their heart and soul into their sport. Both work hard. Both try to challenge themselves. Both want to reach their goals.

UNIT 3: EARLY TO BED EARLY TO RISE

Listening One, Page 57, Preview

DR. MICHAEL HOWELL: A couple of key things to think about when you're dealing with adolescents and sleep issues is that adolescents have a tendency to be a bit of night owls. They tend to like to go to bed later and sleep in later, and this is more than just a behavioral choice on their part. Their brains actually act differently. And this has been noticed not only in human adolescents but also in animal models of adolescents. You'll see they actually like to stay up later and go to bed later. This is particularly troublesome in middle school and high school when, at the same time this is happening in their brains, the school times actually start earlier. So they both like to go to bed later but then are forced to wake up earlier, and it often leads to sleep deprivation.

Page 58, Listen

DR. MICHAEL HOWELL: A couple of key things to think about when you're dealing with adolescents and sleep issues is that adolescents have a tendency to be a bit of night owls. They tend to like to go to bed later and sleep in later, and this is more than just a behavioral choice on their part. Their brains actually act differently. And this has been noticed not only in human adolescents but also in animal models of adolescents. You'll see they actually like to stay up later and go to bed later. This is particularly troublesome in middle school and high school when, at the same time this is happening in their brains, the school times actually start earlier. So they both like to go to bed later but then are forced to wake up earlier, and it often leads to sleep deprivation.

The only way that you're able to consistently reset your circadian rhythm so that you're able to go to, so that adolescents are able to go to sleep at an earlier time and wake up earlier is 1) through consistency, 2) with sunlight—about 20, 30 minutes first thing in the morning, helps reset the circadian rhythm—and 3) you can use a little bit of low-dose melatonin, which is just an over-the-counter vitamin supplement, about six hours prior to bedtime. Those are the only things that have been proven clinically to help people fall asleep earlier.

What most studies have demonstrated is that you need to recover typically about half of the sleep that is lost. So in an adolescent who is, who could otherwise sleep two more hours a day during the week, that'll add up over five days to 10 hours. So over the course of a Saturday and Sunday, if that's the time that they have in the morning to the sleep in, they'll need to catch up five hours.

I think one of the first things to recognize is that sleepiness is not laziness. I mean, there's often times when we think of children or adolescents who are sleeping in class. It is not typically due to slothfulness or just laziness or disinterest. It is actually an intrinsic loss of sleep. I mean, there are perfectly good examples of kids who are lazy and won't do anything, but that is different from kids who are actually not able to maintain wakefulness. So it's not only school start times, but it's also activity start times. So it's not unusual for an adolescent who is both a swimmer as well as in orchestra to have to be at school, and to start at six o'clock in the morning. This can be extremely devastating to one's wakefulness. Now that being said, most adolescents are able to tolerate it pretty well, but for some, it can be just quite devastating.

Page 60, Make Inferences

Excerpt One

DR. MICHAEL HOWELL: I think one of the first things to recognize is that sleepiness is not laziness. I mean, there's often times when we think of children or adolescents who are sleeping in class. It is not typically due to slothfulness or just laziness or disinterest. It is actually an intrinsic loss of sleep. I mean, there are perfectly good examples of kids who are lazy and won't do anything, but that is different from kids who are actually not able to maintain wakefulness.

Excerpt Two

DR. MH: So it's not only school start times, but it's also activity start times. So it's not unusual for an adolescent who is both a swimmer as well as in orchestra to have to be at school, and to start at six o'clock in the morning. This can be extremely devastating to one's wakefulness.

Listening Two, Page 63, Comprehension

LIAN: This is Lian, and, like many of our listeners out there, I'm tired. I'm tired in the morning, I'm tired in the afternoon, and I'm really tired at night. And, frankly, I'm tired of being tired. My excuse is that I have two small children who sleep a little and wake up a lot. Dr. Walsleben, why are we all so tired?

DR. JOYCE WALSLEBEN: We're probably tired because we don't make sleep a priority. And I think, as a young mother and a career woman, your days are pretty well filled, and I would suspect that you probably think you can do without sleep or at least cut your sleep short, and one of the things that happens is we forget that sleep loss accumulates, so even one bad night, teamed with another will make an effect on our performance the following day. The other aspect, which you did touch on, is that even though we may sleep long periods of time, the sleep may not be really of good quality.

L: How serious a problem is sleep deprivation?

DR. JW: Well, it can be very serious, because lack of sleep can affect our performance. It's not . . . We can get cranky and all of that, but if our performance is poor, and we are in a very critical job, we can have a major incident. And there have been many across society in which sleep and fatigue were issues. The *Exxon Valdez* was one in which the captain got a lot of attention, but the mate who was driving the ship had been on duty for 36 hours. But you can read your local papers; every weekend, you'll see a car crash with probably a single driver, around 2 or 3 A.M., no reason why they'd happen to drive off the road, and we all believe that that's probably a short sleep event that occurred when they weren't looking for it.

L: Dr. Walsleben, I know how this sleep deprivation affects me. By the end of the day, with my children, I'm tired and cranky, I'm not making good parenting decisions, I don't have a lot to give my husband when he comes home, and then I just feel too tired to exercise. So I think, "Oh, I'll eat or I'll have a big cup of coffee, and that will give me the energy that I don't have naturally." Are these pretty common effects of sleep deprivation amongst your patients?

DR. JW: They're very common, and so many people accept them.

L: I would even say by Friday afternoon, I'm afraid to get behind the wheel of a car, because I just feel like I am not a safe driver on the road. That's how tired I am by Fridays.

DR. JW: I think it's great of you to have recognized that, and that's a real, major concern for most of America's workers. By Friday, everyone seems to be missing, probably, five hours of sleep.

Page 65, Listening Skill

Exercise 1

DR. JOYCE WALSLEBEN: . . . Lack of sleep can affect our performance. It's not . . . We can get cranky and all of that, but if our performance is poor, and we are in a very critical job, we can have a major incident.

Exercise 2

Excerpt One

DR. JW: The *Exxon Valdez* was one in which the captain got a lot of attention, but the mate who was driving the ship had been on duty for 36 hours. But you can read your local papers; every weekend, you'll see a car crash with probably a single driver, around 2 or 3 a.m., no reason why they'd happen to drive off the road, and we all believe that that's probably a short sleep event that occurred when they weren't looking for it.

Excerpt Two

LIAN: Dr. Walsleben, I know how this sleep deprivation affects me. By the end of the day with my children, I'm tired and cranky, I'm not making good parenting decisions, I don't have a lot to give my husband when he comes home, and then I just feel too tired to exercise.

UNIT 4: ANIMAL INTELLIGENCE

Listening One, Page 84, Preview

ALEX GOODWIN: We've assembled a fascinating group of scientists who make a living working with smart birds, smart chimps, and smart dolphins. All three of them are pushing the edge of the envelope in the animal intelligence field, and they're here to share what they've learned.

Page 85, Listen

ALEX GOODWIN: Welcome, all three of you, to *The Infinite Mind.*

DR. IRENE PEPPERBERG: Hi.

DR. STAN KUCZAJ: Hi.

DR. SALLY BOYSEN: Thank you.

AG: Glad to have you. Now let me start with a quick question for each of you. Off the top of your head, what's the smartest thing you've ever seen one of your animals do? Think—you know, something that made you step out and say, "Wow, that's amazing." Dr. Boysen, what about you?

DR. SB: Oh! You would start with me. I, I guess probably the most remarkable thing I've seen lately is an older chimpanzee that we have in the colony who's now 40. We had an arrival of an ex-pet chimp who'd been living in a home for 20 years, and she really has difficulty kind of getting around the lab. She has some retinal damage from diabetes. And, quite literally, I, I think that Sara, the older chimp, recognizes that this other chimpanzee, Abigail, kind of just doesn't get it. And we've seen her literally move through the facility, put her arms around Abigail, and lead her down to the right door, for example, in the evening when she's supposed to come in for dinner. This is very remarkable behavior for, for a chimp that was born, raised in captivity, who was not socialized with chimps, and yet she really seemed to understand that Abigail needed her assistance. So I think it's, it's, it was a pretty remarkable thing to observe.

AG: Dr. Pepperberg, what about you?

DR. IP: Ours is very different. I believe one of the things that we found that is, that's really very exciting is Alex's ability to use information that he's learned in one context and transfer that to a completely different context. So, for example, he was trained to respond "Color," "Shape," "Matter," or "None" when objects were shown to him and he was asked, "What's same?" or "What's different?" And then we trained him on a task on relative size. So we'd ask him, "What color bigger?" or "What color smaller?" And the very first time we showed him two objects of the same size and asked him, "What color bigger?" he looks at us, and he says, "What same?"

AG: OK.

DR. IP: And—yeah. And then we asked him, "OK. Now you tell us, you know, what color bigger?" And he said, "None." And he had never been trained on this.

AG: That is amazing. Dr. Kuczaj, what about you?

DR. SK: Well, I have two examples that I'd like to mention. Both of these are spontaneous behaviors involving killer whales. In one example, a young whale was playing with a large disk, which ended up on the bottom of a pool, and it couldn't figure out how to get the disk off the bottom of the pool. And, spontaneously, it blew air bubbles out of its blow hole, which raised the disk off the floor so it could grab it. Another thing that we've observed is, with a number of killer whales, is they'll use fish to bait seagulls. As the seagulls will get close enough so that then they can try and catch and often succeed in catching the gull.

AG: OK. Now, Dr. Pepperberg, parrots are particularly intriguing, of course, because they actually vocalize to some extent a kind of communication. Can you really talk to them like you talk to a human? I mean, what's, what's it like?

DR. IP: Well, you can talk to the birds the way you talk to a very young human. They don't speak to us in complete sentences. They don't have the same type of language as we do. We don't even call it language. We just call it two-way communication. But you can come into the lab, you can ask Alex what he'd like to eat, where he wants to go. And he answers numerous questions about colors, shapes, materials, categories, similarity, difference, numbers. So it's, it's like working with a small child.

AG: And you gave us one example. What else has, has Alex learned to do?

DR. IP: Well, one, one thing he can do is to answer multiple questions about the same objects, and that's important because it shows that he understands the questions themselves. He's not simply responding in a rote manner to the particular objects.

ALEX: Some water.

AG: I think Alex is trying to butt in here. Dr. Pepperberg . . .

DR. SK: Good.

AG: . . . do you want to give Alex the floor here?

DR. IP: Alex, do you want to do some work, huh? Here. Listen. What's here?

ALEX: Beeper.

DR. IP: Very good. It's a little toy telephone beeper. Good birdie. OK. Let's go back to this other thing. What's here? How many?

ALEX: Two.

DR. IP: Good. Can you tell me what's different? What's different?

ALEX: Color.

DR. IP: Color, very good. And what color bigger? What color bigger?

ALEX: Green.

DR. IP: That's right. Saw two keys. One was blue and one was green, and they were the same shape and different color and different size. Very good. He's been asking for water, grapes, go shoulder, all sorts of things while we've been doing this.

ALEX: Some water.

AG: At any rate, we really appreciate all of you appearing on *The Infinite Mind*, and we'll, we're going to be coming back to this issue. So thank you all very much.

DR. IP: You're very welcome.

DR. SK: Thank you.

DR. SB: Thank you.

AG: Alex, thank you, too.

Page 87, Make Inferences

Excerpt One

DR. SALLY BOYSEN: And, quite literally, I, I think that Sara, the older chimp, recognizes that this other chimpanzee, Abigail, kind of just doesn't get it. And we've seen her literally move through the facility, put her arms around Abigail, and lead her down to the right door, for example, in the evening when she's supposed to come in for dinner. This is very remarkable behavior for, for a chimp that was born, raised in captivity, who was not socialized with chimps, and yet she really seemed to understand that Abigail needed her assistance.

Excerpt Two

DR. IRENE PEPPERBERG: So we'd ask him, "What color bigger?" or "What color smaller?" And the very first time we showed him two objects of the same size and asked him, "What color bigger?" he looks at us, and he says, "What same?"

ALEX GOODWIN: OK.

DR. IP: And—yeah. And then we asked him, "OK. Now you tell us, you know, what color bigger?" And he said, "None." And he had never been trained on this.

AG: That is amazing.

Page 89, Note-taking Skill

Excerpt One

LIZ PENNISI: And what the chimp readily figures out is that if it kind of sneaks around a barrier that the human can't see, it can get the food.

Excerpt Two

LP: And so they started a series of experiments. Most of them take advantage of what they call *caching behavior* in which a scrub jay, for example, or a crow, will take a tidbit of food, a piece of nut, or whatever, and bury it.

Excerpt Three

LP: So what, one of the prevailing standards is something called "theory of mind," and that is when you can assess what somebody else is thinking, can judge what somebody else might be doing, can take that information and use it at a later time.

Listening Two, Page 90, Comprehension

LIZ PENNISI: A lot of the work is done in chimps and other apes because they're our closest relatives, and the idea is to put the chimps into a situation that they react to. And it turns out that competition for food is what motivates them to perform. So there's been a series of experiments. One of the more recent ones has to do with putting a chimp head-to-head with a human, and the chimp wants to reach for food and the human has the ability to pull the food away. And what the chimp readily figures out is that if it kind of sneaks around a barrier that the human can't see, it can get the food. What that experiment is showing is that the chimp understands that the human is watching them and understands how to manipulate the situation to get what it wants.

HOST: So I guess there's also been some interesting things done with birds as well, though, which aren't quite as close to us on the evolutionary relationship. We've had at least one study just this year that suggests that birds can remember, plan, or even, you know, perhaps, anticipate the future. Is that correct?

LP: Right. What happened is, about 10 years ago, a couple of researchers realized that some of the skills that you see in chimps and social animals, including us, might also exist in social birds. And so they started a series of experiments. Most of them take advantage of what they call *caching behavior* in which a scrub jay, for example, or a crow, will take a tidbit of food, a piece of nut, or whatever, and bury it. And all the experiments are based on the idea of, "OK, if some other bird is watching you bury the food, what do you do?" And what they've discovered is that the bird is aware when somebody else is watching. The bird takes evasive action—it will go behind a barrier so that the onlooker can't see what it's doing. It will bury the food in one place and then come back and move it to another place.

HOST: And I guess part of it sort of plays into this whole question of what cognition really is. I mean, isn't that sort of an extra layer of controversy or disagreement on this whole question?

LP: Oh right. I mean the definition of cognition and intelligence, even, if humans have to be the most intelligent beings, then we have to define intelligence in terms of what we can and cannot do. So what, one of the prevailing standards is something called "theory of mind," and that is when you can assess what somebody else is thinking, can judge what somebody else might be doing, can take that information and use it at a later time. And at one point no animal was supposed to have any of that, and of course the experiments with chimps and even with the birds are showing that, well, they know about deception, they know when someone can see something they're doing, and they know how to manipulate that—what that person can see.

HOST: Well, Liz, it sounds like there's a lot going on on this front. Thanks for coming in today and chatting with us about some of it.

LP: Well, thank you.

Page 91, Listening Skill

Exercise 2

LIZ PENNISI: About 10 years ago a couple of researchers realized that some of the skills that you see in chimps and social animals, including us, might also exist in social birds. And so they started a series of experiments. Most of them take advantage of what they call *caching behavior* in which a scrub jay, for example, or a crow, will take a tidbit of food, a piece of nut, or whatever, and bury it. And all the experiments are based on the idea of, "OK, if some other bird is watching you bury the food, what do you do?" And what they've discovered is that the bird is aware when somebody else is watching. The bird takes evasive action—it will go behind a barrier so that the onlooker can't see what it's doing. It will bury the food in one place and then come back and move it to another place.

UNIT 5: THE GOLDEN YEARS

Listening One, Page 110, Listen

ROBIN ROBERTS: Who doesn't want to live forever? The *Longevity Project* is an eye-opening book based on a one-of-a-kind study, following 1,500 people over eight decades. This book changes everything we've thought about how to live a long, productive life. We are joined now by doctors Howard Friedman and Leslie Martin. Thank you. You said I can call you Howard and Leslie?

HOWARD FRIEDMAN: Yes.

RR: All right. Thank you, thank you, thank you. This is just remarkable. Howard, first of all, tell us a bit about the study.

HW: Well, this is really a breakthrough study because it's the first scientific study that followed people from when they were children, back in 1921, throughout their whole lives: when they went through adolescence, as they went through young adulthood, as they got married, had their own children, went into their careers, aged, to see why some people thrived, lived long, stayed healthy. Other people kind of fell off the healthy path and succumbed and died before their time.

RR: But to have that body of information is just unheard of. And Leslie, is there a best indicator, one thing that really stood out, about why people lived long?

LESLIE MARTIN: The best, more consistent predictor was actually conscientiousness. So, a conscientious person is someone who is dependable and organized, prudent. They think ahead. They're persistent, so when they start something, they stick to it. That. And it might sound like this is a boring person. These aren't boring people.

RR: No, no, no.

LM: When you have those qualities, you tend to get more opportunities, and you have opportunities to do really cool, fun stuff.

RR: All right. Well, let's have a little true and false here because that will help us get the message across a little bit more. Let's start with you first, Howard. True or false? Carefree folks live longer than worry warts.

HF: What do you think?

RR: I think it's a little good to worry.

HF: It is. It turns out . . .

RR: Kind of keeps your mind going.

HF: Right. It's very important—[Buzzer]

RR: So it's false! Carefree people do not live longer than worry warts.

HF: Right. We found, in fact, that people who . . . take it easy, don't work so hard, don't stress yourself. We found people didn't work themselves to death. They really worked themselves to life. The people who were committed to their careers, worked hard, stayed involved, and succeeded in their careers actually stayed healthy and lived longer.

RR: Because how many times we hear of somebody that they have been working all their life, and everyone is like, "Retire!" And then they retire, and they die soon thereafter because they don't have—

HF: Well, because they lose their social ties, they lose their friends, and they lose their reason to get up in the morning. So it's important, if you like your job, keep working.

RR: All right, Leslie, I got a question for you here.

LM: OK.

RR: Gardening and walking are better for your health than vigorous exercise. True or false?

LM: [Bell] True. In a sense. We're certainly not saying that if you love jogging, you need to stop that, or if you love vigorous exercise, you shouldn't do it. It's certainly good for you. But the thing is, we know we should be active, and yet so many of us are not active because we try to do things that really don't match with our style, and that we don't enjoy. We get bored or we feel overwhelmed. And so we quit. And so what we recommend is that people find something that they enjoy. And if it's gardening or hiking or tennis

or woodworking, whatever it is, that's the thing you're going to be able to do consistently, and the consistency is what really matters.

RR: Do what you love. All right, Howard, we got a final question for you. Folks who have their nose to the grindstone all the time live longer than slackers. I think we pretty much know the answer to that.

HF: Yes, definitely true. [Bell] The prudent, hard-working, conscientious people who stuck with it, that stick-to-it-ive-ness factor, really was one of the best predictors of living a long and healthy life.

RR: All right. Well, thank you Howard . . . (video fades out)

Page 115, Note-taking Skill

WOMAN: My father always said he wanted to travel, but he couldn't go anywhere for many years because he was working in an office and only got a few weeks off every year. But when he retired, he decided that it was time for action. He and my mother spent a few months researching places to visit in Latin America. I was working in Argentina at the time, so I encouraged them to come and visit me. They jumped on a plane and came down for a month, and they loved it. After that great experience, they decided to go to Chile and Uruguay. In total, they spent three months away from home, and, as a result, they've become even more interested in traveling. Next, they plan to go to Cambodia and Vietnam because they've heard the countryside is spectacular!

Listening Two, Page 116, Comprehension

TOBEY DICHTER: I'm Tobey Dichter and I just turned 65. I am the founder of Generations Online.

[Background] Have you ever used the internet? You have?

TD: Generations Online is a national non-profit that introduces the internet and email to people over 65.

[Background] Click two times on the left. Just the left.

TD: We place it in places where they live and congregate. So senior centers, low-income housing.

TD: This happened when the internet was starting to take on. I think my mother really kind of inspired this. I guess I was blessed. The older people in my life, like my mother, who died at age 85—they set the parameters for me. So I thought, it's really cool to be old and wise and witty. And then, as you met more and more older people, you realized that some just don't age as well. And that's what started me on the discovery. I was just curious. I would start to ask older people, you know, "Oh, do you use the internet? You must love it!" "Oh no, dear, I'm too old." "Oh no, I'm too dumb." It broke my heart.

Woman 1 (Dorothy Gray): I'm Dorothy Gray, 82 years old. It's not hard to catch on. Most things you do, cooking, or whatever, you follow directions. So this, same with this. Follow directions, you learn how to use it.

TD: I had this wonderful job, big office. But this thing was tugging at me. And finally I left, after 30 years. I never looked back.

Woman 2: Pero, por eso, yo quiero ser independiente.

Woman 2 Translator: My daughter and my granddaughter are always the ones doing everything in the computer for me. I would like to be more independent and get my own information, so that way I don't have to bother them.

Woman 2: Tú sabes, . . .

TD: It's hard enough to be old. It's much harder when everybody else is communicating in a certain fast way, and you're the only one left off. And I've had so many elders say to me: "They're leaving us behind." And there's too much to catch up to. There's way too much vocabulary—there are too many techniques.

Woman 3: I can type in my name . . . Oh, this is the email here right now.

Woman 4: I learned the mouse, what is it, touching it and directing him . . . I can direct him to do what I want.

TD: We had one woman in the focus groups who says, "Www means I'm never going to see it."

Woman 3: It's good for you to know. It keeps your mind active, keeps you active . . . and the other thing good with the computer (is) you can do a lot of networking.

TD: I think working on this has changed me radically. It's given me a purpose that's driven not by the end product, but by the joys of each and every individual. I wouldn't want to be left off, and so we can't, we can't leave them off.

Page 117, Listening Skill

Exercise 1

Tobey Dichter: The older people in my life, like my mother, who died at age eighty-five—they set the parameters for me. So I thought, it's really cool to be old and wise and witty.

Exercise 2

Excerpt One

TD: Generations Online is a national non-profit that introduces the internet and email to people over sixty-five.

Excerpt Two

Woman 3: It's good for you to know. It keeps your mind active, keeps you active . . . and the other thing good with the computer (is) you can do a lot of networking.

Page 128, Pronunciation

Exercise 2

1. Why did you go there?
2. What did you see at the parade?
3. You can come, can't you?
4. They won't let you in without an ID card.
5. How do you get there?
6. Where do you live?
7. You can't come, can you?
8. Where do you go after class?
9. What do you think about that?

UNIT 6: GIVING TO OTHERS: WHY DO WE DO IT?

Listening One, Page 136, Preview

STACY PALMER: At least half of Americans say they volunteered at some time in the past year. Seventy-five percent of people said they made some kind of a cash donation.

Page 136, Listen

ALEX GOODWIN: Probably most gestures of everyday kindness and generosity are never recorded. But when it comes to organized charities, fundraisers make it their business to know who is giving and why. Welcome, Ms. Palmer.

STACY PALMER: Glad to be here.

AG: What studies have been done on volunteering and charitable giving?

SP: Actually, we don't know all of that much about what really motivates people to give. We know how often they give. And about half of Americans volunteer their time, and 75 percent of people give money.

There have been some polls that give some indication of what, what are some of the kinds of things that make people want to give. And usually, it's the passion for the cause. That's what they really care about. Whatever it is that they're involved with, they care about it a great deal. And that motivates them more than anything else—more than the tax benefits, more than the desire to repay somebody for something. They really care very, very much about whatever it is that they're getting involved in. And that's the biggest motivator.

AG: Do positive appeals work better than negative appeals?

SP: It's hard to tell. It depends on what the issue is. One of the things that politically minded causes often find is that when they have an enemy, they do very well. If they can say that this is the big threat to something, "You better do something now or else something bad will happen," people give in a big way.

AG: Now, what about the difference between volunteering time and volunteering money?

SP: A lot of people have differing attitudes on that, and both are very valuable. But I think people feel better after they volunteer. Writing the check feels good, but I think most people really, when—when they go to volunteer, they see the direct effects of what they're doing. And that's much more rewarding to them.

AG: Now what's the magnitude of this in terms of percentage of the population? I mean, is there a figure at what, you know, at what percentage of the population give either their time and/or their money?

SP: About 50 percent of people say that they volunteer at least at some point, maybe, just, you know, a short-term volunteering project or something like that. It's a smaller percentage that actually volunteers once a week or—or something like that.

AG: Uh-huh. Uh-huh.

SP: But at least half of Americans say they volunteered at some time in the past year. 75 percent of people said they made some kind of a cash donation, and that's often to some kind of a religious institution, which is what commands the biggest share of contributions, but also to multiple other causes. So most people in America do give something.

AG: What about social class? Is that as predictable as it should be?

SP: The very wealthy do give more often, and they give a little bit differently. They tend to like to go to these black-tie benefits and do that sort of thing. And they also like to give with their name attached to it. People who are not in that wealthy class tend to give anonymously more often, and say that that's something that they prefer to do.

AG: Would you say that the less wealthy give a larger percentage of their income?

SP: The evidence is debatable on that, and that's something that economists really disagree on. I think the biggest group of economists think that the poor do give proportionately more, but there's a strong argument to be made on the other side that the wealthy are giving proportionately more. So that's something that is continuing to be studied, and we hope at some point we'll get a more definitive answer with better data. Part of it is, how do you count what's giving? Is it giving when somebody helps their neighbor and gives, you know, a bunch of their winter clothing to somebody next door? Should you count that as part of charitable giving? It's not part of formal giving . . .

AG: No.

SP: . . . but it's certainly something that one would consider generous. The other problem is getting people to accurately say what it is that they've given in response to what they're being asked. Do you remember what you gave over the past year, honestly? Might you exaggerate it when somebody asks you, "Were you a giving person last year?"

AG: Sure.

SP: All of those things are what researchers are trying to factor out so that they get honest answers.

AG: Other than the, the thing we talked about a minute ago about, you know, caring about the cause, are there other reasons that people give? Are there other sort of universals that differentiate a giver from a non-giver?

SP: Usually, it's some kind of moral or religious feeling that also motivates a great deal of people to give. And it seems to come out of a feeling that it's important to, in some ways, give back to society.

AG: Uh-huh.

SP: And that's often part of a family tradition or something that people have been taught all along the way, that that's something that's vital. And one of the things we're seeing a lot of is efforts to teach very young children how to give because it's clear that it is something that can be taught and something that, the more people learn about as part of a tradition, stays with them for all of their lives. So you even see kindergarten classes doing United Way fund-raising events. And I think we'll be seeing much more emphasis on teaching children because we can see that that really pays off. And you see in a lot of schools, too, they—this mandatory service requirement, where they actually have to do community service to graduate. That's part of a way to show people, you know, "Here. I worked on a housing project" or "I helped clean up a river" or "I helped do something. Here's the difference that I made."

AG: Uh-huh.

SP: And that seems to make a huge difference in helping people give all throughout their lives.

AG: Thank you very much, Ms. Palmer, for appearing on *The Infinite Mind.*

SP: Thank you.

Page 138, Make Inferences

Excerpt One

ALEX GOODWIN: Do positive appeals work better than negative appeals?

STACY PALMER: It's hard to tell. It depends on what the issue is. One of the things that politically minded causes often find is that when they have an enemy, they do very well. If they can say that this is the big threat to something, "You better do something now or else something bad will happen," people give in a big way.

Excerpt Two

AG: Now, what about the difference between volunteering time and volunteering money?

SP: A lot of people have differing attitudes on that, and both are very valuable. But I think people feel better after they volunteer. Writing the check feels good, but I think most people really, when, when they go to volunteer, they see the direct effects of what they're doing. And that's much more rewarding to them.

Excerpt Three

AG: What about social class? Is that as predictable as it should be?

SP: The very wealthy do give more often, and they give a little bit differently. They tend to like to go to these black-tie benefits and do that sort of thing. And they also like to give with their name attached to it. People who are not in that wealthy class tend to give anonymously more often, and say that that's something that they prefer to do.

Page 140, Note-taking Skill

ANNOUNCER: Something about winter and all those family gatherings must be inspiring us: Half of all charitable donations are made between Thanksgiving and New Year's. Or, maybe we just realize the tax year is about to end. Some people, though, have the giving spirit year-round. Amy Radil introduces us to an anonymous Seattle resident who's become something of a guerilla philanthropist.

REPORTER AMY RADIL: I had just done a story about a welfare mother who was having trouble feeding her children, when I got a phone message. The woman in the message, let's call her the Mystery Donor, said she would like to do something, anonymously, to help the woman in my story. She ended up paying off a $1,200 light bill to keep the woman's power from being shut off.

Listening Two, Page 141, Comprehension

ANNOUNCER: Something about winter and all those family gatherings must be inspiring us: Half of all charitable donations are made between Thanksgiving and New Year's. Or, maybe we just realize the tax year is about to end. Some people, though, have the giving spirit year-round. Amy Radil introduces us to an anonymous Seattle resident who's become something of a guerilla philanthropist.

REPORTER AMY RADIL: I had just done a story about a welfare mother who was having trouble feeding her children, when I got a phone message. The woman in the message, let's call her the Mystery Donor, said she would like to do something, anonymously, to help the woman in my story. She ended up paying off a $1,200 light bill to keep the woman's power from being shut off. Her career as a benefactor really began after she lost her husband.

MYSTERY DONOR: My husband died about three years ago, and I had access to more money than I needed for expenses. So it was an opportunity to start giving money away.

AR: At age 58, the Mystery Donor lives in a pretty but not extravagant Seattle home. When her husband was alive, they gave money but tended to focus on established charities. Now she acts on her own. Altogether she donates a quarter of her income each year, and she says that amount will increase over time. She says she often gives secretly because she's learned that money can change relationships. Her first secret donation was to a massage therapist she knew.

MD: She was a single mother, and so this was really important work. And she broke her leg. And anybody who's been a single mother as I have knows what a catastrophe looks like on its way. And that looked awful to me. So what I did was to give her some money anonymously through having a cashier's check from the bank sent to her from another town.

AR: These small, personal gifts often go to helping single mothers. Their experience echoes her own years ago.

MD: I know what that feels like to feel desperate and need to care for a child. I was poor as a single mother for a period, looking for a job and had a one-year-old. And I do recall the one night where I had to decide whether I could buy tuna fish or diapers. You know, and it was down to that before I got my next paycheck. Of course, we got the diapers.

AR: She describes the past three years as a learning curve in the art of philanthropy. She contributes hundreds of thousands of dollars each year to her cause of choice: sustainable farming. She belongs to a group, the Women Donors Network, that put her in touch with a University of Montana professor named Neva Hassanein. Hassanein had created a program to help local farmers supply the school's cafeteria food. The Mystery Donor wanted to help expand the program to other institutions. Hassanein says she then proposed having

AmeriCorps volunteers work with other colleges to replicate it.

NEVA HASSANEIN: And so we approached this donor with this idea and she loved it, was very excited. And it was, in fact, her prodding that got us to think a little bit outside the box.

AR: Hassanein says working with these freelance philanthropists has its advantages. They're more flexible and responsive than big foundations, she says, who can sometimes push their own agenda. The Mystery Donor says she may create a foundation one day, but right now she enjoys the freedom that comes from giving on her own.

MD: I really love flying under the radar and writing checks, you know, without having a structure. I certainly consult with a lot of people around what I do to make sure my judgment is as accurate as it can be, but right now this other way is good.

AR: Even when helping someone she knows, the Mystery Donor says she doesn't feel the need to ask whether they've received her gift. She says these gifts are more like being a secret Santa, where secrecy itself is part of the charm. In Seattle, I'm Amy Radil for *Marketplace Money*.

Page 142, Listening Skill

Exercise 1

(See Comprehension, above.)

Exercise 2

Excerpt One

REPORTER AMY RADIL: These small, personal gifts often go to helping single mothers. Their experience echoes her own years ago.

MYSTERY DONOR: I know what that feels like to feel desperate and need to care for a child. I was poor as a single mother for a period, looking for a job and had a one-year-old.

Excerpt Two

AR: The Mystery Donor says she may create a foundation one day, but right now she enjoys the freedom that comes from giving on her own.

MD: I really love flying under the radar and writing checks, you know, without having a structure. I certainly consult with a lot of people around what I do to make sure my judgment is as accurate as it can be, but right now this other way is good.

Page 156, Final Speaking Task, Prepare

ANNOUNCER: A Public Service Announcement. Close your eyes in Chicago and you can hear the sound of zebra braying in Africa. Look hard out your window in DC and you can see the snow-covered peaks of the Andes. Stand on a corner in LA and feel the hot wind of the Sahara brush across your face. The world is that small. We are that connected. Please visit earthshare.org and learn how the world's leading environmental groups are working together, making it so simple for you to make a difference, because we are many and we are one. Please visit us at earthshare.org to learn more. EarthShare. One environment: one simple way to care for it all.

UNIT 7: WATER, WATER, EVERYWHERE?

Listening One, Page 163, Preview

INTERVIEWER JUDY WOODRUFF: Hundreds of millions of people around the world depend on the use of underground rock formations known as aquifers to get the clean water they need. But a pair of new studies show many of the largest aquifers are being depleted at alarming rates. As seen on this map, of the 37 largest ones in the world, 21 are losing more water than is being replaced, with those areas in orange and red showing much more serious problems with depletion. These are located in countries like China, Russia, and Australia, as well as India, where water resources are already a major problem. The reports also identify declining levels for California's Central Valley Aquifer.

Page 164, Listen

INTERVIEWER JUDY WOODRUFF: Hundreds of millions of people around the world depend on the use of underground rock formations known as aquifers to get the clean water they need. But a pair of new studies show many of the largest aquifers are being depleted at alarming rates. As seen on this map, of the 37 largest ones in the world, 21 are losing more water than is being replaced, with those areas in orange and red showing much more serious problems with depletion. These are located in countries like China, Russia, and Australia, as well as India, where water resources are already a major problem. The reports also identify declining levels for California's Central Valley Aquifer. Jay Famiglietti is a lead author on one of the reports from NASA's Jet Propulsion Laboratory, and he joins me now. Welcome, Mr. Famiglietti. Remind us, what is an aquifer and how does it produce the clean water?

JAY FAMIGLIETTI: An aquifer is an underground soil or rock unit that contains, contains water in its, in its pore spaces, and the way we get at that water is by, is by drilling wells and pumping it up from the subsurface.

JW: So what did these two studies find?

JF: We found that in the 37 world's largest aquifers that, that we looked at, that over 21 of them are past sustainability tipping points, meaning that the rate of withdrawal exceeds the rate of replenishment, and of those we found that 13 are in a pretty bad way and threatened to exceed a point at which they, they may not come back.

JW: And why is this happening?

JF: Well, we rely heavily on groundwater, but yet we don't manage it very well. Around the world we use about, about 2 billion people rely on groundwater as a primary water source, and it provides about half of the water that we need to irrigate agriculture. So we rely on it heavily, but we don't manage it very well, and that's true in the United States as well as around the world.

JW: So is this depletion happening at a faster rate than it did historically?

JF: In some places, yes. It's taken a while for the population in a particular region to, to develop, or it's taken a while for the

infrastructure to, to come into place. For example, in northwestern India, the Green Revolution is something that didn't start until the 1960s and the 1970s. Prior to that, there wasn't much groundwater depletion.

JW: Let's talk for a minute about where this is happening. We mentioned on several continents. Where is the problem the worst?

JF: Probably the worst in the Middle East. The Arabian Peninsula and, and even the region above the Arabian Peninsula—Turkey, Syria, Iraq, and Iran—are regions that we've studied before. Northwestern India, and really across northern India and into Bangladesh is, is in pretty rough shape. The North China Plain, the big aquifer system around Beijing. It is true, it's on every continent. The, the Pilbara Mining Region, which is the Canning Basin in northwestern Australia. Several of the aquifers in, in Africa are in rough shape because there's very little rainfall there in the, in the Sahara Desert. So not very much replenishment, and in Argentina, the Guarani Aquifer, and then of course the aquifers in the United States, big ones being in the Central Valley and the High Plains, or the Ogallala Aquifer.

JW: Then, and what about, what about the one in California's Central Valley, what, what shape is that in?

JF: Well, that's in pretty rough shape. This study and other studies that we've done on the aquifer show that we've been losing about five and a half trillion gallons of groundwater per year for the last four years during this drought. And that's because in California right now, there's no, there's no snow in the mountains. There's no, no rainfall happening. There's very little water in our reservoirs. So we have to rely on this groundwater and it's, it's disappearing pretty rapidly.

JW: Is there a way of knowing when this water is going, how much more water there is, when it's going to run out? And is there anything that can be done about this?

JF: So that's an excellent question. And that was really the topic of the, of the second paper. And so we, we tried to expose the fact that we really don't know how much water we have in the world's major aquifers. Again, it's true in the United States and it's, it's true around the world. We know that we're past the sustainability tipping points and all kinds of ecological damage is occurring. And we know that the water tables are falling and wells are running dry. So I think it's very important that we think very carefully about exploring the world's major aquifers to understand how much water is actually there.

JW: Well, it's a grim, grim set of findings that I know a lot of people are going to be paying close attention to. Jay Famiglietti, we thank you for being with us.

JF: Thank you very much.

Page 166, Make Inferences

Excerpt One

INTERVIEWER JUDY WOODRUFF: And why is this happening?

JAY FAMIGLIETTI: Well, we rely heavily on groundwater, but yet we don't manage it very well.

Excerpt Two

JW: So is this depletion happening at a faster rate than it did historically?

JF: In some places, yes.

Excerpt Three

JW: Let's talk for a minute about where this is happening. We mentioned on several continents. Where is the problem the worst?

JF: Probably the worst in the Middle East.

Page 169, Note-taking Skill

Excerpt One

REPORTER: With support from the National Science Foundation, this team is working to develop solar panels like these, designed to mount on the side of a building and take greywater recycling to a new level.

Excerpt Two

MARIA PAZ GUTIERREZ: Here you see we will collect the greywater through the day. It's

filtered, and then it's brought into these facades within a panel. It's warmed through the day, and then we reuse it, so pass it under the slabs of the floors and then use it as thermal energy.

Listening Two, Page 169, Comprehension

MARIA PAZ GUTIERREZ: What matters to you is exactly that boundary position . . .

REPORTER: Architect Maria Paz Gutierrez is a woman on a mission.

MPG: Can you show me a bit of what you're working on?

REPORTER: Not just to mentor a new generation of students here at the University of California-Berkeley, but to design a new generation of affordable, sustainable building technologies aimed at conserving an increasingly precious resource: water.

MPG: So, this research began by trying to address a very key environmental and socioeconomic and cultural issue that we face today, which is the issue of water scarcity around the world.

REPORTER: Right now an average family of four in the U.S. uses more than 250 gallons of clean water per day. Most of it goes right back out to the sewer. More than half of *that* is so-called "greywater."

MPG: Greywater is all the water that we have used for activities with the exception of water from toilet flushing, and in some parts of the world, also the water from kitchen sinks.

STUDENT: When some of them were like shifted this way a little bit . . .

REPORTER: With support from the National Science Foundation, this team is working to develop solar panels like these, designed to mount on the side of a building and take greywater recycling to a new level. And they're designed to be multi-purpose, too. The water that flows through them will be heated by the sun during the day, and then circulate through the building to warm it when it's cold.

MPG: Here you see we will collect the greywater through the day. It's filtered and then it's brought into these facades within a panel. It's warmed through the day, and then we reuse it, so pass it under the slabs of the floors and then use it as thermal energy.

REPORTER: The key is photocatalytic disinfection technology. Glass surfaces inside the panels, which can look like spheres, or louvers, are coated with nanoparticles that chemically react to sunlight. The process generates molecules called O-H radicals that kill microbes, like e-coli. The processed greywater isn't clean enough to drink, but fine for flushing toilets or washing clothes.

SLAV HERMANOWICZ: Many people considered water in the 21st century to be an equivalent of oil in the 20th century.

REPORTER: Environmental engineer Slav Hermanowicz and his students are building panel prototypes that they test in the lab and also outdoors.

SH: Instead of using water only once—and that's the norm in pretty much all [the] developed world—we want to use it at least twice. And in this way we can cut the water demand, we can use solar energy, which is free, and we can also potentially capture that energy for other usage.

REPORTER: Gutierrez says this technology could be ready for commercialization within the decade, at a price point that would be practical for use in water-stressed areas all around the globe.

MPG: The end user will benefit because we'll pay less money in electricity, in the water usage. The city will have savings because you'll have less water to treat. The environment will benefit because we're not going to be contaminating aquifers. So there are advantages that work across scales, from the local to the global scale.

REPORTER: Engineering sustainable communities, using the energy of the sun to conserve water and generate power. We can all take a shine to that. For *Science Nation*, I'm Miles O'Brien.

Page 170, Listening Skill

Exercise 1

MPG: So, this research began by trying to address a very key environmental and socioeconomic and cultural issue that we face today, which is the issue of water scarcity around the world.

Exercise 2

Excerpt One

SLAV HERMANOWICZ: Instead of using water only once—and that's the norm in pretty much all [the] developed world—we want to use it at least twice. And in this way we can cut the water demand, we can use solar energy, which is free, and we can also potentially capture that energy for other usage.

Excerpt Two

MARIA PAZ GUTIERREZ: The end user will benefit because we'll pay less money in electricity, in the water usage. The city will have savings because you'll have less water to treat. The environment will benefit because we're not going to be contaminating aquifers.

UNIT 8: VIDEO GAMES: FRIEND OR FOE?

Listening One, Page 189, Preview

REPORTER: We spend more than 3 billion [pounds] a year on gaming, more than we spend on film or music. And gaming has shed its nerdy image to become an essential part of youth culture. As a parent, I often wonder what effect it will have on my children. It's an immersive, interactive, cinematic experience, but is it too much for some people to handle?

Page 190, Listen

Part One

REPORTER: In the past five years, computer gaming has exploded in popularity.

TEEN A: "I love playing video games."

TEEN B: "I play games every day."

TEEN C: I've been waiting for this game for a really long time."

REPORTER: We spend more than 3 billion [pounds] a year on gaming, more than we spend on film or music. And gaming has shed its nerdy image to become an essential part of youth culture. As a parent, I often wonder what effect it will have on my children. It's an immersive, interactive, cinematic experience, but is it too much for some people to handle? It's a fate 20-year-old Leo, not his real name, is trying to avoid.

LEO: You substitute the real world for this world. I mean, two years I've been playing, 12 hours of the day, online, for two years if you want to look at it that way. It was fun while you're playing, but then when you think about the derogatory effect it's having on your life, then, then obviously, you don't feel so good.

REPORTER: His university work is suffering. He's lost contact with his friends and damaged his relationship with his family.

LEO: I would never inflict this game on anyone. This game is just a disease. It's just horrible. It's very hard to explain properly. You really, it's one of those things you really have to experience.

REPORTER: He's now decided to go cold turkey and stop playing the game.

When Allison Dando's son, Chris, started refusing to go to school, she had no idea why.

ALLISON DANDO: Initially, we didn't connect it to the computer game playing at the start because it was just something that every boy did, and particularly a lot of the boys that we knew, and friends of ours. Yeah, we had the internet, yeah, both the children had computers in their bedroom, but there was nothing that particularly alarmed us.

CHRIS: It brought you into another world. Like, you're being what you wanted to be.

REPORTER: He was playing for up to 20 hours a day.

CHRIS: I remember there was one point where, I think, our internet just went down, and I started sweating, and I actually started shaking, just because I couldn't play it.

AD: Once I understood that this game was online, I'm saying, "Right. OK, well the answer to it is we'll cut off the internet;

that's it." And the response was just an outpouring of violence. He just went berserk.

CHRIS: I put on a boot and I kicked a hole in my sister's door. I just smashed anything I could see.

AD: It was really scary.

CHRIS: It got to the point where, you know, my dad almost had to pin me down on the ground.

AD: That was the point where we started to really understand from a parental point of view, "Gosh, this is dangerous! This is a dangerous tool in our house."

Part Two

REPORTER: I went to meet a world authority on the psychological impact of computer games.

PROF. MARK GRIFFITHS: The good news is that for the vast majority of people, video games is something that's very positive in their life. But we have to take on board that there is a growing literature that suggests for a small but significant minority, things like gaming can be potentially problematic. My research has consistently shown people seem to display the signs and symptoms you get with the more traditional addictions.

REPORTER: He says there isn't enough research to be certain how serious the problem is.

PROF. MG: People put money into alcohol and tobacco addiction, maybe even into gambling addiction, but in gaming addiction, it's kind of so new, people don't really see it as an important research area to look into.

REPORTER: The little research that has been done suggests it's online games that cause the most concern. One award-winning games designer thinks it's time the industry accepts that some online games may encourage obsessive playing.

ADRIAN HON: I think people don't necessarily understand how powerful some game mechanics can be. It's one thing to think, "OK, I'm playing too much." But it's another thing to just stop playing because some games are designed in a manner that you just don't want to leave.

REPORTER: He says powerful psychological techniques are used.

AH: The first one is by using this idea called a variable rate of reinforcement, which is basically like a jackpot. So it's a slot machine.

REPORTER: The idea was developed after scientists discovered rats, taught to feed themselves by pressing a lever, would press it obsessively when the food appeared randomly.

AH: And people have found that this worked on humans as well. If you go and give people a lever to press or a button to press and give them random rewards based on pressing that, you know, they'll do it all the time.

REPORTER: In games, instead of food, you randomly get extra lives, or extra in-game features to keep you playing. The idea is to create a compulsion loop to keep us coming back for more. It's simple but powerful, and it's thought to explain why people get addicted to slot machines. I don't want to stop my son from gaming, but I'm going to keep an extra close eye on him to make sure he games safely.

Page 196, Note-taking Skill

Excerpt One

JANE MCGONIGAL: You know, what I've discovered is that games do a better job, in many ways, of providing the things that we crave most, you know, whether it's a sense of satisfying hands-on work where we can really see the outcomes of our actions, or a chance to succeed and get better at something—to start out being really bad and then have this sense of mastery as we get better and better.

Excerpt Two

JM: Gamer addiction is not about, necessarily, the quality of the games being somehow fundamentally . . . they just grab us, and we can't escape. It's really about what they offer us that the real world sometimes does a terrible job of offering us. And it is,

hopefully, our goal to take those things that we get from games and find ways to have them in our real lives, too.

Listening Two, Page 197, Comprehension

JANE MCGONIGAL: There are a couple of concerns that come up often when we talk about video games. The first is addiction, and that's definitely a real problem.

You know, what I've discovered is that games do a better job, in many ways, of providing the things that we crave most, you know, whether it's a sense of satisfying hands-on work where we can really see the outcomes of our actions, or a chance to succeed and get better at something—to start out being really bad and then have this sense of mastery as we get better and better. Gamer addiction is not about, necessarily, the quality of the games being somehow fundamentally . . . they just grab us, and we can't escape. It's really about what they offer us that the real world sometimes does a terrible job of offering us. And it is, hopefully, our goal to take those things that we get from games and find ways to have them in our real lives, too.

The other big concern that people have about games is violence, of course. And there's no evidence that gaming makes you more violent. In fact, a study came out just last week showing that gamers who play violent games that require strategy with your teammates or cooperation with other players to beat the bad guys are actually much more cooperative in the game and in real life—that they're actually honing skills of cooperation, not skills of violence. This makes perfect sense because when you're playing a game with other players, you're not actually being violent, right? You have to actually work with the other players. You have to trust them to finish the game. You have to work with your teammates. You have to communicate. There's no actual violence involved, right? The actual effort involved is highly collaborative, highly trustworthy, highly social.

So, the message needs to be, "This is training for real life." You know, yes, games are escapist in that we do get to escape reality when we play them, but they're not just escapist. They're also returnist. We return to our real lives with real ways of thinking about what we're capable of, real ways of solving problems more creatively. And this is the great news for the gamer generations: that we have spent our lives planting this seed, planting this capability. And now we can take those skills and abilities to real challenges, whether they're things like overcoming concussions the way that I used my gamer way of thinking to deal with that. Or tackling global challenges like climate change, and curing cancer, and overcoming political corruption. There are games to do all of these things now that you can play. You can bring your gamer abilities and help save the real world. So if you have a gamer in your life, or if you are a gamer, the good news is you are ready, they are ready to do extraordinary things in their real life.

Page 198, Listening Skill

Exercise 1

JANE McGONIGAL: You know, yes, games are escapist in that we do get to escape reality when we play them, but they're not just escapist. They're also returnist. We return to our real lives with real ways of thinking about what we're capable of, real ways of solving problems more creatively.

Exercise 2

Excerpt One

JM: The other big concern that people have about games is violence, of course. And there's no evidence that gaming makes you more violent. In fact, a study came out just last week showing that gamers who play violent games that require strategy with your teammates or cooperation with other players to beat the bad guys are actually much more cooperative in the game and in real life.

Excerpt Two

JM: Gamer addiction is not about, necessarily, the quality of the games being somehow fundamentally . . . they just grab us, and we can't escape. It's really about what they offer us that the real world sometimes does a terrible job of offering us.

THE PHONETIC ALPHABET

	Consonant Symbols		
/b/	**b**e	/t/	**t**o
/d/	**d**o	/v/	**v**an
/f/	**f**ather	/w/	**w**ill
/g/	**g**et	/y/	**y**es
/h/	**h**e	/z/	**z**oo, bu**s**y
/k/	**k**eep, **c**an	/θ/	**th**anks
/l/	**l**et	/ð/	**th**en
/m/	**m**ay	/ʃ/	**sh**e
/n/	**n**o	/ʒ/	vi**s**ion, A**s**ia
/p/	**p**en	/tʃ/	**ch**ild
/r/	**r**ain	/dʒ/	**j**oin
/s/	**s**o, **c**ircle	/ŋ/	lo**ng**

	Vowel Symbols		
/α/	f**a**r, h**o**t	/iy/	w**e**, m**ea**n, f**ee**t
/ɛ/	m**e**t, s**ai**d	/ey/	d**ay**, l**a**te, r**ai**n
/ɔ/	t**a**ll, b**ou**ght	/ow/	g**o**, l**ow**, c**oa**t
/ə/	s**o**n, **u**nder	/uw/	t**oo**, bl**ue**
/æ/	c**a**t	/ay/	t**i**me, b**uy**
/ɪ/	sh**i**p	/aw/	h**ou**se, n**ow**
/ʊ/	g**oo**d, c**oul**d, p**u**t	/oy/	b**oy**, c**oi**n

CREDITS

VIDEO CREDITS

Unit 1: ABC News Internet Ventures
Unit 2: ABC News Internet Ventures
Unit 3: AP/BO Clips
Unit 4: ABC News Internet Ventures
Unit 5: AFP/BO Clips
Unit 6: NBC Universal Archives
Unit 7: Science360/BO Clips
Unit 8: ABC News Internet Ventures.

TEXT AND AUDIO CREDITS

Unit 1
Pages 5–8, 224–225, classroom audio, and MyEnglishLab "Focused Listening": Listening One: The Music in My Head. Blue Jay: Julliard called this kid the greatest prodigy in 200 years," *CBS News*, May 3, 2013. Copyright © 2013 CBS News. All rights reserved. Reproduced by permission.
Pages 11–12, 225–226, classroom audio and MyEnglishLab "Listening Skill": Listening Two: What Makes a Prodigy? An interview Dr. Gráinne McLoughlin. Used with permission.

Unit 2
Pages 32–34, 226–227, classroom audio and MyEnglishLab "Focused Listening": Listening One: Artist Opens Others' Eyes. A report about artist Carol Saylor. Wider Horizons is a project of WHYY, Inc. and Coming of Age, published by Carol B. Saylor on YouTube, Mar 14, 2012. Used with permission from Carol B. Saylor. URL: https://www.youtube.com/watch?v=U3_66z-WPHM

Unit 3
Pages 57–60, 229–230, classroom audio and MyEnglishLab "Focused Listening": Listening One: How Can Teenagers Get Enough Sleep? Michael Howell, "Expert Alert: Healthy sleep schedule key for students to hit the ground running." © 2010 Regents of the University of Minnesota. Used with permission.
Pages 63–65, 230–231, classroom audio and MyEnglishLab "Listening Skill": Listening Two: Get Back in Bed! Satellite Sisters: "Get Back in Bed," An interview with Dr. Joyce Walsleben, Director of New York University's Sleep Disorder Clinic. © Mudbath Productions. Used with permission.

Unit 4
Pages 84–88, 231–233, classroom audio and MyEnglishLab "Focused Listening": Listening One: Who's Smart? A radio interview featuring these psychology professors, Dr. Sally Boysen, Dr. Irene Pepperberg, and Dr. Stan Kuczaj from "The Infinite Mind: Animal Intelligence" excerpt from "The Infinite Mind" public radio series, programs on "Animal Intelligence" and "Altruism," produced by Lichtenstein Creative Media, © 2007, 2013 Lichtenstein Create Media, Incorporated.
Pages 89–91, 233–234, classroom audio and MyEnglishLab "Listening Skill": Listening Two: What Motivates Animals? A podcast interview with Liz Pennisi, a writer for *Science* magazine. Republished with permission of American Association for the Advancement of Science(AAAS), from Science Podcast Cloaking Devices, Animal Cognition, Ancient Beads and More? Science Podcast, 23 June 2006; permission conveyed through Copyright Clearance Center, Inc.

Unit 5
Pages 114–117, 235–236, classroom audio and MyEnglishLab "Focused Listening": Listening One: The Longevity Project. An interview with Howard S. Friedman and Leslie Martin, Forever Young:Myth-Busting Longevity. ABC News. Used with permission from ABC News Internet Ventures.
Pages 114–117, 235–236, classroom audio and MyEnglishLab "Listening Skill": Listening Two: Tobey Dichter, Generations Online. Longevity – Coming of Age: Interview with Tobey Dichter, Founder of Generations Online and Dorothy Gray. Wider Horizons is a project of WHYY, Inc. and Coming of Age. Used with permission.

Unit 6
Pages 136–138, 237–238, classroom audio and MyEnglishLab "Focused Listening": Listening One: Why We Give. "The Infinite Mind: Animal Intelligence" excerpt from "The Infinite Mind" public radio series, programs on "Animal Intelligence" and "Altruism," produced by Lichtenstein Creative Media, © 2007, 2013 Lichtenstein Create Media, Incorporated.
Pages 141–144, 238–240, classroom audio and MyEnglishLab "Listening Skill": Listening Two: The Mystery Donor. Amy Radil's "Sometimes charity is better a mystery" from American Public Media's Marketplace © 2007. Used with permission. All rights reserved.

Unit 7
Pages 163–166, 240–242, classroom audio and MyEnglishLab "Focused Listening": Listening One: Water Shortage: Past the Tipping Point? From PBS NEWSHOUR, "Is the world's fresh water supply running out" (June 17, 2015). Used with permission from Newshour Production LLC.
Pages 169–171, 242–243, classroom audio and MyEnglishLab "Listening Skill": Listening Two: Putting Water to Work. Transformational Building Design Energizes Water Recycling—Literally! Science360/BO Clips

Unit 8
Pages 189–194, 243–245, classroom audio and MyEnglishLab "Focused Listening": Listening One: The Darker Side of Video Games. Addicted to Games? *Panorama*, 6 December 2010. Copyright © BBC Worldwide Americas Inc. All rights reserved. Reproduced by permission.
Pages 196–199, 245–246, classroom audio and MyEnglishLab "Listening Skill": Listening Two: Truths and Myths in Gaming. Jane McGonigal: Truths & Myths in Gaming, June 2, 2012. Copyright © Big Think, Inc. All rights reserved. Reproduced by permission.

PHOTO CREDITS

Cover
Maik Hoehne/Shutterstock; Katjen/Shutterstock.

Frontmatter
Page vi (p. 2–3): VGstockstudio/Shutterstock; vii (p. 4): Dean Drobot/Shutterstock; vii (p. 5): Douglas Mason/Getty Images; vii (p. 10): Gorodenkoff/Shutterstock; ix (photo on cell phone): VGstockstudio/Shutterstock; xi (p. 26): Ljupco Smokovski/Shutterstock; xiv (Unit 1 opener): VGstockstudio/Shutterstock; xiv (Unit 2 opener): Alexandr Zadiraka/Shutterstock; xv (Unit 3 opener): Dean Drobot/Shutterstock; xv (Unit 4 opener): Anna Segeren/Shutterstock; xvi (Unit 5 opener): Pressmaster/Shutterstock; xvi (Unit 6 opener): Fotos593/Shutterstock; xvii (Unit 7 opener): gg-foto/Shutterstock; xvii (Unit 8 opener): Pixel-Shot/Shutterstock.

Unit 1
Pages 2–3: VGstockstudio/Shutterstock; 4: Dean Drobot/Shutterstock; 5: Douglas Mason/Getty Images; 6: Fullempty/Shutterstock; 8–9: Watchara/Shutterstock; 10: Gorodenkoff/Shutterstock; 13: Allen.G/Shutterstock; 14: Dragon Images/Shutterstock; 16: Vgm/Shutterstock; 17 (parent): Amble Design/Shutterstock; 17 (teacher): Image Source/Getty Images; 17 (prodigy): Lightfieldstudios/123RF; 18 (Kendra Bauer avatar): Kurhan/123RF; 18 (proudpapa123 avatar): Jon Barlow/Pearson Education Ltd; 18 (m_vasquez avatar): Diego Vito Cervo/123RF; 18 (avs_fan17 avatar): Ivan Ryabokon/123RF; 23: Siamionau Pavel/Shutterstock; 26: Ljupco Smokovski/Shutterstock.

Unit 2
Pages 28–29: Alexandr Zadiraka/Shutterstock; 30: Miunicaneurona/Shutterstock; 31 (Helen Keller): Wallace/Mirrorpix/Newscom; 31 (coin): RadlovskYaroslav/Shutterstock; 32: Courtesy of Carol Saylor; 34: Marino Bocelli/123RF; 36: Robin Marchant/Getty Images; 38: 101akarca/Shutterstock; 41: M.Sobreira/Alamy Stock Photo; 42–43: AridOcean/Shutterstock; 50 (left): Wally McNamee/Corbis/Getty Images; 50 (right): Bryan Bedder/Getty Images.

Unit 3
Pages 54–55: Dean Drobot/Shutterstock; 57: ESB Professional/Shutterstock; 61: Sargis Zubov/Shutterstock; 64: Fizkes/Shutterstock; 67: Fizkes/Shutterstock; 68: Stan Honda/AFP/Getty Images; 78: Rawpixel.com/Shutterstock.

Unit 4
Pages 80–81: Anna Segeren/Shutterstock; 82–83 (chimpanze): Protasov AN/Shutterstock; 82–83 (background): Lukasz Szwaj/Shutterstock; 84: Juniors Bildarchiv GmbH/Alamy Stock Photo; 85: Daulon/Shutterstock; 88: Kondratuk Aleksei/Shutterstock; 90: Thomas W. Woodruff/Shutterstock; 93: Steve Meese/Shutterstock; 94: Mark Bridger/Shutterstock; 96–97: Laly Harris/Shutterstock; 100: Eric Isselee/Shutterstock.

Unit 5
Page s106–107: Pressmaster/Shutterstock; 108: Odua Images/Shutterstock; 110: Paula Solloway / Alamy Stock Photo; 112–113: Stefan Schurr/Shutterstock; 114: Carterdayne/E+/Getty Images; 121: Goran Bogicevic/Shutterstock; 122: Jeanne McRight/Shutterstock; 123: Dmytro Zinkevych/Shutterstock; 126: Lisa F. Young/Shutterstock.

Unit 6
Pages 132–133: Fotos593/Shutterstock; 134 (top): Pierre Villard/Sipa/Shutterstock; 134 (bottom): Amit Shabi/Getty Images; 135: Justin Sullivan/Getty Images; 136: ESB Professional/Shutterstock; 139: Flamingo Images/Shutterstock; 144: Rawpixel.com/Shutterstock; 148 (top): Jim West/Alamy Stock Photo; 148 (bottom): Brendan Fitterer/Tampa Bay Times/ZUMA Press Inc/Alamy Stock Photo; 149: Rawpixel.com/Shutterstock; 152: Africa Studio/Shutterstock; 158: Rawpixel.com/Shutterstock.

Unit 7
Pages 160–161: gg-foto/Shutterstock; 166–167: Panyajampatong/Shutterstock; 168: Sergey Merkulov/Shutterstock; 169 (top): Robert Paul Van Beets/Shutterstock; 169 (bottom): Taras Dubov/Shutterstock; 172: Rawpixel.com/Shutterstock; 174: Karuna Tansuk/Shutterstock; 176 (fish): Nitsuki/123RF; 176 (green field): David Litman/Shutterstock; 176 (brown field): Tanja Esser/Shutterstock; 176 (brush fire): Photo Cornwall/Alamy Stock Photo; 176 (dried reservoir): Robb Kendrick/National Geographic Image Collection/Alamy Stock Photo; 176 ((tap with dirt): Takiwa/Shutterstock; 176 (cows): Thechatat/Shutterstock; 182 (pool in desert): MaRabelo/iStock/Getty Images; 182 (water fountain): Coleman Yuen/Pearson Education Asia Ltd; 182 (kanagroo): John Carnemolla/Shutterstock; 182 (woman collecting water): Sean Sprague/Alamy Stock Photo; 182 (dried lake bed): Zorro12/123RF; 182 (man drinking water): Dmitry Kalinovsky/123RF.

Unit 8
Pages 186–187: Pixel-Shot/Shutterstock; 189: Svyatoslav Lypynskyy/123RF; 195: Antoniodiaz/Shutterstock; 199: MONOPOLY919/Shutterstock; 203: REDPIXEL.PL/Shutterstock; 206: Aapsky/Shutterstock; 208: Leonel Calara/Shutterstock; 214: Bodnar Taras/Shutterstock.

ILLUSTRATION CREDITS

Aphik Diseño, ElectraGraphics

NOTES

NOTES

NOTES